John Mark Dempsey, PhD
Editor

Sports-Talk Radio in America
Its Context and Culture

Pre-publication
REVIEWS,
COMMENTARIES,
EVALUATIONS . . .

"*Sports-Talk Radio in America* is very readable and most interesting. The material is well researched. This book would be a good supplement to a sports media or sportscasting course."

Frank Chorba, PhD
Professor,
Department of Mass Media,
Washburn University

"This book's addictive mixture of sports-talk radio history, communication theory, and research makes it a hard-to-put-down, entertaining read. The stories concerning the ethical considerations of sports-talk radio have already sparked intense debate in my classroom. After I finished the book I had an intense urge to listen even more to sports-talk radio. I don't want to miss any moments like those highlighted by the contributors."

Marilee M. Morrow, MA
Assistant Professor
and News/Sports Director,
Department of Communication
and Media Studies,
Marietta College

Sports-Talk Radio in America
Its Context and Culture

THE HAWORTH PRESS
Contemporary Sports Issues
Frank Hoffmann, PhD, MLS
Martin Manning
Senior Editors

Minor League Baseball: Community Building Through Hometown Sports by Rebecca S. Kraus

Baseball and American Culture: Across the Diamond edited by Edward J. Rielly

Dictionary of Toys and Games in American Popular Culture by Frederick J. Augustyn Jr.

Football and American Identity by Gerhard Falk

Basketball in America: From the Playgrounds to Jordan's Game and Beyond edited by Bob Batchelor

Sports-Talk Radio in America: Its Context and Culture edited by John Mark Dempsey

Sports-Talk Radio in America
Its Context and Culture

John Mark Dempsey, PhD
Editor

The Haworth Press®
New York • London • Oxford

For more information on this book or to order, visit
http://www.haworthpress.com/store/product.asp?sku=5335

or call 1-800-HAWORTH (800-429-6784) in the United States and Canada
or (607) 722-5857 outside the United States and Canada

or contact orders@HaworthPress.com

PUBLISHER'S NOTE
The development, preparation, and publication of this work has been undertaken with great care.
However, the Publisher, employees, editors, and agents of The Haworth Press are not responsible
for any errors contained herein or for consequences that may ensue from use of materials or information contained in this work. The Haworth Press is committed to the dissemination of ideas and
information according to the highest standards of intellectual freedom and the free exchange of
ideas. Statements made and opinions expressed in this publication do not necessarily reflect the
views of the Publisher, Directors, management, or staff of The Haworth Press, Inc., or an endorse-
ment by them.

Cover design by Lora Wiggins.

Library of Congress Cataloging-in-Publication Data

Sports-talk radio in America : its context and culture / John Mark Dempsey, editor.
       p. cm.
    Includes bibliographical references and index.
    ISBN-13: 978-0-7890-2589-0 (hard : alk. paper)
    ISBN-10: 0-7890-2589-2 (hard : alk. paper)
    ISBN-13: 978-0-7890-2590-6 (soft : alk. paper)
    ISBN-10: 0-7890-2590-6 (soft : alk. paper)
    1. Radio broadcasting of sports—United States. 2. Radio and baseball. I. Dempsey, John Mark,
1954-

GV742.3.S68 2006
070.4'49796—dc22

                                                                            2005035144

CONTENTS

ABOUT THE EDITOR

John Mark Dempsey, PhD, is Associate Professor of Radio/Television at Texas A&M University-Commerce. He is the author of *The Light Crust Doughboys Are on the Air!,* a history of the legendary Texas radio band that launched the career of Bob Willis, and *The Jack Ruby Trial Revisited: The Diary of Jury Foreman Max Causey.* Dr. Dempsey works in radio as a news anchor and producer for the Texas State Network in Arlington, and is play-by-play announcer for the Texas A&M baseball and basketball teams.

CONTRIBUTORS

Ron Bland is a lecturer in the University of Texas at Arlington (UTA) Communications Department. He is the advisor of UTA Radio, a twenty-four-hour student Internet radio station. He is chairman of Collegiate Broadcasters, Inc. At this writing, he is working toward his doctoral degree at the University of North Texas.

Paul F. Gullifor, PhD, was born and raised in South Bend, Indiana. The Irish-Catholic son of a high school coach, Gullifor is a lifelong Notre Dame sports fan. After graduating from St. Joseph's High School in South Bend in 1978, he earned a BA in broadcasting (1981) and an MS in broadcast management and programming (1982) from Indiana State University. He earned a PhD in communication from the University of Missouri in 1988. He is currently a tenured professor in the Department of Communication at Bradley University in Peoria, Illinois, where he teaches a variety of courses in electronic media. His research interests are in broadcast history and programming, particularly sports programming, and he has published in these areas. His first book, *The Fighting Irish on the Air: The History of Notre Dame Football Broadcasting,* published by Diamond Communications, was released in September 2001. Most recently, his second book, *Courting Success,* with Notre Dame Women's Basketball Coach Muffet McGraw, was released in November 2003. He enjoys coaching basketball in his spare time, and has coached grade school boys and girls, and high school girls teams. He lives in Peoria, Illinois, with his wife Shelley, and their three children—Sarah, Daniel, and Allison.

Michael L. Hilt, PhD, is Professor and Graduate Chair (PhD, University of Nebraska, 1994). He is co-author of *Crime and Local Television News: Dramatic, Breaking, and Live from the Scene* with Jeremy H. Lipschultz (Mahwah, NJ: Lawrence Erlbaum, 2002). Hilt is the author of *Television News and the Elderly: Broadcast Managers' Attitudes Toward Older Adults* (New York: Garland, 1997).

Sports-Talk Radio in America
© 2006 by The Haworth Press, Inc. All rights reserved.
doi:10.1300/5335_b

Alma Kadragic, PhD, teaches print and television journalism as an associate professor in the College of Communication and Media Studies at Zayed University, Abu Dhabi, United Arab Emirates. She considers sports a continuing thread in her career. Kadragic began reporting at the City College of New York, where she joined the sports staff of CCNY's *Campus* student newspaper. Her knowledge of sports helped her get started at ABC News, where she spent sixteen years as a producer and bureau chief in New York, Washington, London, and Warsaw, Poland. She also founded and operated a public relations and marketing company in Poland, and has managed such clients as Little League Baseball. She contributed to this book while living in Orlando, Florida, and working as a newspaper and magazine reporter and part-time instructor for area universities.

Jeremy H. Lipschultz, PhD, is Reilly Professor and Director (PhD, Southern Illinois University, 1990) of the School of Communication at the University of Nebraska at Omaha. Lipschultz is the author of *Broadcast Indecency: FCC Regulation and the First Amendment* (Boston: Focal Press, 1997) and *Free Expression in the Age of the Internet: Social and Legal Boundaries* (Boulder, Colorado: Westview Press, 2000).

Troy Oppie is a 2003 graduate of Pacific Lutheran University with a degree in broadcast and print communication. He's a lifelong KJR listener (since the third grade) and participated in an internship with KJR's morning show in the summer of 2001. Oppie is a sports reporter and weekend anchor for KECI-TV in Missoula, Montana. Previously, he worked as a jazz DJ for Seattle's KPLU, a broadcast associate (graphics producer) and audio engineer at Fox Sports Net in Bellevue, Washington, and a private personal technology technician in Seattle.

Douglas Pils, MA, is a sports copy editor for the San Antonio *Express-News.* He lives in San Antonio with his wife Honny and son Cole. Pils worked for the Associated Press in Little Rock, Arkansas, for two years, and from 1992 to 2002 he worked for five Texas newspapers—*The Dallas Morning News, Arlington Morning News, Corpus Christi Caller-Times, Waco Tribune-Herald,* and *New Braunfels Herald-Zeitung.* Pils was a Mayborn scholar at the University of North Texas, where he received a master's degree in journalism from the Mayborn Institute of Journalism in 2002. He has undergraduate degrees in journalism and economics from Texas A&M University.

William Raffel, PhD, JD, is an assistant professor of communication at Buffalo State College after earning a PhD and JD from the University at Buffalo. Bill served as the news director of WNCE-TV in Glens Falls, New York, and was a news reporter/producer for public radio stations WEBR and WBFO in Buffalo. He currently hosts *The Celtic Kaleidoscope* and produces music specials for WBFO. Sports-related accomplishments include producing Ithaca College Football broadcasts for WICB-FM, and interviewing tearful Buffalo Bills fans for national radio networks after two of the infamous Super Bowl losses.

Max Utsler, PhD, has spent most of the past twenty years teaching journalism at the University of Kansas (KU), except for 1995 when he served as Executive Producer of Sports at KPNX-TV in Phoenix. He graduated from Knox College where he played varsity football and baseball. He earned a master's degree in journalism at the University of Missouri (MU) while serving as a graduate assistant in baseball. After finishing his doctorate in education at Missouri and teaching at MU for eleven years, he joined KSDK-TV in St. Louis as an assistant news director. He came to KU in 1983.

Shelley Wigley, MA, is an assistant professor in the College of Mass Communications at Texas Tech University. She holds a bachelor's degree in broadcast journalism from Oklahoma State University (OSU), a master's degree in mass communication from OSU, and is currently finishing up a PhD in the Department of Communication at the University of Oklahoma. Her professional experience includes nine years of work in nonprofit and government public relations. She also is a former newspaper features reporter/editor and television associate producer. An avid sports-talk radio listener since 1995, Wigley's master's thesis focuses on women who listen to sports-talk radio. Her research interests include inoculation, crisis communication, corporate social responsibility, and men's and women's nontraditional use of media.

"Sign On"

When the first all sports-talk radio stations hit the air in the late 1980s, the skeptics stood in line to cast doubt on the format's viability. Who would listen to nothing but talk of back-door sliders, picks-and-rolls, and the cover-two defense day after day? How long before these jock talkers ran out of anything remotely interesting to say? (The notion of sports-talk's alter ego, "guy talk," had yet to emerge).

And yet *Birmingham* (Alabama) *News* columnist Bob Carlton admits his hopeless addiction to sports-talk radio. He writes of traveling the backroads of rural Alabama, feverishly scanning the dial for a fix, when he picked up a remote station carrying the syndicated *Jim Rome Show,* also known as "The Jungle":

> "Romey," as his, uh, "clones," call him, was talking "smack" [loosely defined: jocular sports banter] with Virginia Tech football coach Frank Beamer. But it didn't matter who was in "the house." At that point, I would have listened even if Romey was ranting about synchronized swimming.
>
> Carlton lost the station's signal, and suffered something close to withdrawal symptoms as he hurtled across the Alabama countryside. As he approached Birmingham, he picked up the show on another station and listened to the entire broadcast again, this time in tape delay.[1]

For better or worse—and that is very much a matter for debate—millions of mostly male listeners like Carlton indulge their obsession with sports to the exclusion of virtually all else available on the dial—music, news, and (mostly conservative) political talk.

While some stations and hosts earnestly stick to expert postmortems of the local team's latest debacle (losing always makes for more animated, passionate talk) or predictions for the next all-important game, the trend is toward attitude, the more attitude the better, as ex-

Sports-Talk Radio in America
© 2006 by The Haworth Press, Inc. All rights reserved.
doi:10.1300/5335_01

1

emplified by the hipper-than-hip Rome. While Rome is often a prob-
ing interviewer in the best tradition of broadcast journalism ("It
seemed to me if they were going to entrust me with the public airwaves and pay me to do the job, I'd better ask those questions people
at home want asked," he said), he made his name by getting into an
on-the-air scuffle with oft-inured Los Angeles Rams quarterback Jim
Everett, after repeatedly referring to Everett as "Chris," an obvious
reference to female tennis star Chris Evert and a taunting slight to
Everett's manhood.[2]

Although Rome and others often are deliberately provocative,
some observers, such as Steve Mirsky in *Scientific American,* have
criticized sports talk for its general obtuseness. He described listening to a show in which the host argued that the Boston Red Sox payroll had grown so much that the archrival New York Yankees no longer had a significant advantage over the Sox: "A Boston caller
disagreed, saying, 'The Red Sox's payroll is only $120 million, and
the Yankees is $180 million. You know what percentage $120 million
is of $180 million? Seventy-five percent.' The host did not dissuade
the caller."

The article went on to describe a discussion between the two hosts
of the same program concerning a Ku Klux Klan initiation ceremony
in which a Klansman fired a gun into the air, with the falling bullet
critically injuring a spectator. Mirsky described the hosts bickering
over the pronunciation of the Klan's infamous name. One of them
pronounced the name "Klu" Klux Klan, but repeatedly insisted he
didn't mispronounce it. The argument went on for some time, leading
Mirsky to proclaim his surprise that two men who made a living at
watching baseball trajectories would be astonished at how fast falling
objects return to the earth.[3]

Besides its inclination to inanity, sports talk also has a dark side, a
reputation for loutish chatter, not all of it coming from uninformed
callers. As *Los Angeles Times* writer Paul Brownfield noted: "Sports
talk radio has always been a haven for the lunatic fringe, a low-rated
medium for men dominated by trumped-up controversy manufac-
tured daily. But it has also given inconsolable, and triumphant, fans a
place to go."[4]

The reputation for crudity is not an entirely undeserved. Brad
James, program director of WDAE in Tampa, Florida, said his station
bills itself as "locker-room talk." WDAE's hosts, like those of many

sports-talk stations, think nothing of referring to private body parts. When someone calls the station andd complains, he asks them:

> "When you're watching TV at home, [is] your child sitting next to you while you're watching the Playboy Channel?" We're an adult, male sports radio station. And sometimes, you might hear one of our hosts [use profanity]. If you've got your child sitting next to you, then change the channel.

Of course, James' contention, while frequently made by those who push the envelope of good taste, ignores the well-established difference between over-the-air broadcasting, which uses the public airwaves, and cable programming, which travels over privately owned lines. Still, he proudly noted that his station has never been fined by the FCC.[5]

Atlanta Journal-Constitution writer Mike Tierney spoke for those who find sports talk far too "laddish," as the Brits say: "Sports talk is a guys-night-out concept, intended to capture the atmosphere of men hunkered around a bar, yapping and hoping for a beer-ad catfight between two centerfold prospects to break out."[6]

Julie Kahn, the general manager of sports-talk station WEEI in Boston—the rare female sports-radio chief executive—takes the sexual talk in stride. She says some listeners take it too literally. "I think it's part theater, I think it's part parody," she said. "A lot of people get up in the air because they don't realize these guys are acting. . . . They're going overboard to be entertaining."[7]

Sometimes the remarks listeners find offensive are not sexual, but racial in nature. A firestorm erupted in Boston when two hosts on WEEI joked that a gorilla that had escaped from a zoo was actually a student in a local racial-desegregation program. The controversy attracted the attention of the city council. "In listening to WEEI . . . I was really concerned this was a pervasive culture within the station," said City Councilor Michael Ross. "We cannot afford to let this continue in a city like Boston."[8] Kahn does not defend the racial comments. "That wasn't parody. That was just an out-and-out mistake," she says.[9]

Such complaints are usually directed at stations that flavor their sports-oriented programming with a generous amount of politically incorrect "guy talk." Other stations take a more purist approach to sports. ESPN Radio general manager Bruce Gilbert said his company's radio broadcasting is different. With hundreds of affiliates across the country, ESPN has no need to "be in the gutter," according to Gilbert. ESPN even has its own rules for broadcasts.[10]

The program director of KFNZ in Salt Lake City, Jeff Rickard, said that although the station engages in "guy talk," the objective is not to appeal to a lowest common denominator. Yet KFNZ has carried segments such as an interview with the winner of a Las Vegas dwarf-tossing contest and its Web page features a link to "Smokin' Hot Babes!!!" "We're not stupid," Rickard explained.[11]

Even when sports-talk stations keep the focus tightly on sports, critics often condemn it for a lack of fairness and journalistic standards. As *Toronto Star* reporter Chris Zelkovich wrote in an article on sports talk: "In Buffalo, when the Bills lose, talk radio becomes a blood sport."[12]

As early as 1987, the dawn of sports talk, players and coaches were complaining about what they believed was unfair coverage. Future baseball Hall of Famer Eddie Murray, nearing the end of his career with the Baltimore Orioles, became the target of talk-show hosts and fans, quit talking to the media, and finally demanded to be traded (the Orioles obliged his request after the 1988 season). *Washington Post* sportswriter Norman Chad, commenting on Murray's treatment, referred to one Baltimore host, Stan "The Fan" Charles, as "a mountain of out-of-control outrage." Charles explained: "My show is a barometer of what the fans are thinking. . . . My approach is I'm going to be here a lot longer than any of the players."[13] Indeed, Charles continued as a host on Baltimore sports-talk radio through 2001.

In 1997, the Philadelphia Flyers of the National Hockey League and their star player Eric Lindros sued sports-talk station WIP for defamation after a host reported that Lindros missed a game because of a hangover. As athletes' complaints against sports-talk stations go, the case was not a particularly egregious one. A year earlier, another NHL star considered suing a Pittsburgh sports station whose host "jokingly suggested" that the player pushed his team to acquire another player because the wives of the two players were lesbian lovers. The WIP host actually cited four unnamed sources, including two in the Flyers organization. Still, Fordham University sports-law professor Mark Conrad reflected on the reckless reputation of sports-talk radio, and asked if WIP's minimal adherence to journalistic standards helped the station's defense. "Probably, because if the standard of sports talk stations is not to do any checking, one can argue that WIP acted more responsibly in this situation than is the norm," Conrad argued.[14]

The bitter criticism of sports-talk hosts and callers is sometimes directed not at professionals, but college athletes. In university towns without pro teams, fans focus as intensely on the college teams as the followers of big-league teams obsess about the pros.

University of Arkansas head football coach Houston Nutt warned his players:

> I tell our players you've got to be careful and selective on what you read, what you hear. A lot of times people may try to bring you down and they don't mean to. A lot of times it's just misinformation or information that's not totally true.

Former Auburn University head football coach Terry Bowden—himself now a sports-talk host in Orlando—said he avoided listening to sports-talk radio when he coached the Tigers from 1993-1998. "I wouldn't dare listen because it can be so negative," he said.[15]

Women's college basketball is rarely a hot topic on sports-talk radio, but many hosts took umbrage when a Manhattanville (Westchester, New York) College player, Toni Smith, turned her back on the flag in protest of the coming war in Iraq in early 2003. Tony Bruno of Fox Sports Network and others called for the athlete's scholarship to be taken away. *St. Petersburg Times* columnist John C. Cotey blasted sports-talk radio hosts for not respecting the player's First Amendment rights: "In the testosterone-filled world of sports talk radio, history has shown us we should expect nothing more than knee-jerk, screaming voices calling for Smith to be stripped of her scholarship, beaten up, ridiculed and thrown out of the country."[16]

A 1994 ESPN television *Outside the Lines* program on sports-talk radio contained a segment on the topic of fairness, including comments from a sports-talk host, Andy Furman on WLW in Cincinnati. Furman accused a former Reds pitcher of having an extramarital affair, and based the allegation on the call of an anonymous woman who claimed to have had sexual relations with the pitcher. When asked why he hadn't asked the pitcher about the story, Furman seemed genuinely puzzled by the question. "Good point, I don't know. Just to con[firm]...? I mean, I don't know why. I just knew in my heart that I had the story and that was it. You mean to ask him what he thought of it, would he want to comment on it? Why would I call him?"[17]

* * *

The relationship between sports-talk radio and local newspapers is decidedly conflicted. On one hand, many sportswriters double as sports-talk hosts, arguably bringing a greater sense of journalistic propriety to radio. On the other hand, sportswriters (and other newspaper reporters) are among the sharpest critics of sports-talk radio.

Salt Lake Tribune writer Linda Fantin noted: "Traditional rivals in print and broadcast media openly promote one another and downplay their divided loyalties." (However, one Salt Lake sports-talk station, KFNZ, has dropped sportswriters as hosts. General manager Rickard said he wants employees whose first loyalty is to the station, not part-timers who are "indentured to other masters.") University of Utah mass communications professor Jim Fisher worries that sportswriters serving as sports-talk hosts reduces the diversity of opinions being heard. Defenders of sportswriters as radio hosts argue that their presence on the air gives readers a "direct line" to journalists, increasing the sportswriters' accessibility to the public.[18]

When venerable *Boston Globe* sportswriter Bob Ryan found himself in hot water for suggesting that the wife of New Jersey Nets basketball star Jason Kidd deserved to be "smacked" for allegedly drawing media attention to herself, Tierney noted: "A possible contributing factor to the faux pas is Ryan spreading himself too thin. He so permeates the airways that his main job, full-time, is easily overlooked: Sportswriter for the *Boston Globe*." While Ryan's careless remark came on local television, Tierney noted: "The smaller the audience, the more slanderous the yakkers tend to become. And radio tends to trump TV for offensiveness."[19]

St. Louis Post-Dispatch sports-media columnist Dan Caesar ventured these guidelines for sports-talk hosts, some of whom would do well to heed Caesar's words:

- Be as informed as your listeners: . . . Too often, guys sound like they pulled into the parking lot five minutes before air time and jumped behind the microphone with absolutely no preparation. There is a word for this: unprofessional.

- Put the listeners first: When a local team is playing on the West Coast, it is of utmost importance that hosts of morning drive-time shows watch the telecast. . . .
- Go to events, develop sources: Is it too much to ask for hosts to go to games, talk to players and team officials, do interviews in the locker rooms and develop sources so all-sports stations can actually break stories once in a while? . . .
- Listen to your station: This sounds as basic as it gets, but it's amazing how often a host has no knowledge of what was on the air on his station earlier in the day. . . .
- Don't promote other stations: Taking shots at shows and individuals on other stations not only doesn't serve the listeners—who cares about personal feuds—it gives free advertising to the competition. . . . [20]

* * *

Sports talk is part of a trend called "narrowcasting." No longer do radio stations attempt to reach the broadest possible audience, as in the original concept of "broadcasting." Instead, they attempt to dominate a particular niche of the overall audience, by appealing to factors of age, income, gender, and culture.[21] Craig Hanson, president of Simmons Media, the owner of sports-talk station KZN in Salt Lake City, referred to sports-talk as "the niche of the niche."[22]

By the year 2000, the *Broadcasting and Cable Yearbook* noted seventy distinct radio formats in use.[23] The number of stations using the sports-talk format went from virtually none (save WFAN) in 1988 to more than 600 in 2000.[24]

The explosion of the sports-talk format accompanied the evolution of the AM radio band. Until 1941, all U.S. commercial radio stations were heard on AM channels. In that year, the FCC established the FM band. For a variety of reasons (including World War II and the emergence of television), FM radio did not rise as a serious competitor to AM until the 1970s. Because of its superior fidelity, FM gradually became the choice of music listeners.[25]

Of course, all-sports never would have seen the light of day had all-news and all-talk formats not blazed a trail. Gordon McLendon, better known as a pioneer of Top 40, launched the first commercially successful all-news station, XTRA, in 1961. Actually a Mexican station located in Tijuana, XTRA blasted its robust signal into Southern California (not entirely coincidentally, XTRA is now a sports-talk station). By 1966, *Broadcasting* magazine declared all-news to be a viable format choice.[26]

Throughout the 1950s, free-standing talk shows became increasingly familiar to radio listeners. In 1959, KLIQ in Portland, Oregon, introduced the all-talk format, followed quickly in 1960 by KABC in Los Angeles. By 1965, interest in the new format was great enough for the National Association of Broadcasters to host a well-attended talk-radio clinic in Chicago.[27]

The roots of sports talk go back at least to 1964 when Bill Mazer hosted the first telephone call-in sports-talk show on WNBC-AM, 660 kHz., in New York. At the time, the station had just adopted the all-talk format. Known for an encyclopedic knowledge of sports, Mazer accepted challenges from callers asking questions on everything from lacrosse to weightlifting.[28]

An abortive attempt to launch the all-sports format came in 1981, when the Enterprise Radio Network started a national sports radio network. New York's WWRL was one of the affiliates, but as New York Daily News writer David Hinckley cracked, "Few sports fanatics were fishing up around 1600 on the AM dial to hear a chat about Alabama's football prospects." The network collapsed in less than a year.[29]

Not until July 1, 1987, did the first station adopt the all-sports talk format. Emmis Broadcasting, bought country-music station WHN-AM in New York and broadcast at 1050 kHz.[30] Later, the company bought WNBC (which began in 1922 as historic WEAF and became the flagship station for the National Broadcasting Company in 1926) and changed the station's call letters to WFAN.[31] "Friends in the industry thought I was stark-raving crazy," said Emmis founder Jeff Smulyan. The plan to change formats wasn't well received within his own company. "Nobody wanted to do it," Smuylah said.[32]

WFAN had something that WWRL did not: legendary radio personality Don Imus. "The I Man" was not known as a sports expert, but he had a vast and loyal fan base. WFAN also took over WNBC's strong and well-established frequency and acquired the rights to the NHL's Rangers and the NBA's Knicks.[33] So successful was WFAN that in 1996, Emmis sold the station to Infinity Broadcasting for $70 million, what was then a record price for a standalone AM station.

Industry sources recently estimated that WFAN is now worth at least four times that amount.[34] WFAN, despite a relatively small share of the twelve-plus audience in New York, became the top-billing radio station in history in 1997, crossing the $50 million dollar barrier.[35] As of early 2004, more than a dozen major-market stations were each generating more than $10 million per year in advertising revenue.[36]

WIP in Philadelphia soon followed WFAN in adopting the sports-talk format, and by the early 1990s, with AM radio's move to talk programming well established, stations all over the U.S. were adopting the all-sports format.[37]

While major-market stations may be able to afford a staff of "live" local hosts, medium- and small-market stations generally cannot. And so the introduction of ESPN Radio in 1992 was a crucial development in the emergence of sports talk. An extension of the iconic ESPN cable-television sports channel, ESPN Radio started with an impressive 147 affiliates in forty-three states and grew from there. In the beginning, the network offered limited programming of about sixteen hours per week.[38] Today, ESPN Radio claims 700 affiliates, with more than 200 carrying its programming twenty-four hours per day.[39]

* * *

The nature of narrowcasting and broadcasting on the AM band mean that sports-talk stations typically draw less than 3 percent of the listening audience in major markets. Ratings for the highest-rated sports-talk stations in the top ten U.S. markets in spring 2004 bear this out (see Table I.1).[40]

Why would so many stations adopt a format that wins such a small slice of the pie? The answer is that the target for sports-talk radio is not the largest possible share of the overall, age-twelve-and-older market. Rather, it is the affluent twenty-five to fifty-four male market that sports radio seeks (and finds).[41] Indeed, the Simmons Market Research Bureau finds that listeners to sports talk are 74 percent more likely to earn $100,000 or more per year than members of the general population.[42] This often translates into clout with advertisers. "Most sports radio stations are not big ratings stories," said the president and general manager of sports-talker WQXI in Atlanta. "But if they're good, they can sell much, much higher than their ratings suggest."[43]

TABLE I.1. Ratings: Sports-talk stations in the top U.S. markets, 2004.

Market	Station	12+ rating	Rank in market
1. New York	WFAN	2.4	17
2. Los Angeles	KSPN	0.5	27
3. Chicago	WSCR	1.3	21
4. San Francisco	KNBR	3.1	9
5. Dallas-Fort Worth	KTCK	3.1	11
6. Philadelphia	WIP	2.8	17
7. Houston	KILT	1.5	18[a]
8. Washington, DC	WTEM	1.2	16
9. Boston	WEEI	5.8	3
10. Detroit	WXYT	1.7	16

Source: RadioandRecords.com
[a]Ratings for winter 2004.

Since 1999, listening to sports-talk radio has increased 25 percent, according to Arbitron, from about 2 percent of the overall share of the audience to about 2.5 percent. Only urban (hip-hop, R&B) and religious stations have shown faster growth. Meanwhile, traditional formats such as adult contemporary, country, oldies and album rock have all declined. George Hyde, the executive director of the Radio Advertising Bureau, said sports talk has an advantage over other formats. While music on radio largely serves as background ambience, sports talk provides "foreground" programming that demands the listener's attention.[44]

The general manager of all-sports KTCK in Dallas-Fort Worth, Dan Bennett, said sports talk has much broader appeal to advertisers than many think. "The misunderstanding about this format is that there are some people who think it's all sports bars and gentlemen's clubs," he said. "That couldn't be further from the truth. We have captured the mainstream advertisers in a big way."[45]

*   *   *

This book, the first known work devoted to the all-sports radio format, provides a close-up look at individual sports-talk stations around the country, including major-market, medium-market and small-market stations.

The differences between these stations are nearly as numerous as the similarities. Some are ratings successes; some are struggling. Some focus on sports in a relatively straightforward, traditional way; others trend more toward irreverent guy talk. Some are in "major-league" towns; some in college towns. Some are in cities that are wild about sports; some are in cities that are mostly indifferent toward sports. The more successful stations tend to have a strong local foundation and their programming is deeply rooted in the traditions of their communities.

Although sports-talk radio definitely has its detractors, who criticize it on the basis of its content, the format has found a solid niche in the increasingly fragmented world of radio among often difficult-to-reach young men. The sports-talk format has the advantage of an audience that is passionate about sports and their teams. That loyalty is often transferred to the local sports-talk stations, leading to higher-than-average time-spent-listening numbers, and so the format is attractive to advertisers.[46]

In many ways, the "guy talk" tag is more accurate than sports talk. Rick Scott, president of RSA Sports International, a Washington, DC, sports-radio consulting firm, said it's actually men's entertainment. "It's been referred to as a sports bar on the radio or a Tupperware party for guys. Good sports radio is way beyond that. It's about entertaining personalities that are fun to listen to."[47]

In the end, the success of the sports-talk format can best be explained by the unusual bond between the hosts and their niche audience. Close to 10,000 fans turned out for an appearance by Jim Rome in Madison, Wisconsin. "I think one of the reasons the show works is because I'm one of them and they recognize one of them," said Rome. "The only difference between me and them is that I have a radio show and somebody pays me to express my opinions. They're my people. These are my people."[48]

NOTES

1. Carlton, Bob. "Sports talk radio addict faces the truth." *Birmingham* (Ala.) *News,* October 20, 2002, 1-F.

2. Wolfley, Bob. "Rome has a take on many issues." *Milwaukee Journal-Sentinel,* December 6, 2002, C-2.

3. Mirsky, Steve. "It is high, it is far." *Scientific American* 290(2) (February 2004): 98.

4. Brownfield, Paul. "Joe McDonnell and Doug Krikorian speak to a certain kind of fan: The die-hard obsessed with LA teams." *Los Angeles Times,* February 1, 2004, E-1.

5. Harmon, Rick. "Sports radio not for kids or squeamish, director says." *Tampa Tribune,* Nation/World, February 1, 2004, 4.

6. Tierney, Mike. "Listen, babblers: Shut your mouths." *Atlanta Journal-Constitution,* May 8, 2003, F-1.

7. Doyle, Bill. "Keeping male order: WEEI stays course with woman GM." *Worcester* (Mass.) *Telegram & Gazette,* February 19, 2004, D-1.

8. Johnson, Dean. "Controversial hosts spark new firestorm." *Boston Herald,* January 9, 2004, E-31.

9. Doyle.

10. Harmon.

11. Fantin, Linda. "Air wars: Salt Lake City radio stations battling for sports listeners." *Salt Lake Tribune,* June 9, 2002, C-1.

12. Zelkovich, Chris. "Want nasty talk radio?" *Toronto Star,* November 28, 2003, E-1.

13. Chad, Norman. "Criticizing Orioles a nightly ritual on Baltimore's call-in radio shows." *Washington Post,* July 17, 1987, B-2.

14. Conrad, Mark. "Malicious sports talk radio?" *Mark's Sportslaw News.* Accessed July 27, 2004. Available at http://www.sportslawnews.com/archive/articles%201999/Lindros.html.

15. Fires, Rick. "Call-in criticism can take toll on players, coaches." *Arkansas Democrat-Gazette,* August 13, 2000, C-9; Brown, Scott. "What's all the talk about? Brevard's sports fans keep in touch through radio shows." *Florida Today,* February 3, 2004, 1-D.

16. Cotey, John C. "In protest of talk radio." *St. Petersburg Times,* February 28, 2003, C-2.

17. *Outside the Lines.* ESPN television program. Video recording. 1994.

18. Fantin.

19. Tierney.

20. Caesar, Dan. "Hosts of sports-talk shows should follow a few basics." *St. Louis Post-Dispatch,* May 29, 2004, Sports, 3.

21. Ganzert, Charles F. "Narrowcasting." In *Museum of Broadcast Communications Encyclopedia of Radio,* Volume 2, edited by Christopher H. Sterling, 985-986. New York: Fitzroy Dearborn, 2004.

22. Fantin.

23. Ganzert.

24. Eastman, Susan Tyler. "Sportscasters." In *Museum of Broadcast Communications Encyclopedia of Radio,* Volume 3, edited by Christopher H. Sterling, 1311-1320. New York: Fitzroy Dearborn, 2004.

25. Huff, W.A. Kelly and Christopher H. Sterling. "AM Radio." In *Museum of Broadcast Communications Encyclopedia of Radio,* Volume 3, edited by Christopher H. Sterling, 83-85. New York: Fitzroy Dearborn, 2004.

26., Ellis, Sandra L. "All news format." In *Museum of Broadcast Communications Encyclopedia of Radio,* Volume 1, edited by Christopher H. Sterling, 37-40. New York: Fitzroy Dearborn, 2004.

27. Ellis, Sandra L. and Ed Shane. "Talk radio." In *Museum of Broadcast Communications Encyclopedia of Radio,* Volume 3, edited by Christopher H. Sterling, 1369-1374. New York: Fitzroy Dearborn, 2004.

28. Sandomir, Richard. "It's talk tumult: ESPN vs. WFAN." *New York Times,* August 7, 2001, D-6; "Inductees, The Jewish Sports Hall of Fame: Bill Mazer." Accessed July 7, 2003. Available at http://www.jewishsports.org/html/inductees_m_0.html.

29. Hinckley, David. "Big town replay sports and the sporting life in New York City: All Sports WFAN." *New York Daily News,* July 9, 2003, 23.

30. Petrozello, D. "AM savors sound of success." *Broadcasting and Cable,* October 10, 1994, 45-47; Ditingo, V.M. *The Remaking of Radio.* Boston: Focal Press, 1995.

31. Allen, Craig and Christopher H. Sterling. "WNBC." In *Museum of Broadcast Communications Encyclopedia of Radio,* Volume 3, edited by Christopher H. Sterling, 1542-1543. New York: Fitzroy, 2004.

32. Brown, Scott. "What's all the talDearbornk about? Brevard's sports fans keep in touch through radio shows." *Florida Today,* February 3, 2004.

33. Hinckley.

34. Adams, Russell. "Sports talk radio: On the air and on a roll." *Street and Smith's Sports Business Journal* 6(41), February 2, 2004.

35. Battema, Douglas L. "Sports on radio." In *Museum of Broadcast Communications Encyclopedia of Radio,* Volume 3, edited by Christopher H. Sterling, 1320-1823. New York: Fitzroy Dearborn, 2004.

36. Adams.

37. Petrozello; Ditingo.

38. Battema.

39. "Frequently asked questions." Available at: ESPNRadio.com. Accessed July 20, 2004.

40. "Ratings." *Radio and Records.* Available at http://www.radioandrecords.com/RRRatings. Accessed July 26, 2005.

41. Battema.

42. Adams.

43. Ibid.

44. Ibid.

45. Ibid.

46. Eastman.

47. Brown.

48. Libit, Daniel. "For one Saturday, no place like Rome: Nearly 10,000 show at the Alliant Center to see the syndicated sports-talk show host." *Wisconsin State Journal,* December 8, 2002, D-1.

Chapter 1

KTCK, "The Ticket," Dallas-Fort Worth: "Radio by the Everyman, for the Everyman"

J. M. Dempsey

When KTCK, 1310 AM "The Ticket"—Dallas's highest-rated, and oldest, sports-talk station—took the air in 1994, it earnestly endeavored to cover the local sports scene, with a little bit of postmodern, Seinfeldian attitude. It wasn't long, however, before the attitude tail began to wag the sports dog. Today, The Ticket is all irony, all the time. Oh, yes, they also talk about sports, between hip takes on rock music, movies, and, most of all, sex. It's all carefully calculated to satisfy the discerning tastes of the twenty-five- to fifty-four-year-old male.

In the highly fragmented world of major-market radio, a successful station need only capture a tiny slice of the overall audience. In Dallas-Fort Worth, the nation's fifth largest radio market, urban (hip-hop, R&B) station KKDA-FM consistently scores the number-one position among listeners age twelve and up with about 6 percent of the audience. No station comes close to pleasing all listeners; indeed, to attempt to do so would be a disastrous mistake. So it is not surprising that The Ticket—owned by Susquehanna Radio Corporation—has its detractors:

> I'm a 43-year-old male, and I listen to talk radio constantly. Except for Norm [Hitzges, late-morning Ticket host], The Ticket sucks! That's just inane trash. It's just boring prattle. So they have an opinion—so what? [The Ticket prides itself on

doi:10.1300/5335_02

"HSOs"—hot sports opinions.] They don't have the clarity of thought to allow them to express the REASON for that opinion. And really, who cares what their opinion is? They're all assholes![1]

But The Ticket has successfully carved out a niche that allows it to claim the top spot in the ratings for adult males: "The Ticket succeeds like it does because it never takes sports or itself too seriously. It's radio by the everyman for the everyman."[2]

The Ticket's faithful listeners, known as P-1s ("first-preference" listeners whose primary station is KTCK), strongly identify with the station and its personalities. Indeed, by identifying its listeners with the radio-ratings term "P-1" (otherwise unknown to the listeners), The Ticket uses a deliberate strategy of creating a virtual community of adult men joined together by their common interests, including The Ticket itself.

The sports-talk format enjoys an audience that is passionate about sports. The loyalty that listeners feel for their teams is often transferred to the local sports-talk stations, leading to higher-than-average time-spent-listening numbers and making the format attractive to advertisers.[3] Nationally syndicated sports-talk host Jim Rome, asked to describe his audience, said: "I think they are rabid. I think they are passionate. I think they are loyal."[4]

Social-identity theory[5] explains how individuals attach part of their identity to the groups to which they belong. The related self-categorization theory[6] further describes how people at times identify themselves as unique individuals and at other times as members of groups, and that each identity is equally meaningful. Each theory helps to explain the success of The Ticket.

FIGURE 1.1. KTCK logo.

In the context of radio, one study found that workers in the "textile belt" of the South during the period between 1929 and 1934 who lived in close proximity to radio stations had a greater sense of group identity and were more likely to strike. The study found that radio messages helped to shape the workers' sense of collective experience.[7]

These theories have often been used to show the power of group identity in a sports context. For example, Platow and colleagues (1999) found that fans of a team are more likely to make charitable donations to solicitors who identify themselves as fans of the same team.[8] Hirt and Zillman (1992) found that fans' perceptions of their own competencies are affected by their teams' fortunes, with some fans perceiving themselves as less capable following losses by their favorite teams.[9] On the other hand, End et al.[10] (2002), Lee[11] (1985), and Cialdini et al.[12] (1976) have studied the psychology of sports fans "basking in the reflected glory" of their favorite teams.

As with college and professional sports teams, The Ticket engenders strong identification among its listeners. It does this by conjuring a community of listeners joined not only by their interests, but also by attitudes and a common vernacular unique to the station.

* * *

Each weekday morning, perched atop a sleek office tower in tony, uptown Dallas, a radio odd couple named Dunham and Miller (also known as "the Musers" for their oddly philosophical bent; see Figure 1.2) help thousands of sleepy P-1s start their days with a heavy dose of sarcasm-laced sports japery. To be fair, it is Craig "Junior" Miller who specializes in the sideways remark. Junior is the originator of the one of The Ticket's most popular "bits" of fanciful irony: "The Girl on TV Who is So Good Looking We Need To Watch Out For Her Because She's So Good Looking." Junior is tall, lean, athletic, and decidedly single. His partner George (sometimes known as "Jub Jub") Dunham, is tall, bearlike, agreeably ponderous in bearing and manner, and decidedly married. As the pair's station bio explains: "George is married with three sons. Junior is single with three girlfriends." Dunham and Miller are lifelong friends, and started working together in radio at the University of North Texas station, KNTU-FM, during the early 1980s.[13]

FIGURE 1.2. "The Musers," KTCK, "The Ticket," Dallas-Fort Worth: (left to right) George Dunham, Gordon Keith, and Craig Miller. Courtesy KTCK.

"There's a lot of diversity in our talent," KTCK general manager Dan Bennett said. "George and Craig are very different people. George is the settled-down, married guy with kids, and Craig isn't [laughing at his understatement]. If all we did was hire a bunch of guys who were all alike, it wouldn't be a very dynamic show."[14]

Dunham said:

> There are people who connect to me who don't connect to Craig. And there are people who connect to Craig who don't connect to me. Craig will say something and I'll say, "Gee, I don't know where Craig's coming from with that. I don't have much to add to this conversation." But the single guy, who doesn't have three kids like I do, does. The next day, if I talk about what a beating Little League Baseball can be, the nineteen-year-old may say, "Well, this is boring," but the dad who's slumped over the wheel because he was up until ten-thirty coaching baseball the night before can relate to that.
>
> Sometimes it almost sounds contrived that he takes this stance and I take that stance, but it's just that way. I don't see things the way he sees them. It's funny: We're really unique in

that most radio talk-show co-hosts have not been friends for twenty years. We used to see things exactly the same. We thought U2 was the spokesman for our generation, and we were going to change the world.

Dunham said creativity has always been an important part of his and Miller's success going back to their college days. "No one would call," George remembered of their college-radio talk show.

So we would "order" phone calls from the other guy. I'd host one week, and Craig would host the next. And before the other person would leave the station, we'd say, "All right, I want a concerned country guy asking about the North Texas defense, I want an older guy asking about the Cowboys, and I want a young guy asking about the Mavericks." They would be left on carts [tapes], and we'd say, "All right, let's go to the phones. Mike in Denton . . ." "Hey, how you doing, enjoy the show." "Thanks." "My question is . . ." It was ridiculous.[15]

* * *

The Ticket's environs are very much what its listeners would imagine. The office is businesslike, yet decidedly casual, unquestionably male dominated. Dallas-area sports memorabilia is abundant—an autographed Michael Irvin Cowboys jersey hangs framed on one wall, a give-away Texas Rangers replica jersey is tossed haphazardly over the top of a cubicle, a high school football helmet sits on the floor by someone's desk. A full-page *Dallas Morning News* "High Profile" article on Dunham and Miller looks out from a metal frame. Newspaper sports pages, sports magazines, and classic rock LPs are scattered everywhere. A personal photo of Alice Cooper is proudly displayed on someone's desk.

Still, Bennett said the casual attitude conveyed on The Ticket is deceptive.

"I think they [listeners] would be surprised to know how much the guys prepare," he said.

This is the hardest-working on-air staff I've ever been around. When people listen to The Ticket, they think it's a bunch of guys shooting from the hip and it's anything but. It's really what we like to call sometimes "organized chaos." But there's a tremendous amount of organization that goes into it. Our guys get here hours and hours before their airshift, and put in tons of time before and after their airshift in preparation. There are a lot of people who think we just wing it, and that's not true.

In the control room, a corporate message from parent company Susquehanna hangs above the window looking into the announcer's booth where Dunham and Miller reside: "It begins and ends with product." But the solemn admonition is overwhelmed by the flippant tone of a collection of bumper stickers that adorn the room: "Support National Thong Awareness Week" . . . "The problem is Jerry [Jones, Dallas Cowboys owner]." A display box for miniatures mounted on the wall is festooned with unwound audiotape. Among the throwaway sports novelties and buttons in the boxes, a small photo of a busty blonde with her teeth blacked out.

Board operator "Big Strong" Jeremy is the supreme master of a digital world. (In The Ticket's endlessly ironic world, Jeremy is often addressed as "Big Strong.") He sits surrounded by an array of five computer terminals. A virtual audio meter constantly pulses, green and yellow, while seconds resolutely tick away on a digital clock. By touching one of the multicolored boxes on a screen, he can instantly fire off a "drop," in Ticket parlance a rapid-fire nonsequitur that can be lobbed into any discussion at any appropriate (or inappropriate) time. "I just know where they [the drops] are," Jeremy said. "I can find 'em quickly if I have to."[16]

George said The Ticket's distinctive drops, like everything else on the Musers and the other shows, have evolved. Dunham reflected:

It just started with contrived movie clips, funny sounds, stuff out of the production library. I don't know when it started that we would play something that, when you took it out of context and played it, it sounded really weird. That's why you always hear "mark." If someone says something that's really strange, we started marking it and playing it back, basically to make that person look as bad as possible. If you do it right, it sounds like the guy is saying it live, and then everyone goes, "My gosh, why would he say *that*?" It's part of the madness.

A favorite drop is the distinctive voice of The Ticket's late-morning host Norm Hitzges. Norm, a veteran Dallas broadcaster in his fifties, is much older and more earnest than the other Ticket hosts, and faithfully sticks to sports as a topic for discussion, often building elaborate statistical arguments for his points. Hitzges' high-pitched, giggling laugh is unmistakable, and turns up as a drop in programs around the clock on The Ticket.

Jeremy, a heavy-set but powerful-looking young man, has his own mike and inserts his own comments from time to time, as does producer Mike "Fernando" Fernandez, who sits at a table to Jeremy's right, surrounded by this day's local papers, current magazines, and sports media guides. Fernando will spend a good deal of the morning on the phone, making last-minute arrangements for show segments and fielding calls from listeners.

It is George who takes the lead in directing the show. The Ticket is enormously self-referential—the quirks and foibles of its hosts and announcers are eagerly pounced upon by other personalities, and endlessly ridiculed. As this morning's proceedings are beginning, George ambles into the control room to consult with Jeremy. "George, what were you looking for from yesterday?" Jeremy asks. "When Rich [Phillips, "Ticker" sports-headline announcer] jumps on me about the cigarette thing," George replies. Told the recording has been found, George responds, "We'll use it at six-ten."

On this summer Friday, the Dallas Stars' season has ended with an early exit from the NHL playoffs, the Dallas Mavericks have recently been ousted from the NBA playoffs, the Texas Rangers are in the middle of one of their season-killing losing streaks, and the Dallas Cowboys are weeks away from going to training camp. And so Dunham and Miller will operate in free-association mode for much of the morning. But, in reality, a good deal of planning, or at least premeditation, goes into what may seem a stream-of-consciousness approach to the casual listener.

Dunham said:

> I'll see something or experience something and I'll write it down or keep in my mind: "We've got to talk about that." I have a notebook that I keep for the show and I'll write some things down, but a lot of it's just mental. Yesterday, I knew what at least three-fourths of our show was going to be today. I knew we were going to do that thing on Rich.

* * *

"That thing on Rich" is a postmortem of the previous day's verbal dust-up between Phillips and Dunham, the playback that George had earlier arranged with Jeremy. The segment is seemingly unrelated to anything that might be of any direct interest to the P-1s, and only tangentially related to sports, yet somehow listeners find this sort of endless carping between the station's on-air personalities deeply entertaining. This particular episode involved Dunham's needling of Phillips, a NASCAR fan and a smoker, for NASCAR switching from Winston cigarettes to Nextel as the major sponsor for its series of stock-car races. "Was it just me, or did Rich bite my head off yesterday?" George asks.

[Recording from previous day's program is replayed:]

GEORGE: I think Rich is bitter today.

JUNIOR: Why?

GEORGE: Because the news is sinking in that there will be no more free cigarettes at NASCAR events.

RICH: [in a testy tone of voice] They don't have free cigarettes at NASCAR events.

GEORGE: They do to the media when you go out there.

RICH: No, they don't anymore.

GEORGE: Oh, they don't?

RICH: [impatiently] How many NASCAR events have you covered, George?

GEORGE: Zero.

FERNANDO: [*Dallas Morning News* columnist] Tim Cowlishaw says they have free cigarettes in the press box at Daytona.

RICH: [wearily] Well, they don't do that at the Texas Motor Speedway [in Fort Worth].

GEORGE: Well, according to Rich, we haven't covered races, so therefore, we can't speculate.

RICH: That's right, you don't know what goes on out there [end of recording].

Now it is time for Junior to fan the flames of indignation:

JUNIOR: Whoa! Wow! Man, I don't remember that being that strong! Rich! [Drops: "Go to hell!" "Kiss my ass!" "Bite me!"]

GEORGE: I thought Rich and I were buds, and I was just joking around, and Rich just bites my head off.

JUNIOR: Man, I'll say!

GEORGE: It wasn't really that big a deal, but I just sensed a biting tone to Rich, and I thought, man, I wonder if Rich is mad at me for something I don't know about. So it bothered me throughout the day. . . . Well, I tune in later in the day, and I'm listening to "the Throwdown" [a segment on the "Bad Radio" show that features Phillips] . . . .

JUNIOR: [rapidly losing interest] Give me a gun. [Drop: gunshot] Missed.

JEREMY: Damn it.

Now George, though interrupted in mid-sentence by Junior and Jeremy, drops what passes for a bombshell in the endlessly self-referential world of The Ticket:

GEORGE: [with rising, incredulous Seinfeld-like inflection] . . . and I catch the end of a segment where Rich is talking about how he's quit smoking cigarettes!

JUNIOR: What?

JEREMY: What?

FERNANDO: What?

GEORGE: Yeah! And it made me feel better in one sense. I was like, oh, that's why he bit my head off when I brought up cigarettes this morning. Well, that's fine, that's cool. Then I thought, "Hey, wait a minute, if you're going to tell someone, why not tell us?" The show that you do everyday, from five-thirty to ten!

RICH: It's because I have segments to burn this week [on the "Throwdown"], buddy!

GEORGE: You can burn this at six-ten [a.m.] and at two-ten in the afternoon!

FERNANDO: It's good to recycle, buddy [indeed, The Ticket's hosts thrive on "repurposed" bits from other shows].

RICH: Well, we're recycling now and I knew it would make it back around the next morning.

GEORGE: Well, that is BS, that's what that is, and you should have told us on, like, Monday. I swear to you, I would have tried to be really supportive toward you. I think it's a good thing.

RICH: I've been playing it very understated because today will be day number thirteen and I've had one cigarette in the last thirteen days [drop: polite applause].[17]

The bit goes on for many more minutes. Such self-absorbed diversions, which not many years ago would have been considered the height of self-indulgent unprofessional broadcasting, are a staple of Ticket programming. The P-1s have rewarded The Ticket by consistently making it the top-rated station among twenty-five- to fifty-four-year-old men in the Dallas-Fort Worth market. In three of the five quarterly ratings periods from winter 2003 through winter 2004, KTCK was number one among men twenty-five to fifty-four, pulling as high as an 8.5 percent share of the audience. It was number two in the other two periods.[18]

Said George following the show:

> You've got to understand, the only thing sportswise that's going on right now is baseball. So today was a little bit unusual in that we goofed off a little more today than we normally do. This morning we probably had three segments that were not sports that are normally sports. Our first segment of the day is almost always sports. But today, there was just nothing going on. Now, for *BaD Radio* [The Ticket's ironically named early-afternoon show] when they go in today, they may have seen something in last night's Rangers game that really is a talking point for them. I'd say normally we're about 80 percent sports. Now the 20 percent sometimes seems like more because it gets more laughs and gets more reaction. Sports are our basis, but we're in the entertainment business too.

Bennett said casual observers misunderstand The Ticket and sports-radio. Sports-talk listeners do not "watch sports sixteen hours a day, eat Cheetos, drink beer and live in their mother's basement," he said. Very few listeners, he said, "care who the backup fullback at SMU is."[19]

Indeed, the GM said it is critical that sports-talk stations take a light approach to sports. He said:

> We have figured out the formula in sports-talk radio that you have to do more than "X's and O's." If you've ever been to a sporting event with a bunch of guys they do more than sit around and talk about statistics. They notice the women that walk by, they like to drink beer. They enjoy the ambience that is sports. We've tried to capture that on the air. We've certainly been criticized by the so-called "sports purists," but I think we've proved them wrong.

Dunham said:

> In my travels, I've probably listened to three or four-dozen all-sports stations and I've not heard one do what we do, because we have a tight-knit group, and for the most part we've been together for a long time. There's a real fraternity to it.
>
> Probably the thing I'm most proud of here at The Ticket is we are the only morning sports-talk show that's number one with men twenty-five to fifty-four. We've done it twelve out of the last sixteen [ratings] books. There's a ton of morning sports shows out there, but none of them have done it.

* * *

KTCK Program Director Jeff Catlin said The Ticket grew organically:

> In the beginning of the Ticket, we didn't really do anything consciously. We didn't know if we were going to have any listeners at all, let alone be able to create some group of them on purpose. But early on, we did find out that we were on to something. We didn't work to mold our group of listeners into P-1s; they did it themselves.

Catlin said the connection between The Ticket's hosts and the listeners is genuine:

> What I do believe happened, is that our hosts and our listeners were of the same ilk. There were no dividing lines between who was on the air and who was listening. At events and remotes, our hosts were not only accessible, but we enjoyed hanging out with the listeners and for some reason they enjoyed hanging out with us. That is where the bond began and continued.

The Ticket is relatively free from the pervasive influence of consultants, Catlin said. "We don't really use any consultants in the traditional sense of the word. We are programmed locally and all programming and business decisions are made by the local program director, sales manager and general manager."

Even The Ticket's trademark use of the term "P-1s," while an obvious reference to ratings jargon, came about fortuitously. Catlin said:

> The term "P-1" came out on the air once and just stuck. It was not planned, and in fact, consultants told us we shouldn't use radio/ratings terms on the air, because our listeners weren't smart enough to get it. Well, they were wrong! "P-1s" is a standard term on the station that we know has been copied (less successfully) by other stations across the country. But you can't manufacture it, it has to be real.[20]

* * *

The listener to The Ticket must learn a special vocabulary unique to the station and its listeners. The terms have developed naturally over the station's ten year history, as distinctive words and phrases casually dropped once or twice by hosts have been adopted and enshrined in the station's everyday parlance. Ticket-speak conveys the station's ironic, "everyman" attitude, and is echoed by those who identify themselves as P-1s. The "Ticktionary" is posted on the station's Web page:

- "Burnin' Segments: This is what we do all day. Whatever it takes, it's all about taking up time and getting through the day."

- "Emergency Brake: When an action, comment or statement totally disrupts the natural flow of the show, it's considered an 'emergency brake.'"
- "Failed Bit Warning: When conditions are right for a failed bit, the National Weather Service might find it necessary to issue a 'Failed Bit Warning' so the P-1s, P-2s, and P-3s can take appropriate action."
- "Man Crush: One male being in awe of another male for any reason."
- "Wheels-off: When something goes terribly wrong, the wheels are off."
- "Whip: When something or someone 'beats you down' [another Ticket term that means a particular subject has gotten tiresome], it's a 'whip.'"[21]

* * *

So you don't forget the station you're listening to, write it down someplace safe—like the band of your underwear. Sports Radio 1310, The Ticket. (Station identifier at start of a segment)

Coming out of a spot break, which—including the "Ticker" and the sultry-female-voiced "Stick It Up Your Tailpipe" traffic report, typically can last eight minutes or more—the show's witty observer of current affairs, Gordon "Gordo" Keith weighs in.

Keith brings a talent for satire and mimicry to the show. He mimics the voices of Dallas-area sports figures with dead-on accuracy. He once wrote and performed a skit in which former Cowboys quarterback Quincy Carter and owner Jerry Jones sat together in a hot tub. The "fake" Jones—notorious in Dallas for his ego and alleged visits to the plastic surgeon—repeatedly asked Carter if he, Jones, had the body of a man in his sixties. Like many of Keith's bits, it flirted with the perverse.[22]

It's Gordo's role to interpret the "real world" (as distinguished from the world of sports and popular culture) to the P-1s. Junior introduces Gordo's philosophical "Observation Deck."

With schlocky lounge-style music playing underneath, Gordo wryly reports on a study in which those responding in eleven countries said the United States is an "arrogant superpower," an "antagonistic bully" that is a "greater threat than North Korea."

"So are we a bully to them when these countries call us when they have a natural disaster? The billions and billions we give in aid and supplies and food, is that arrogant?" George asks.

Gordo replies: "It is human nature to get what you can from someone and then flip them off as you run away if you don't like them."

"So is that what you've done to management all these years?" George rejoinders.

"Absolutely, I take their money then flip them off," Gordo replies. "Big Strong" Jeremy lobs in a drop (flavored with a heavy rural twang): "All these candy-asses that don't stand up for our country need to get the hell out."

*   *   *

During the previous break, George once again had entered the control room and asked Jeremy, "Hey, can you find the girl in the next seven minutes who got everything wrong?" He's referring to a live bit from the day before, somewhat like Jay Leno's "Jaywalking" segments, in which a young woman, questioned by Gordo, spectacularly strikes out on a series of oh-so-easy questions.

GORDO: How many stripes are on our American flag?

WOMAN: I'm going to say . . . 10?

GORDO: Who is on Mount Rushmore?

WOMAN: I don't know.

GORDO: How many stars are in our solar system?

WOMAN: I don't know.

GORDO: Just hazard a guess.

WOMAN: I'm going to say . . . 20?

"The scary thing about this is, their votes count just as much as your vote," Junior muses.

"How did she make it through third grade?" George marvels.

*   *   *

On this sluggish sports day, Dunham and Miller dutifully address a few sports topics, including the annual arrival of *Texas Football* magazine on the newsstands, the traditional sign that football season is once again in sight, and the possibility of Utah Jazz star Karl Malone joining the Mavericks.

George quotes an online column by ESPN's Stuart Scott: "I guarantee any NBA vet who has achieved individual greatness but doesn't have a ring would sacrifice points and the spotlight to get a championship." Dunham uses Scott's column as a springboard for a discussion on Malone and the Mavericks.

Noting that Malone would probably have such a decision to make, George asks: "Generally, I think most athletes would play for the ring, especially if they've had a long career and made a lot of money. But, Fernando asked me this question: Can you name the player in any pro sport who's taken significantly less money to play for a title? I couldn't off hand."

After mulling over the late-career moves of NBA stars Bob McAdoo and Bill Walton, Junior diffidently replies: "I'm sure that it's happened. I can't come up with it." The topic generates a full bank of phone calls from listeners, most of which do not get past producer Fernando. "Really? I'll check that out, thanks. . . . Well, he got traded so his contract was the same. . . . He never played for the Bulls. You got that one wrong." No conclusions are reached, but the segment is filled in reasonably engaging fashion. (For the record, Malone ultimately signed with the perennial champion Los Angeles Lakers, making only a fraction of what he had been making previously with Utah.)

By and large, The Ticket is milder in its criticism of sports figures than many other sports-talk stations around the country. Dunham is sympathetic to pro athletes who get harshly treated on the air. He said:

> Some of the criticism [of sports-talk] is legitimate. Some of the things that are said on sports-talk radio about athletes or coaches are not fair. I think I would be frustrated by it. A lot of the stuff I hear on other stations is really manufactured. [Adopting a gruff, phony broadcast voice] "Hey, let's get on the air and rip on this guy." If we don't really feel something, we're not going to say it. As much goofing around as we do, we try not to start rumors. If we are going to talk about sports, we try to be accurate about it. Like if we get an e-mail, "Hey, I saw a prominent Dallas Cowboy at a topless bar last night," we won't use that. We have boundaries. Sometimes that may make for boring radio because we may not have much to say. Sometimes we say things to get a reaction, but usually the reaction we're looking for is laughter.

Dunham said the Musers and The Ticket achieved a higher standing with their listeners following the terrorist attacks of September 11, 2001. He reflected:

> I think September eleventh showed a lot of people that we are real. Whatever you think of what kind of people we are, that morning we reacted the same way that everyone else did. Two of us cried on the air. We were overcome by it. We were live on the air and watching those stinking buildings crash down. We didn't know if fifty thousand people were going to be killed or how many.

Fort Worth Star-Telegram broadcasting writer Robert Philpot commented: "I heard from a lot of people who thought that The Ticket gave the best radio coverage [of September eleventh]." *Dallas Observer* writer Eric Celeste praised The Ticket's "pitch perfect coverage of the terrorist tragedy: heartfelt, comforting, angry, honest."[23]
Dunham said:

> We still have people coming up to us and saying, "You know, I was listening that morning and I'll never forget it." I hate to bring it up, because I don't want to say, "Hey, that was our real coming-out party." We'd been around for a long time before that. But you talk about honesty and connection [with the listeners]. We connected with a lot of people that morning who probably didn't think we were capable of it.

* * *

The day's bland sports agenda will only take the Musers so far, and soon they move on to another deeply philosophical topic—Junior's theory that eating bagels absorbs intestinal gas. Junior has received an e-mail from P-1 "Sherman" on the subject:

GEORGE: In his [Junior's] little simple mind, he thinks it's just like dipping a bagel into a glass of water.

JUNIOR: It soaks up the acid or whatever in that gas-producing food makes you produce gas. . . . Well, Sherman the P-1 did an experiment. Four days eating the same food he eats every morning without a bagel, and four days, same food, with a bagel. And here are his findings . . .

GORDO: I don't want to hear the findings.

JUNIOR: The four days without a bagel: Day one, twelve farts.

GORDO: I'm out of here.

JUNIOR: Day two, eleven farts.

GEORGE: This is abrasive.

GORDO: Disgusting. That word is just shocking.

[Drop: WFAA-TV sports anchor and weekly Ticket host Dale Hansen: "My dog farts when I'm not in the house."]

Junior relates the results of the P-1's study ultimately showing a 14 percent decrease in bowel emissions after consuming a bagel for breakfast.

George said he's sometimes uneasy with being part of some of the more outrageous bits.

> As we want people to see us for what I think is honest on the air, where do you draw that line? I'm probably not the same person off-the-air that I am on-the-air. I probably say some things on the air that I wouldn't say otherwise. I'm not that type of person necessarily. I think that holds true for Gordon and Craig. Especially Gordon. He says outrageous things, but he's not going to act on them.

* * *

Getting ready for his daily "Muse in the News" segment, Gordon Keith sweeps into the control room to snag a Krispy Kreme doughnut from an open box and swap jibes with Big Strong Jeremy. "So who does 'Big Dick' [Hunter] have on his show tonight?" Keith asks.

"Porn-star Bob Crane's son," Jeremy ad libs, trading on Hunter's penchant for guests with connections to, if not outright involvement in, pornography on his show, *Big Dick's Wild Ass Circus*. For example, one guest was a female porn star who says she "partied" with two Dallas Stars all night before a playoff game.

With a kitschy 1960s Herb Alpert tune playing underneath the segment, Gordo reports the news that intelligence analysts now believe

Saddam Hussein is alive, in this summer prior to his ignominious capture in a "spider hole." "I came to that conclusion months ago when you two were trying to proclaim him dead. No way," Junior intones. "He's so alive it's not even funny. He's like a cockroach."

A report that an Ohio trucker had been arrested for helping al-Qaeda plan more terrorist attacks soon wanders into a fervent debate on the merits of the 1970s hit, "Convoy," as Jeremy quickly replaces the Tijuana Brass background music with C.W. McCall's novelty tune. Gordo is distracted. "Oh, listen to this song!" he exclaims. "It's a horrible song! Why do you like this?" Junior interjects.

Dunham gamely comes to the song's defense: "It was good for the time."

Junior: "It's so anemic!"

Keith replies: "No, it's powerful!" (He slips into a distorted citizens-band radio voice and free-associating 1970s Paul McCartney lyrics, "Hello, Uncle Albert and Auntie Gin, open the door now and let 'em in.")

"Thanks for listening to our continuing coverage of al-Qaeda activities," Junior tells the listeners.

A few days earlier, a Fort Worth woman had been arrested for putting her two small children out of the car and leaving them at a busy intersection. A listener's e-mail to Miller suggesting an alternative to "The Girl on TV Who is So Good Looking . . ." bit finds its way into the segment. The e-mail facetiously suggests a bit called: "'The-Girl-on-the-Lake-Worth-Highway-who-abandons-her - two -children-on-the- median-in-rush-hour-traffic-with-blatant-disregard - for -their-well-being-who's-so-good-looking-you've-got-to-watch-out-for-her-because-she's-so-good-looking.' See page two of the *Dallas Morning News* today in the Metro section."

Junior responds: "She did a very evil thing, there's no doubt about that. But is she not hot?"

George disapproves, but Gordo rebukes him: "If women can marry serial killers, can we just say some criminal is good looking, George? I want fairness for men in this case."

After stories about Iranian protestors setting themselves on fire (accompanied by the 1960s hit "Fire" by The Crazy World of Arthur Brown) and a Florida boy being killed by an alligator, the "Muse in the News" segment ends with the "WOWY (Which one would ya?)"

daily birthday segment. "We have a fifty-year-old and a thirty-six-year-old," Gordo advises George and Junior.

"All right, I'll take 36," Junior says, warily.

"Well, George, you'll be making love to the most beautiful song-bird in the world and hottest woman ever in rock and roll: Cyndi Lauper is fifty today. . . . And Junior, you're going to have to settle for the tore-up, ugly actress known as Nicole Kidman [again, a heavy dose of Ticket irony]. What a glorious, glorious morning this is."

Former KTCK program director Bruce Gilbert, sensitive to criticisms of an overemphasis on sex, said he believes many children don't understand the meaning of what's being said. "There is a way to talk about things so that if your 12-year-old son is listening, it goes over his head," Gilbert contended.[24]

Bennett said The Ticket hosts are on a very loose leash when it comes to sex talk.

> It becomes a matter of interpretation. Do we sometimes go up to the line? Absolutely. Have we occasionally stepped over it? Yeah. But you can't micromanage these guys to the point that I'm going to make them play every [comedy] bit for me so I can approve it first. You have to have a little bit of faith in what they're doing.

The Ticket, like many other sports-talk stations, hires beautiful young women, usually Dallas-area college students, to serve as "Ticketchicks" at station events.

In the niche-oriented environment of modern radio, Bennett said the audience essentially precensors The Ticket. Said Bennett:

> [We get complaints] occasionally, but not as often as you think. I think because people who tune into The Ticket know what to expect and they know it's going to be edgy with a little innuendo. Normally, not always, the complaints come from older people, the fifty-plus demo most of the time. We're not surprised by that. We're probably not doing it right if we don't get some complaints.

Compared to most other shows on The Ticket (for example, the nighttime show, *Big Dick's Wild Ass Circus*), the morning-drive Dunham and Miller show is mild. But George, the family man with three sons, admitted to a certain amount of discomfort over some of The Ticket's raunchier bits, even on his own show. He said:

> I hope they're not listening. I wouldn't recommend it for seven- or eight-year-olds, some of the subject matter we have. My oldest is sixteen now, and I think about it sometimes. Next year he'll be driving to school and listening to some of the things we're talking about. I probably feel a little more relaxed about it now because they're not as little.
>
> I've always tried to keep this separate from my home life. We don't talk about the station at our house. It's my job. It's paid the bills. It's hopefully going to give them a good education. I don't want them to do this. I'd rather them do something much more productive and respectable than this. It's great job, but it's a bad business.

*   *   *

Producer Mike Fernandez's job often requires him to make arrangements for the show on the fly. Stories on the former eighteen-year-old pitching phenom for the Texas Rangers, David Clyde, appear in today's local newspapers. Clyde pitched for the Rangers just days out of a Houston high school in 1973, giving them their first sell-out after moving to Texas from Washington, DC, and tonight, Clyde will return to Arlington to throw out the first pitch before the game with the Houston Astros.

Relying on his extensive collection of otherwise well-guarded phone numbers, Fernandez reaches former Ranger outfielder and general manager Tom Grieve, now a commentator on the team's local telecasts. "Tom, I'm wondering if you might have a couple of minutes to go on 'Dunham and Miller'?" Fernando asks Grieve. "Dynamite! I want you to talk about David Clyde."

The normally placid, amiable Grieve's voice rises as he remembers Clyde's mishandling by the Rangers. "The only reason David Clyde was pitching in the majors at 18 years old is because [Rangers owner] Bob Short needed the money," Grieve says with genuine outrage, thirty years after the event. Grieve remembered that Clyde fell into bad habits trying to fit in with his much-older veteran teammates, leading to a short and disappointing career.

Via text messages to Dunham and Miller, Fernando suggests questions for Grieve: "Was there any resentment [toward Clyde] on the part of the other players?" "Can something like this happen now or would the clubs protect the youngsters?" But the interview is flowing well, and George and Junior ignore the questions.

Quickly returning to the show's satiric tone, Miller notes that the Rangers and the Astros will be playing for the "Silver Boot" trophy in their relatively new interleague series.

"The most coveted trophy in sports," Junior notes solemnly.

"Next to the Stanley Cup," Gordo adds.

At the conclusion of the segment, Fernando returns to the phone. "Tom, what a powerful interview!" he exclaims. "Holy cow! We archive interviews for the end of the year. That's going on the tape."

George asserts: "We can be informative. We try to be balanced."

* * *

The Musers take relatively few listener phone calls, preferring to rely on their own innate ability to entertainingly comment on the events of the day. For one segment, however, George invites calls. He confides:

> I think it's a sign of getting older, but I've become fascinated with the products available to buy on television. The power wheelbarrow. That thing looks awesome! All those heavy things you carry in the wheelbarrow, and you start getting shake wheel, and you end up dumping them out. Not with the *power* wheelbarrow!

George goes on to say he's very happy with some knives he bought from a television ad.

"How often do I have to cut into a Coke can with a butcher knife?" Gordo asks.

"Our knives always went dull," George replies. "These knives stay sharp, and you can cut through a Coke can then slice up a tomato, just like that."

"Really, and have Coke-tomato salad," Gordo deadpans.

A caller informs the Musers: "My dad ordered those knives. They're great knives, but when he got the credit-card bill, the shipping and handling was one hundred, twenty-five dollars."

"Well, they're dangerous to handle, so you pay extra," Junior helpfully explains.

George reflected:

> This is how we've done it from the start. We'll talk about something that may not be sports. It's "top-of-mind" with us. That's how people think. There are big sports fans who don't always talk about sports when they're with their friends. I think if you're forcing yourself to talk sports, sometimes you're painting yourself into a corner. I want to talk about something that the average male eighteen to thirty-five wants to talk about in the morning. Most of the time it's sports. But sometimes it's, "Hey, you ever bought anything on TV before?"
>
> I think some of our best segments are when we hit on something that people think about but don't talk about. Kind of like *Seinfeld*. How about the guy who talks too close to you?"

* * *

Some of Gordon Keith's satirical segments require a considerable amount of preparation. Moments before a skit featuring a confrontation between The Ticket's resident sports psychologist, "Dr. Carlton Maxwell" and the station's elderly maintenance man, "Clarence Murphy," Gordo first enters the control room to consult with Jeremy. He's prepared various sound effects and voices in advance. They can be activated at the touch of the computer screen. "Here's what we're going to do," Gordo says. "Start with the 'door open' and 'applause.' Throw the 'old-man' voice in, and make it sound natural. We're going to fail, but we'll try," he says jauntily. The connection to sports is tenuous, but critical.

Often, Keith's bits feature satirical representations of real-life sports-scene characters, such as Dallas Cowboys owner Jones. Taking part in a football trivia quiz, Jones, as expertly portrayed by Keith, couldn't name legendary Cowboys coach Tom Landry, except as "that guy I fired." In another bit, Keith portrays former Cowboy Deion Sanders, claiming Jesus told him to pay just $1,500 of a $4,500 car repair bill. He explains: "In Revelations it says: Do not trust a hay-sucking hick to restore your car."

Miller intros the bit: "He teaches psychology at the University of Texas at Dallas, right here in the Metroplex: It's our old buddy, Dr. Carlton Maxwell. . . . You are here today to discuss the Rangers' los-ing skid, they've lost sixteen of eighteen. What kind of psychological effect does that have on a team?"

"It has an *appreciable* effect," Keith, as "Dr. Maxwell," says in a fey voice. "I'm so proud of this [holding up a media guide as if it's a new book], we're hoping it will overtake *Living History,* the book by Hillary Clinton. This is called *Losing Sixteen Out of Eighteen: A Sea-son in Hell.*"

"How timely!" George marvels.

"It's really only good for today," Junior observes.

"That's right, it has a very short shelf life, so pick it up today, we want to pass a million," "Dr. Maxwell" replies.

The segment ends as maintenance man "Clarence Murphy" bursts in and insults "Dr. Maxwell." "Why do we have to have some 'bum lover' on a manly show like this?" Keith-as-"Murphy," demands, in a coarse, "Yosemite Sam"-type voice.

Jeremy drops in a prerecorded line of Keith speaking in "Dr. Maxwell's" decidedly prissy voice: "Sir, I'm offended by that."

On the air, the fight that ensues between "Murphy" and "Dr. Maxwell" comes off smoothly, with no seams showing. The skit ends with Gordo banging a chair on the floor, shouting off mike, and slam-ming the door as he exits.

"Boy, that's oil and water," George concludes.

The Ticket and other raucous sports-talk stations often are criti-cized by real psychologists and other critics for their lack of political, or social, correctness. Is a character like "Dr. Maxwell" a reaction to that? "Sometimes it inspires us to do characters like that," Dunham said. "To kind of poke fun back at them. We've come up with a lot of characters that annoy us: The generic white businessman, the over-talker, the overexplainer. Characters that you meet every day."

Corby Davidson, a member of Greg Williams' and Mike Rhyner's popular KTCK afternoon-drive show *The Hardline* (motto: "Stay Hard"), is known for his performance-art interviews of unsuspecting athletes, in which he satirizes foolish reporters. Sample question from Davidson's "Obvious Man": "Is it just me, or are most of the running backs around here black?"

Gordo's skit with "Dr. Maxwell" and "Clarence" is followed by an interview with the venerable Dave Campbell, the distinguished, highly respected publisher of *Texas Football* magazine, the "bible" of the sport in the Lone Star State. George laughed,

> Sometimes it sounds like you're really grinding the gears. You go from "Clarence" and "Dr. Carlton Maxwell" getting in a fist fight to Dave Campbell. That's just weird. But it's had five or six minutes [during a spot break] to breathe a little bit, and then we're back into it.

* * *

The success of The Ticket is as improbable as it is remarkable. Critics have noted that since it went on the air in 1994 with "serious" sports journalist Skip Bayless as its original morning-show host, the station has gradually drifted from "sports talk" to "guy talk." But thousands of listeners in Dallas-Fort Worth have responded with a passionate devotion to the station. When The Ticket's on-air personalities staged a "Charity Challenge on Ice" hockey game at Dallas' Reunion Arena, 17,000 fans turned out. "It's almost like a cult," media buyer Joan Tibbets said.[25]

The Ticket's move away from pure sports-talk has attracted competition from two other stations in the Dallas-Fort Worth market, KESN 103.3 FM (an affiliate of the ESPN Radio network) and KFXR 1190 AM, an outlet of the Fox Sports Radio network. Tibbets noted: "My 46-year-old husband is sort of my focus group of one. He listens [to The Ticket] all the time, but he can be put off by some of the more juvenile antics that go on."

There may be a market in Dallas-Fort Worth for more sports-intensive radio talk, but, at the time of this writing, KESN and KJOI had made barely a dent in the Dallas-Fort Worth ratings. "History says there's not that great of a market for pure sports talk," Dunham noted.

The success of The Ticket is not easy to duplicate. Gilbert left KTCK for ESPN Radio in 2002. ESPN radio is more tightly focused on sports than The Ticket, but Gilbert still admires KTCK's approach. Before leaving, Gilbert said that The Ticket's format works primarily because of the on-air talent. The fact that the hosts are from the area and are personal, revealing, and passionate about what they do contributes to the station's success, he added. This may seem facile to other stations, but Gilbert contended that trying to do a "one-eighty" and changing formats to duplicate what The Ticket does simply "doesn't work, especially if people already have a reputation in the market for one thing or another."[26]

Bennett said The Ticket may have dominated the male-oriented radio market in Dallas-Fort Worth for a long time, but he knows the station can never afford to prop its feet up and relax. He said:

> One of the things we've learned is that you have to constantly reinvent. I think our guys have understood that. With a male-oriented audience, you have to understand men. An example I used with the guys the other day, if you think about it, the male audience is one of the most fickle there is.

> I picked up the paper the other day and found out that Halle Barry, arguably one of the most beautiful women in the world, is divorcing her husband because she found out he was cheating on her. Now think about that. Here's a guy who's married to Halle Barry, and he's bored! Guys are fickle and they get bored incredibly easily.

> Every year when we put on our "Ticketstock" event, which is our big signature event, we don't lay the room out with the booths and displays the same every year. There's a reason we do that. We don't want guys to walk in and say, "Oh, yeah, just like last year." I think there are a lot of radio stations that aim at men that don't understand that dynamic. You have to reinvent, you've got to keep it new, and if you don't, they get bored and go away.

* * *

KTCK, The Ticket, has been successful in creating an environment in which listeners, as described in social-identity and self-categorization theories, become part of a social group known as "P-1s," faithful listeners to The Ticket.

One explanation for the success of The Ticket is the apparent lack of contrivance in its programming. As Program Director Jeff Catlin said: "We didn't work to mold our group of listeners into P-1s; they did it themselves. . . . There were no dividing lines between who was on the air and who was listening." The organic nature of The Ticket's programming makes it difficult to emulate, as Catlin observed.

As General Manager Dan Bennett observed, twenty-four- to fifty-four-year-old men (The Ticket's demographic) talk about many things besides sports, even at a sporting event. The Ticket has successfully captured the "ambience"—the attitude—of casual "guy talk" in its programming.

As previously noted, KTCK's morning hosts, George Dunham and Craig Miller, grew up in the Dallas area, indeed, they are best friends from their college days. Most of the other hosts also have deep North Texas roots. Older on-air personalities such as Norm Hitzges, and Mike Rhyner and Greg Williams (the "Hardline"), if not Dallas-area natives, have spent almost all of their adult lives in the area. This familiarity with the area is likely another important factor in the audience member's tendency to identify themselves as "P-1s," faithful listeners.

Unlike many other sports-talk stations, KTCK has managed to find success without holding the rights to broadcast the games of any big-league sports franchise. The station broadcasts Southern Methodist University football games and Dallas Desperados Arena Football League games. KTBK, 1700 kHz., licensed to Sherman, north of Texas, simulcasts The Ticket programming, but provides broadcasts of the Frisco RoughRiders Class AA minor-league baseball games.

Dunham reckoned that, in the final analysis, sport is life and life is sport, at least in the virtual community of the airwaves known as The Ticket: "It sounds real corny, but we talk about life. We're all trying to make a buck, and if we're dads, we're trying to take care of our kids and we hope for the best. We kind of talk about that."

NOTES

1. Posting on "dfw.general" newsgroup. Accessed June 24, 2004. Available at http://groups.google.com/groups?hl=en&lr=&ie=UTF-8&group=dfw.general.

2. "dfw.general" newsgroup.

3. Eastman, Susan Tyler. "Sportscasters." In *Museum of Broadcast Communications Encyclopedia of Radio,* Volume 3, edited by Christopher H. Sterling, 1311-1320. New York: Fitzroy Dearborn, 2004.

4. Wolfley, Bob. "Rome has a take on many issues." *Milwaukee Journal-Sentinel,* C-2, December 6, 2002.

5. Tajfel, H. and Turner, J.C. "An integrative theory of intergroup conflict." In *The Social Psychology of Intergroup Relations,* edited by W.G. Austin and S. Worschel. Monterey, CA: Brooks-Cole, 1979.

6. Turner, J.C., Hogg, M.A., Oakes, P.J., Reicher, S.D., and Wetherell, M.S. *Rediscovering the Social Group: A Self-Categorization Theory.* Oxford: Blackwell, 1987.

7. Roscigno, Vincent J. and Danaher, William F. "Media and mobilizations: The case of radio and southern textile worker insurgency." *American Sociological Review 66*(1) (February 2001): 21-48.

8. Platow, Michael J., Durante, Maria, Naeidra, Williams, Garrett, Matthew, Walshe, Jarrod, Cincotta, Steven, Lianos, George, and Barutchu, Ayla. "The contribution of sport fan social identity to the production of prosocial behavior." *Group Dynamics 3*(2) (June 1999): 161-169.

9. Hirt., E. and Zillman, D. "Costs and benefits of allegiance: Changes in fans' self-ascribed competencies after team victory versus defeat." *Journal of Personality and Social Psychology 63* (1992): 724-738.

10. End, Christian M., Dietz-Uhler, Beth, Harrick, Elizabeth A., and Jacquemotte, Lindy. "Identifying with winners: A reexamination of sport fans' tendency to BIRG (bask in reflected glory)." *Journal of Applied Social Psychology 32*(5) (May 2002): 1017-1030.

11. Lee, M.J. "Self-esteem and social identity in basketball fans: A closer look at basking in reflected glory." *Journal of Sport Behavior 8* (1985): 210-224.

12. Cialdini, R.B. et al. "Basking in reflected glory: Three (football) field studies. *Journal of Personality and Social Psychology 34* (1976): 366-375.

13. "Dunham and Miller: The Musers." KTCK Web page. Available at http:// theticket.com/. Accessed July 29, 2004.

14. Bennett, Dan. Interview by author. Tape recording. November 25, 2003. Except where otherwise noted, all comments from Bennett come from this interview.

15. Dunham, George. Interview by author. Tape recording. June 20, 2003. All comments by Dunham come from this interview.

16. Observational material, including in-studio comments, comes from the author's visit to the KTCK studios, June 20, 2003.

17. *Dunham and Miller Show.* KTCK, Dallas, Texas. Tape recording. June 20, 2003. All recorded excerpts come from this recording.

18. "Arbitron Maximi$er V.9 trend report, Dallas-Fort Worth." Courtesy of Arbitron and KTCK.

19. Brown, Scott. "What's all the talk about? Brevard's sports fans keep in touch through radio shows." *Florida Today* February 3, 2004, 1-D.

20. Catlin, Jeff. E-mail to author. July 15, 2004.

21. "Ticktionary." KTCK Web page. Available at http://theticket.com/. Accessed July 29, 2004.

22. Brown.

23. Celeste, Eric. "How did the juvenile jokesters at The Ticket respond to real-life terror? Real well." *Dallas Observer* September 27, 2001.

24. Barron, David. "Success in talk radio? Yeah, that's The Ticket." *Houston Chronicle* August 20, 2001, Sports, 2.

25. Scott, Dave. "Sports talk radio: How much is too much?" *Dallas Sports Guide.* Available at http://www.gordonkcith.com/wordpress/index.php?p=30. Accessed April 12, 2006.

26. Barron.

Chapter 2

WEEI, Boston:
"Men Are Adults, Too"

Ron Bland

WEEI 850 AM in Boston, by most measures, is the number-one sports talk station in the country. While most sports stations rely heavily on the male audience, WEEI set the standard by being the highest-rated station in both males and females in the coveted twenty-five- to fifty-four-year old demographic.[1]

Although WEEI is happy to have the ladies listening, the target audience is definitely men. "We have a saying here that 'Men are adults, too,'" said Julie Kahn, general manager of WEEI, "and adults 25-54 are the primary buying demo. Give us credit for delivering more of them than anybody."[2]

The winter 2006 ratings credit WEEI with a 4.4 rating, making it the sixth highest-rated station in the Boston market. Even more impressive, WEEI is the only sports station in the country in the top fifteen markets to crack the list of top-ten stations in its market at the time of this writing. WIP in Philadelphia was the second highest-rated sports station in the country during the same ratings period. Yet the difference between WEEI's 4.4 and WIP's 3.3 is considerable. WIP is the number eleven station in Philadelphia.[3]

The strong listenership remains loyal across individual dayparts. The *Dennis and Callahan* morning show was second only to Howard Stern in the twenty-five to fifty-four demographic and third behind a news-talk station and Stern in the overall (twelve-and-older) popularity contest. Glenn Ordway's afternoon show was again the top choice with twenty-five to fifty-four listeners, while the station's midday show was second only to a soft rock station in that age group.[4]

Although New York's WFAN-AM was indeed the first all-sports radio station in the country, Boston is the true cradle of sports talk. The city is generally credited in the industry with having the first weekly sports-talk show, the first nightly sports show, and the first call-in sports show.

It began in the early 1960s, when WHDH-AM's Don Gillis would tape a group interview with area sportswriters on a Friday night and play it on Saturday night. A few years later, WBZ's Guy Mainella became the first to play host to a nightly show about sports.

But neither show put callers on the air. That came on June 17, 1969, with the "Sports Huddle" on the very end of the AM dial—WUNR-AM 1600. The show featured three area insurance agents—Eddie Andelman, Mark Witken, and Jim McCarthy—talking sports, doing skits, and taking calls. The popular show worked its way through numerous Boston stations until the group broke up in the mid-1990s.[5]

The original WEEI signed on as one of New England's broadcasting pioneers in 1924. The call letters stood for "Edison Electric Illuminating" and served as a public relations vehicle for the Edison Company. This station, owned by CBS for forty-two years, pioneered the talk-radio format in Boston.[6]

In 1990, Boston Celtics Broadcasting bought the station and but kept the all-news format until 1991, when WEEI became the first sports-talk station in Boston. WEEI carried the Celtics broadcasts as well as the Boston Bruins.[7]

In August of 1994, WEEI moved its programming and call letters to 850 kHz., formerly home to WHDH. The following year, WEEI became the flagship station for Boston Red Sox games.

In 2000, current owner, Entercom, closed down local operations at WWTM in Worcester, changed the call letters to WVEI, and began simulcasting the Boston signal to central Massachusetts, the same role WWTM formerly played for the old WEEI. Then in 2004, Entercom bought Providence's WWRX (103.7 FM), changed the call letters to WEEI-FM, and began simulcasting the WEEI signal to Rhode Island and eastern Connecticut.[8]

"When WEEI began the sports-talk format in 1991, we wanted to dominate men 25-54," said WEEI program director Jason Wolfe.

Clearly, they have accomplished that goal by ranking number one in the Boston market in the twenty-five to fifty-four male demographic for the five ratings periods leading up to summer 2004.[9]

Sports-radio programming consultant Rick Scott boiled down the keys to WEEI's success to "great personalities, strong leadership and a great market for sports in Boston. It's just a package that's really come together; they're very good at what they do."[10]

Others in the country have recognized the success of WEEI as well. In 2004, the National Association of Broadcasters nominated WEEI for a Marconi Award. Established in honor of radio inventor and Nobel Prize winner Guglielmo Marconi, the award was created to recognize excellence in radio.

The most impressive aspect of this nomination is that WEEI was not grouped among similar stations in the News/Talk/Sports category. Instead, the station was nominated in the more competitive Major Market Station of the Year category.[11]

WEEI's success must be credited to the personalities that dominate other Boston stations during every daypart. "We are personality-driven, number one. We take advantage of the live, local, credible and knowledgeable hosts that have incredible personalities that the listeners want to listen to," said Wolfe.

Said Kahn:

> I love the opinions our broadcasters have and how passionate they are, and God knows, they cause me trouble sometimes, but they're a highly talented group who spew out millions of words without a script. . . . These guys are live and flying for four hours every day.[12]

John Dennis and Gerry Callahan have been hosting mornings on WEEI since 1997. Both bring a strong New England background to their show.

Dennis began his career at WDAF in Kansas City. He became the youngest sports director at an NBC affiliate when he took the job at the age of twenty-two. Three years later, he moved to Boston's WNAC-WHDH television. There, he served as a weekend sports anchor and sports director, winning eight Emmy awards in his twenty-one years at Channel 7.[13]

Gerry Callahan is a Boston native who began a newspaper career in 1983. He worked for the *Boston Herald* for several years before leaving to become a senior writer at *Sports Illustrated*. He recently returned to the *Herald* where he is currently a columnist in addition to hosting his radio program.[14]

Glenn Ordway is the host of the afternoon *Big Show*. Ordway was a commentator for Boston Celtics radio broadcasts for thirteen years, an analyst for Boston Bruin hockey for two years, and has worked in Boston sports radio for decades. WEEI signed Ordway to a five-year contract in late 2003 that many speculate will lead to regional syndication of his afternoon program. The "Big O" has hosted *The Big Show* on WEEI since 1995.[15] Ordway is so much an icon in Boston sports circles that he appeared as himself in a 1991 episode of NBC's *Cheers*.[16]

Ordway interacts with a regular group of sportswriter co-hosts on *The Big Show*. Most listeners appreciate the inside knowledge that the writers can share. "The writers have the information," said one fan. Another said: "I really like listening to the sportswriters. I think it's smart for the shows to have them on. They have inside information, a finger on the pulse (of the Boston teams)." All the while, "Ordway holds the show together very well."[17]

Middays, Dale Arnold, the Boston Bruins play-by-play announcer, teams with Bob Neumeier, a twenty-year veteran of the Boston market.

Arnold has been a New England sports broadcaster for over twenty years. He currently serves as the New England Sports Network's play-by-play man for Boston Bruin home games. In addition to the Bruins, Arnold has also announced the New England Patriots and Boston College.[18]

Neumeier began his career in Boston in 1981 as a reporter and weekend anchor at WBZ television. He also served as the voice of the Boston Bruins for a five-year stint in the 1990s.[19] More recently, Neumeier has worked for NBC Sports and was assigned as the trackside reporter for the track-and-field competition during the 2004 Summer Olympics in Athens. According to the *Dallas Morning News'* Barry Horn: "It could be the toughest gig at the Games." Horn was referring to the combination of regular track stories and the continuing controversies concerning performance-enhancing drugs.

Horn, the *News'* sports-media columnist, devoted an entire column about Neumeier, naming him as the potential reporting star of the games. Asked before the Games began, which broadcaster might enter as an unknown and emerge a star, David Neal, executive vice president of NBC Olympics, nominated Neumeier.

Neal labeled Neumeier's reportorial instincts as "absolutely impeccable."

"The stuff he's done on the air for us in relatively small viewership situations leading up to the games, leaves no doubt in my mind that he's going to be an impact personality for us once we get to Athens," Neal said.[20]

Finally, Ted Sarandis wraps up the day at WEEI from 7 p.m. until midnight. Sarandis, a Boston native, came to WEEI in 1992 and has been a fixture in the play-by-play booth for many college teams over the past twenty-five years. He has broadcast games for Northeastern, Holy Cross, University of Massachusetts, and Harvard. He also hosts Red Sox and NFL wrap-up shows on both radio and television.[21]

Such a seasoned lineup of hosts brings the station credibility in the market. Every WEEI personality has been covering sports in the Boston market for more than two decades, but the team is also entertaining. In addition to taking calls, they do parodies and imitations of local sports figures and even write songs about the hot topic of the week.

What they don't do is to recycle the minutiae of every game. "We're not going to spend half the morning dissecting why the manager decided to bunt again in the ninth inning. This is what makes it interesting to listeners beyond the core audience," according to Wolfe.

However, after the Red Sox had several runners thrown out at home, WEEI produced a song to the tune of "Grandma Got Run Over by a Reindeer" in honor of the Sox's third-base coach, Dale Sveum.[22]

Although middays and evenings are "kinder and gentler" according to Dean,[23] the mornings and afternoon shows tend to paint with a broader brush. Both drive-time shows still are 90 percent sports, but they both delve into the topical stories of the day that may or may not be related to sports. According to morning host John Dennis, "Mornings we tend to blend 'guy radio,' sports, and water cooler topics":

> Early on in our incarnation, we did a segment between seven-thirty and eight o'clock, called Headlines. Bawdier, more risqué, noticeable headlines of the day, and we would react in a smart-ass fashion, mock ridicule, etc. That segment was rated higher than anything we were doing. There was a need in embracing

guys wanting to hear other stuff. Hanging chads, election topics, the Roman Catholic Church, Cardinal Bernard "Pimp," anything that was in the forefront of people in Boston, is fair game for our discussion. The backbone is sports, but you can only talk sports for a while. The [2000] election, it's good for us, because it allows us to do more than should they trade A-Rod?

Dennis said the goal at WEEI is to make interesting radio.

We are as much as two guys can be—intelligently opinionated, occasionally maddening, 100 percent of the time interesting, at least that's our goal. We're never "namby-pamby," we never straddle the fence, we pick a side and we defend it to the death. People can relate to how Gerry defends some issues, some people can relate to me. But we've been around long enough that we aren't some pretty boys that are trying to tell people they know what's going on. We're knowledgeable, in terms of attacking issues, and never saying I'm not sure how I feel about that. Even when I'm not, I pick a side and then wade into the waters to defend that side.[24]

Of course, live, open microphones do occasionally generate some controversy. And WEEI has its detractors.

In a story heralding the move of veteran sportsman Eddie Andelman from WEEI to rival WWZN (1510 the Zone), the Web site *Visiting New England* referred to "WEEI's nasty, crude, locker-room sports-talk style (or lack of)."[25]

During his first show on WWZN, Andelman promised to "get rid of the lunacy and idiocy of sports radio and have a little class." He took another veiled shot at WEEI when he stated, "You are not going to leave my show hating your mother like you do on other stations."[26] This isn't news in the Boston market. While still employed at WEEI, Andelman said, "I don't like a lot of things they do. I have a different philosophy." In fact, the *Boston Globe* management grew concerned with some of the station's programming and banned its writers from appearing on the station.[27]

According to Wolfe, "*The Globe* management felt the morning show and afternoon show were not the tone for the way they wanted their people promoted, so we said we don't need you at all, because we're not going to let any entity dictate where they will appear."[28]

No doubt, hosting a live program can be perilous, but a few controversies have made news. The most widely reported incident came in October 2003 when Dennis and Callahan compared a gorilla who escaped from a local zoo to an African-American high school student:

CALLAHAN: They caught him at a bus stop, right—he was, like, waiting to catch a bus out of town.

DENNIS: Yeah, yeah—he's a Metco gorilla.

CALLAHAN: Heading out to Lexington.

DENNIS: Exactly.[29]

Metco is a voluntary desegregation program that buses inner-city Boston students to suburban schools.[30]

These few seconds incited reactions from local leaders to the state attorney general's office and resulted in both hosts being suspended for two weeks. Reactions included editorials and community-leader protests. An editorial in the *Boston Phoenix,* for example, blasted Dennis and Callahan, calling them the "Duo of Dung Radio" and "spewers of hate" who had built their reputation by attacking homosexuals, women, and other groups and individuals supposedly deserving of their degrading comments.[31]

Metco Executive Director Jean McGuire said: "There is a line that has been gone over. It is something to be witty and another one to be forgetful of where you are, and who you are, and what power you have to use the FCC airwaves."[32]

The Massachusetts attorney general sought to investigate. AG Tom Reilly "hasn't just criticized Dennis and Callahan. He has requested a meeting with WEEI management to discuss the incident," according to an editorial in the *MetroWest Daily News.* The paper continued: "It's not the attorney general's job to police what people say on the radio. Nor is it the attorney general's job to fix the 'culture' of a private company that has broken no laws."[33]

While everyone condemned the team, some put the ordeal in perspective. Regis College professor Ernest Collamanti said: "Here are people who make their money by using their mouths. Once he or she is on a roll, I can see where they're so taken with their words, the passion of it takes them away and they make idiotic . . . and insensitive comments."[34]

And, according to Johnson: "It all boils down to the basic law of gravity: When you live your professional life constantly dancing on the edge, it's only a matter of time before you take a nasty fall."[35]

* * *

One of the most popular features on *The Big Show* is the "Whiner Line," a recorded voicemail of listeners giving their thoughts concerning topics on the sports scene. During this time, the station uses preproduced material—sound effects, listener calls, movie bites, arguments between different hosts—or whatever may be appropriate.

The popularity of this segment evolved into the Whiny Awards. In 2003, there were fourteen categories including the Best of the Year, Best Musical Whine, Best Impersonation of a Host, and many more, Wolfe said. The station sold 800 tickets at $150 each and raised $20,000 for amyotrophic lateral sclerosis (also known as Lou Gehrig's disease).

The station is heavily involved in the community. One of its chief fundraisers is the WEEI Jimmy Fund Radiothon. An eighteen-hour day is devoted to raising money for the Jimmy Fund, an organization that does cancer research. Broadcasting from the Red Sox's Fenway Park, the station puts together a lineup of local and national guests from the sports and entertainment world and the money starts pouring in.

The first year of the event, the radiothon raised $325,000. Wolfe said the second year over $1.1 million was raised, with more than $1.5 million raised in 2004. In total, the station works with over twenty agencies in the Boston area in an effort to give back to the community.

In just a decade, WEEI has perfected a formula of compelling entertainment built around personalities with strong and long-standing ties to the Boston area and with community involvement providing promotional muscle. WEEI constantly attempts to find a benefit for the community as the station promotes itself as a "win-win" situation for Boston.

NOTES

1. Johnson, Dean. "Boston radio: As the dust settles, two stations emerge." *The Boston Herald,* July 23, 2004, E-40.

2. Adams, Russell. "Sports talk radio: On the air and on a roll." *Street and Smith's Sports Business Journal,* February 16, 2004.

3. "Radio and records." Available at: www.radioandrecords.com/RRRatings/. Accessed April 5, 2006.

4. Johnson, Dean. "Boston Radio: WEEI sports some key victories in Hub ratings race." *The Boston Herald,* April 30, 2004, O-31.

5. "Boston radio watch." October 4, 1998. Available at: http://commons.some here.com/bostonrw/1998/Boston.Radio.Watch. Accessed July 30, 2004.

6. "The Boston radio dial: WEZE(AM)." Available at: www.bostonradio.org/radio/weze.html. Accessed July 23, 2004.

7. "The Boston Radio Dial: WEEI(AM)." Available at www.bostonradio.org/radio/weei.html. Accessed July 17, 2004.

8. Griffith, Bill. "Radio waves from WEEI." *The Boston Globe.* Available at http://boston.com/sports/other_sports/aricles/2004/03/23/radio_waves_from_weei.

9. Wolfe, Jason. Telephone interview by author. August 16, 2004. Unless otherwise noted, all comments from Wolfe come from this interview.

10. Scott, Rick. Telphone interview by author. August 23, 2004.

11. "2004 NAB Marconi Radio Awards final nominees announced." (NAB press release.) Available at: www.nab.org/newsroom/pressrel/rs2004/marconi_finalists .htm. Accessed July 30, 2004.

12. Tremblay, Bob. "Making waves in sports radio: Newton's Kahn named general manager of WEEI." *MetroWest Daily News,* February 8, 2004. Available at: www.metrowestdailynews.com/businessNews/view.bg?artcleid=59824. Accessed August 2, 2004.

13. "The gang's bios: John Dennis." Available at: www.weei.com/listingsEntry .asp?ID=109243&PT=thegangsbio. Accessed July 28, 2004.

14. "The gang's bios: Gerry Callahan." Available at: www.weei.com/listings Entry.asp?ID=109247&PT=thegangsbio. Accessed July 28, 2004.

15. "A wider look: Glenn Ordway." Available at: www.weei.com/listingsEntry .asp?ID=114060&PT=awiderlook. Accessed July 30, 2004.

16. "Glenn Ordway." *TV Tome.* Available at: www.tvtome.com/tvtome/servlet/ PersonDetail/personid-78403#info. Accessed July 29, 2004.

17. Megliola, Lenny. "Fans view: Sportswriters good on the radio." *Metro West Daily News,* September 15, 2002. Available at http://www.metrowestdailynews .com/sportsNews/view.bg?articleid=49879. Accessed April 12, 2006.

18. "Getting to know Dale and Neumy: Dale Arnold." Available at: www.weei .com/listingsEntry.asp?ID=114040&PT=gettoknowdaleandneumy. Accessed July 28, 2004.

19. "Getting to know Dale and Neumy: Bob Neumeier." Available at: www.weei .com/listingsEntry.asp?ID=114045&PT=gettoknowdaleandneumy. Accessed July 28, 2004.

20. Horn, Barry. "Newbie on track for NBC." *Dallas Morning News,* August 22, 2004, 2-CC.

21. "Ted Nation: Ted-ography." Available at: www.weei.com/tedography.asp. Accessed August 2, 2004.

22. Wolfe.

23. Johnson, telephone interview.

24. Dennis, John. Telephone interview by author. August 18, 2004.

25. "The return of a local sports talk radio legend comes to '1510 the Zone.'" *Visiting New England.* Available at: www.visitingnewengland.com/andelman.html. Accessed July 30, 2004.

26. Molori, John. "Kellogg's in 'The Zone' for a sports radio war." *Engle-Tribune,* March 5, 2002. Available at: www.eagletribune.com/news/stories/20020305/SP_011.html. Accessed August 2, 2004.

27. Megliola, Lenny. "WEEI host steps down." *Metro West Daily News.* December 13, 2001. Available at http://www.metrowestdailynews.com/sportsNews/view.bg?articleid=49066. Accessed April 12, 2006.

28. Wolfe.

29. "The duo of dung radio: John Dennis and Gerry Callahan should be fired." *The BostonPhoenix.com.* Available at: bostonphoenix.com/boston/news_features/editorial/documents/03218005.asp. Accessed July 30, 2004.

30. Dadsetan, Andy. "Black leaders: Radio hosts should resign." *The Daily Free Press,* October 17, 2003. Available at http://www.dailyfreepress.com/media/storage/papers87/news-2003/10/17/News/Black.Leaders.Radio.Hosts.Should.Resign-531799.shtml. Accessed April 12, 2006.

31. "The duo of dung radio."

32. "Radio station gorilla remarks spur advertiser concerns." *The BostonChannel.com.* Available at: www.thebostonchannel.com/news/2538645.detail.html. Accessed July 30, 2004.

33. "Editorial: AG shouldn't try to police talk radio." *MetroWest Daily News.* October 21, 2003. Available at: www.metrowestdailynews.com/opinion/view.bg?articleid=710. Accessed July 30, 2004.

34. Reuell, Peter. "The buzz: Radio host blunders." *MetroWest Daily News,* October 7, 2003. Available at: www.metrowestdailynews.com/columnistws/view.bg?articleid=18920. Accessed July 30, 2004.

35. Johnson, Dean. "Boston radio: Racial comments spurred by talk hosts' culture." *The Boston Herald,* October 31, 2003, S-35.

Chapter 3

WFAN and the Birth of All-Sports Radio: Sporting a New Format

Paul F. Gullifor

This chapter explores the history and current practices of New York radio station WFAN, the world's first all-sports radio station. Since its debut in July 1987, WFAN has remained among the preeminent sports-talk radio stations in the business. Indeed, dozens of radio stations have copied the all-sports format, but few have achieved the success and the notoriety of WFAN. Through interviews with the architects of WFAN, this chapter examines the original decision to convert 660 AM to a twenty-four-hour all-sports station, and attempts to explain the phenomenal success of WFAN, and all-sports radio in general.

HISTORY

Many radio listeners, and certainly most sports fans, know WFAN radio in New York as the world's first all-sports radio station. But this is just one of many historical firsts for this legendary radio station. One would have to go back to the beginning of radio to understand the role of this station in the development of American broadcasting. Indeed, although it weathered several format, call letter, and ownership changes through the years, 660 AM's historical significance is arguably unparalleled.

Sports-Talk Radio in America
© 2006 by The Haworth Press, Inc. All rights reserved.
doi:10.1300/5335_04

It was known in the 1920s as WEAF (which stood for "Water, Earth, Air and Fire"). On August 16, 1922, two years after KDKA in Pittsburgh signed on as America's first radio station, AT&T launched the station in New York. In that same year, WEAF began to engage in a practice known as "toll broadcasting," in which airtime was sold to anybody with a message to distribute. Although this practice seemed innocuous at the time, it actually provided the foundation for commercialism. It is not a stretch to say that WEAF created the very economic model that would come to support first American radio, and later television. In other words, it became apparent soon after WEAF began charging tolls for airtime, that advertisers would provide the financial support for American broadcasting.

However, WEAF's historical contributions do not stop with commercialism. The station whose early slogan was "The Voice of the Millions," was also pivotal in the development of network broadcasting. As early as 1923, WEAF linked with WNAC for the first chain broadcast, which featured five minutes of voice and music. WEAF was sold to the newly formed National Broadcasting Company (NBC) in 1926, where NBC used it as the flagship station for its NBC Red radio network. Programs originated from WEAF and were distributed to other stations on the network. WEAF was moved to 660 AM in 1928 and, to reflect its corporate owner, the call letters were changed to WNBC in 1946. Then, to reflect NBC's parent company, the call letters were changed to WRCA for a brief time in the 1950s, but changed back to WNBC in 1960, where it would continue to occupy 660 AM for the next twenty-eight years.

Throughout the 1960s and 1970s, 660 AM WNBC experimented with a variety of music formats, and was one of the first stations nationally to try all-talk as a radio format. Among the present-day celebrities whose careers flourished at WNBC are Howard Stern and Don Imus. More soon on Imus.

In the meantime, it is important to note that another radio station, WHN, was making a name for itself in New York City. This legendary station, whose call letters represented the Hotel Navarro (the first site of the station's studio) also went on the air in 1922, and its historical importance rivaled that of WNBC. For a while WHN was known as WMGM, but it changed its call letters back to WHN in 1962. WHN was located at 1050 AM where it became a popular country music station, and once claimed to be the most listened to country music station in America. Interestingly, WHN also carried New York Mets baseball. However, on July 1, 1987, owner Emmis Communications changed WHN's call letters again, this time to WFAN. And, with the Mets as its main sports property, 1050 AM WFAN became the world's first all-sports radio station (although country music was abandoned, the genre quickly found a home on WNYW-FM).

Former WFAN General Manager Lee Davis credited the creation of the all-sports format to the current Chairman of the Board, President and CEO of Emmis Communications, Jeff Smulyan.[1] Indeed, Smulyan founded and became the principal shareholder of the Indianapolis-based Emmis Communications in 1980. The company went public in 1994 and currently holds broadcast, newspaper, and magazine properties worldwide. Significantly, Smulyan is also a sports fan who led a group that purchased the Seattle Mariners baseball team in 1989, selling the club three years later. During that time, he also served on the Major League Baseball owner's ownership and television committees.

That first year on the new all-sports WFAN 1050, the on-air lineup consisted of such nationally known sports broadcasters as Greg Gumbel and Jim Lampley, and New York Mets 1969 World Series hero Art Shamsky, to name a few. Emmis Communications decided to make one more crucial move for WFAN. In 1988, Emmis bought WNBC's frequency of 660 AM and moved WFAN and its all-sports format from 1050 to 660 AM, where it remains to this day. This was a significant upgrade. The 660 frequency is a powerful, clear-channel 50,000-watt station as opposed to 1050 AM, which is a directional signal with reduced nighttime power. Today, the WFAN studios are located in Astoria, Queens, and its transmitting tower is located on High Island, located off City Island, an upscale enclave of Bronx County.[2]

As significant as the improved signal was WFAN's move to retain top-flight talent. One critically important personality from WNBC was hired to do mornings on the newly formed WFAN. Don Imus began doing a morning show on WFAN in 1988. It was actually a case of the station joining Imus, rather than the other way around. He already had a legion of followers, and this, according to current WFAN Program Director Mark Chernoff, was critical to WFAN's success. "More than anything else, hiring Imus put WFAN on the map," Chernoff said. "He already had this legion of followers that he brought with him to our format, so he gave us this huge audience."[3]

There was one more ownership change in store for WFAN. In February 1992, Emmis sold WFAN to Infinity Broadcasting for $70 million. Infinity Broadcasting, now CBS Radio, is the second largest owner of radio stations in America. CBS Radio operates 184 radio stations, the majority of them in the top fifty markets, including six in New York City alone.[4]

What happened to 1050 AM, the frequency that WFAN vacated, is an interesting bit of historical irony. For a few years, WEVD, owned by the Forward Association, a newspaper publishing company dedicated to Jewish concerns, occupied 1050 AM, where it was primarily a news and talk station. But in September of 2002, the Walt Disney Company bought WEVD for $78 million dollars. Disney quickly converted the station to all-sports, where it adopted the call letters of WEPN and became the flagship station for Disney's ESPN Radio network. Today, it is known as ESPN 1050 and is a direct competitor of 660 WFAN. Essentially, this put WFAN in the position of competing with its former frequency.

CURRENT PROGRAMMING

Lee Davis, former general manager of WFAN, said ESPN 1050 is just one of several competitors in the New York market. "ESPN 1050 are competitors in the sense that they also do sports, so formatically they are our competitors," Davis said. "Our competitors actually range from stations that play classic rock to other talk radio stations."[5]

Certainly, according to Arbitron's numbers, ESPN 1050 is at best a distant competitor to WFAN. Ratings figures from summer of 2004 show that WFAN delivered a 2.5 share of listeners twelve years old and older, which was good enough for a seventeenth place ranking out of thirty-eight rated stations serving New York. By contrast, ESPN 1050 garnered a 0.5 share during the same period placing them in a tie for thirtieth place in the market.[6] In one year (from summer 2003 to summer 2004) WFAN saw its ratings rise two-tenths of a ratings point, while ESPN 1050's ratings remained the same.

WFAN may well be the most influential all-sports radio station in America. But the key to the station's success, according to Lee Davis, is that WFAN is more than just sports. "We are more than just a sports radio station. We lead our day off with *Imus in the Morning*," Davis reflected. "While Imus will feign some interest in sports, he also has a wide range of topics; politics, books, music. So, we have a very strong mass appeal lead-in with Imus."[7]

Imus in the Morning is now syndicated to more than ninety stations nationally; with an estimated audience of 10 million listeners.[8] Imus has also been simulcast on the MSNBC cable network since 1996. It seems reasonable that such a simulcast could only hurt WFAN by splitting the available audience for Imus. However, according to Davis, this is not necessarily true. He said:

> From a logical perspective it would seem the simulcast can't help because it takes people away from WFAN, but to some degree, I think it does enhance the brand a little bit. It might encourage people to listen to Imus that otherwise wouldn't. So of the pros and cons, it probably splits evenly. Imus does not win the morning-drive radio time slot in New York, but he is still very, very popular. There are really only a handful of big personalities in New York radio, and Imus is certainly one of them.[9]

Davis said WFAN's talent runs deep, far beyond Imus. The station is very happy with the team of Mike Francesa and Chris Russo, better known as "Mike and the Mad Dog," who anchor the afternoon-drive slot. "They've become a must-listen in afternoon drive in New York," he asserted.

> When something happens in sports, they are the two that everyone tunes in to. Imus and "Mike and the Mad Dog" have also been together as our morning- and afternoon-drive hosts since 1989. So, for fifteen years we have had the same morning and afternoon team. I don't know of any New York station that has had a morning and afternoon drive time team on the air as long we have.[10]

The ascension of midday host Joe Benigno, who teams with Sid Rosenberg, is an unusual story. Benigno was one of WFAN's most loyal listeners, and a regular caller of the station who became known as "Joe from Saddle River." His big break came in 1994 when he won WFAN's "Fan Appreciation Day" contest and was awarded a guest host spot on the station. Benigno was quickly recognized for his sports knowledge and was hired as an overnight host at a station in

FIGURE 3.1. *Mike and the Mad Dog,* WFAN, New York: (left to right) Mike Francesa and Chris Russo. Courtesy WFAN.

FIGURE 3.2. *Mike and the Mad Dog,* WFAN, New York: (left to right) Mike Francesa, unidentified guest, and Chris Russo. Courtesy WFAN.

New Jersey before being offered a full-time position on WFAN. He was promoted from overnights to the midday to replace Jody McDonald from the popular *Mac & Sid Show*. These three talk shows, according to Lee Davis, are the strength of the station. He said:

> The single most important programming element the station owns is compelling talk-show hosts. Imus is very important to the radio station, and morning drive is a very important time slot for radio, but "Mike and the Mad Dog" also are a great brand here in New York as well. And Sid Rosenberg and Joe Benigno, our new midday team, are important to us also. They're all very passionate. So I wouldn't limit our strength to just one entity, but our talk shows in general, and our personalities are the strength of the station.[11]

The midday- and afternoon-talk programs, which consist of the reporting and commenting on a range of sports topics, are among the most popular on WFAN. The station is also known for its "20/20" updates, in which sports updates are provided every twenty minutes.

Of course, doing so much talk involves the occasional controversy, and WFAN has seen its share through the years. Imus has been a controversial radio figure for years, especially in the political realm, where he infamously insulted both President Bill Clinton and First Lady Hillary Clinton in their presence at a formal dinner. And then there are times when the sports hosts stray from sports-related topics. For example, it was suggested on the *Mike and the Mad Dog* show that the terrorists attacks of September 11 were motivated by U.S. support of Israel. That assertion resulted in a fiery letter to WFAN Program Director Mark Chernoff from Abraham Foxman, the national director of the Anti-Defamation League:

> Since September 12, ADL offices in the tri-state area have been flooded with calls complaining about comments made by "Mike and the Mad Dog" show hosts Mike Francesa and Chris Russo . . . . We have reached out to you asking for a response to these complaints in order to better inform our constituents about the matter. At this point, we need more than a casual explanation for the comments made by the hosts. The calls continue to come in on a daily basis describing the hosts' continual injection of Israel in connection with the World Trade Center tragedy. We un-

derstand that WFAN's focus is the sports world. At this time we suggest it would be appropriate for Mr. Francesa and Mr. Russo to be instructed that their listeners tune into hear an analysis of the game rather than unfounded presumptions about a horrific act of terrorism. We look forward to your response.[12]

Then there was the time that Sid Rosenberg admitted in his role as sportscaster on *Imus in the Morning* that he was illegally accessing programming from DirecTV by using a modified access card. DirecTV responded by suing Rosenberg alleging violations of the Digital Millennium Copyright Act. The irony of Rosenberg's comments is that they included the theft of copyrighted broadcasts including those of Viacom, the parent company of WFAN.

In addition to on-air talk, play-by-play sports programming is crucial to the success of WFAN. The station is still the home of New York Mets baseball, New York Giants football, New Jersey Devils hockey, and New Jersey Nets basketball. WFAN formerly held the rights to New York Knicks basketball and New York Rangers hockey, but, Davis said, negotiations to renew the deal failed in early 2004. He explained:

> There are two ways to have teams on your radio station. One is for the station to pay for the rights, the other is for the team to pay the station to be on, but the team then sells the advertising inventory. We could not reach an agreement with the Knicks or the Rangers, who are owned by Cablevision. We couldn't come to terms with them, so we decided to take on the Nets and the Devils. The most valuable of these is probably the New York Mets, if for no other reason than the number of games we get. We get 162 games, and New York is certainly a baseball town.[13]

To make matters worse, the rights to the Rangers and Knicks went to competitor ESPN 1050 after sixteen years on WFAN. According to industry reports, Cablevision was paying WFAN a six-digit sum annually to carry the games of the two teams, but Cablevision didn't want to pay those fees anymore.[14]

The New York Yankees are on WCBS, a sister station of WFAN. In an example of corporate synergy, WFAN is also the home of University of Notre Dame football (Notre Dame football is carried by the Westwood One Radio Network, which is also owned by CBS Radio).

According to Davis, this is more than corporate synergy. It's also good programming. "Notre Dame has a tremendous following here in the tri-state area," Davis said. "It is one of the most popular universities in America and it does very well for us also."[15]

Davis also dispelled the common belief that ratings rise and fall with the success of the team.

> In the past, that probably carried more credence. When teams don't perform well, we know where we're going to be in the ratings, so that when teams perform well, it gives us a nice spike in the ratings. We don't fall off the map just because our teams aren't performing well. In fact, the teams around here have had some good runs. And, there are enough sports here, that there is always a good story in New York. There are nine professional sports teams in the area, so chances are at least a couple of them are having a good year.[16]

Although engaging talk shows and play-by-play of big-time sports are at the core of WFAN's success, Davis claimed their commitment to localism is what separates them from the competition. Davis said:

> We are unique in New York radio. We truly are the voice of New York sports. And, of the New York sports fan. No one else in this market can say that. Yes, there is another sports radio station here, but their local programming right now is limited to six hours per day. We talk New York sports all day long . . . and our brand, WFAN, is as strong as any throughout the country.[17]

Davis added that localism gives him comfort when he looks into the future at competitors, including satellite radio.

> As you look into the future the one thing that is very difficult to replicate is our localism. We're local. Satellite radio is not going to do a local radio show like we are. We're in a good position in regards to our niche and serving the needs of our listeners in the tri-state area. The same is true of the all-news stations here that cover local news. We don't panic at all. We just need to serve our listeners' needs. As for opportunities, every day, sports becomes more of a mainstream news subject. That bodes well for us.

There are growing sports also. Women's sports are beginning to take off.[18]

The 50,000-watt clear channel signal, Davis reminded, gives WFAN wide geographical range.

I wouldn't say it's national, but we certainly blanket the northeast and much of the central United States if you're in the right spot. Yet, we focus on New York sports because the ratings service just measures New York. Those national listeners are bonus listeners for our advertisers, but we focus on New York sports because that's where we make our living.[19]

Those bonus listeners attract a large number of upscale advertisers. As noted in the introduction to this book, WFAN became the top-billing radio station in history in 1997. This, according to Davis, should help dispel a common myth about the nature of the sports-radio listener:

Our major advertisers are everybody from Mercedes and BMW to banks to New York Stock Exchange and Medical Centers. There is also Toyota, and other really blue-chip advertisers [are carried] on this radio station. These are upscale, affluent advertisers, which really goes against the perception of the sports audience. WFAN happens to be one of the most upscale stations, in terms of it listenership, in the country. I know a lot of CEOs who love sports, and remember, we have *Imus in the Morning,* which is a very intelligent radio show in terms of both the host, and the guests that he has on. We've had everyone from John McCain to John Kerry on the show. We've also had Bob Schieffer, Tom Brokaw, and Tim Russert. That is a very upscale audience listening to Imus. Sports is a common denominator among men. You can go to a game, and you could have a CEO sitting next to a taxi driver.[20]

WFAN is also proud of its work for charitable causes. Particularly noteworthy is WFAN's annual Radiothon. Begun in 1990, the Radiothon has raised nearly $22 million for the Tomorrow Children's Fund, the CJ Foundation for SIDS and the Imus Ranch in Imus' native New Mexico, where children with cancer enjoy working with horses and cattle.[21]

CONCLUSION

WFAN was the world's first all-sports radio station and, as such, created the blueprint for all-sports formats across the country. Several stations have tried to replicate the format, but few have achieved the success and notoriety of WFAN. A close examination of the program schedule reveals WFAN's formula for success.

First, WFAN explores controversial topics beyond the sports realm. The most visible example of this is *Imus in the Morning,* which is more of a political talk show than a sports show. But even WFAN's sports hosts will occasionally delve into issues unrelated to sports. This willingness to explore a wide range of topics broadens the appeal of the station, and attracts an upscale, affluent audience, an audience that advertisers want to reach.

Second, WFAN offers its listeners an abundance of play-by-play sports. With nine professional sports franchises in the New York area, combined with many college and high school sports teams, no shortage of content is available for WFAN.

Third, and finally, WFAN is committed to localism. Despite a signal that covers much of the continental United States, WFAN has chosen to focus on New York sports. This niche has served the station well, and distinguishes the station from its competitors.

Compelling talk, play-by-play sports broadcasts, and a commitment to localism are WFAN's recipe for success. As the creator of the all-sports format, WFAN has enjoyed much current success, and finds itself well-positioned for the future.

NOTES

1. Davis, Lee. Telephone interview by author. November 16, 2004.

2. "The Boston Radio Archives." Available at www.bostonradio.org/radio/bostonradio.html. Accessed November 27, 2004.

3. Chernoff, Mark. Telephone interview by author. October 21, 2004.

4. "Musicradio 77 WABC: The Greatest Top Forty Music Radio Station of All Time." Available at www.musicradio77.com. Accessed November 27, 2004.

5. Davis.

6. "New York Radio Guide: Where New Yorkers Turn On and Tune In!" Arbitron ratings. Available at www.nyradioguide.com. Accessed November 27, 2004.

7. Davis.

8. "WFAN, Sports Radio, 66 AM." Available at www.wfan.com. Accessed November 27, 2004.

9. Davis.

10. Ibid.

11. Ibid.

12. Letter, Abraham Foxman to Mark Chernoff, September 24, 2001. © 2001 Anti-Defamation League. Reprinted with permission. All rights reserved. Available at http://www.adl.org/media_watch/radio/letter_infin_broadc.htm. Accessed April 12, 2006.

13. Davis.

14. "New York radio shocker: Rangers, Knicks leave WFAN." *Sportsfan Magazine* 5: February 2004. Available at http://www.sportsfanmagazine.com/sfm/articles.html?id=20. Accessed April 12, 2006.

15. Davis.

16. Ibid.

17. Ibid.

18. Ibid.

19. Ibid.

20. Ibid.

21. "WFAN, Sports Radio, 66 AM."

Chapter 4

WQTM, "The Team," Orlando: Sports-Talk Radio in a City Where Sports Are *Not* King

Alma Kadragic

A quick sketch of Orlando and its position among the sports fans of America—and in particular, the football fans of Florida—explains a good deal about sports-talk radio in the fast-growing city because, of course, sports-talk radio reflects its community. Like the city itself, sports-talk radio in Orlando is pleasant, uncontroversial, "wannabe," and growing. The population is increasing, and, in 2004, so is the presence of sports-talk radio.

Because Orlando is not a traditional pro-sports town such as Chicago or Boston, the sports-talk format is not the natural fit in Orlando it is in those markets. And so, the stations attempting the all-sports format in Orlando face a stiff challenge.

ORLANDO AS A SPORTS TOWN

In the 2004 *Sporting News* listing of top U.S. sports cities, Orlando came in at number 40, way behind number 1 Boston; number 2 Oakland-San Francisco-San Jose; number 3 New York-Long Island-New Jersey; and a whole series of much larger markets that make up the top ten. However, after those leaders, Orlando was also behind number 16 Indianapolis; number 19 Nashville; number 32 Buffalo; number 34 Green Bay; number 37 Columbus; and most strikingly number 25 Durham-Raleigh-Chapel Hill. Admittedly, number 25 and number 37

Sports-Talk Radio in America
© 2006 by The Haworth Press, Inc. All rights reserved.
doi:10.1300/5335_05

boast important college sports powers such as Duke, North Carolina, and Ohio State, but they do not house a single major-league professional team.[1]

Unlike Durham-Raleigh-Chapel Hill and Columbus, Orlando is the home of a big-league professional sports team, the Magic in the Southeast Division of the National Basketball Association. Although the fifteen-year-old franchise finished with the worst record in the NBA in 2003-2004, it has had glory days and may again.

In 1994-1995, Shaquille O'Neal led the Magic to the 1995 NBA Finals—where they lost four straight games to Michael Jordan's Chicago Bulls. In addition, Orlando has been the site of spring training for baseball's Houston Astros since 1985 and the Atlanta Braves since 1998. The Citrus Bowl stadium where the Walt Disney Florida Classic, the Capital One Bowl, and the Mazda Tangerine Bowl draw thousands of spectators to support their favorite college-football teams is another Orlando sports property. The rest of the time the Citrus Bowl is the home stadium of the 1-A University of Central Florida Golden Knights, the team that groomed quarterback Daunte Culpepper for the Minnesota Vikings and went into the 2004-2005 season with its first ever big-name coach, George O'Leary, by way of Georgia Tech, Notre Dame (very briefly, thanks to a resume discrepancy), and the Vikings.

Moreover, Orlando has something that much larger cities cannot claim. As one of the top tourist destinations in America, Orlando draws on a pool of 40 million visitors each year who come to the theme parks and make Orlando a jumping off point for exploring the rest of Florida. That should add up to huge attendance figures for the Magic and Golden Knights football, but so far, it hasn't. *The Sporting News'* top-sports-cities ranking may reflect the general lack of sports fans at many big sports events in Orlando and a certain lack of passion in Orlando sports fans.

Orlando—the number 38 radio market in the country—is a community of transients where people tend to move in for a few years and then move out again, leaving for better jobs or greater opportunities in other parts of Florida or outside the state. Since the only major professional sports team is a "teenager" in tenure, the allegiance of Orlando fans is also still developing. The Magic's biggest attendance in recent years has been when the opponents are either the New York Knicks—who bring in the transplanted New Yorkers—or the Los

Angeles Lakers—whose star act drew everywhere, but especially in Orlando during Shaq's regime, and later when O'Neal returned to Orlando as a Laker.

Orlando is a twenty-first-century city emerging from a sleepy town where citrus groves were the major industry until Walt Disney World's Magic Kingdom opened in 1971 and began the tourist boom. For many residents, loyalty to Orlando is a thin veneer. Unfortunately, the evidence of that is the condition of the Magic's T.D. Waterhouse Centre and the Citrus Bowl. Both facilities, once state of the art, need extensive renovation or replacement. Neither has adequate space for corporate boxes to attract the big-money "snob trade" and boost the bottom line. To fix T.D. Waterhouse and the Citrus Bowl, the community would have to reach into its pockets and make a long-term commitment to serious financing.

So far, neither Orlando's mayor nor the chairman of the Orange County commissioners has been ready to pick up the ball. Part of the problem is the generally low level of income in the area—although that isn't the whole story. While tourism employs mainly lower-paid workers, there is a burgeoning high-tech industry with starting salaries double or triple what hospitality workers earn after a few years. Because of its weather and lifestyle, the area is also home to sports stars from Shaquille O'Neal to Tiger Woods and the grand old man of golf, Arnold Palmer. Whole communities of the very rich and famous are part of the local environment as well as many well-off middle-class Americans in their forties and fifties who emigrated to Florida for a more pleasant way of life, joining the retirees who found Orlando much earlier. Some of this is related to Florida's attractive tax code; the state has no personal income tax and is indulgent in taxing business. Blessed with an excellent international airport, Orlando draws many residents who use it on weekends. Monday to Friday they are commuting to business in other parts of the country.

Another important reason why Orlando rates relatively low among top sports cities is that the most popular sport in Florida is football.[2] Professional football exists at three corners of the state along both coasts, in the northeast with the Jacksonville Jaguars; in the southeast with the Miami Dolphins; and in the southwest with the Tampa Bay Buccaneers. In other words, everywhere but in Orlando, landlocked at the center of the state. Topnotch college football is even more widespread with three teams that have been and are always a threat to repeat as national collegiate champion. College football is king in the state capital of Tallahassee with the dominant Florida State Seminoles and includes the Rattlers of historically black university Florida A & M with their own impressive record and fans; in Gainesville, at the University of Florida with its Gators; and in Miami with the University of Miami Hurricanes. Again, none of these teams is in Orlando.

Orlando's only Division 1-A college football team is Central Florida's Golden Knights. Central Florida is ambitious and eager to move up in the NCAA rankings, but it's a long way from the history and reputation enjoyed by the big three of Florida, Florida State, and Miami, in a state and region where people's loyalty to their college's football team lasts a lifetime. Seminole alumni, for example, scattered around the country with no other connection to Tallahassee, maintain condominiums there just to use for football weekends in the fall.[3]

Sports-Talk in Orlando: WQTM 740, "The Team"

Sports-talk radio in Orlando dates back to 1995 when Paxson Communications turned radio station 540 WFLF into what it called "540 The Team." When Clear Channel bought that station along with 740 WQTM in 1997, the sports-talk format continued. In 2001 to make better use of frequencies in the Orlando market, Clear Channel switched The Team to 740 while 540 reverted to a standard talk-radio format. Today 740 The Team is a sports-radio operation focused on attracting the sports-loving male audience twenty-five to fifty-four[4] with a regular diet of nine hours each weekday of locally originated programming punctuated by Fox Sports programs and live broadcasts of games.

The Team produces three major programs that run Monday through Friday for three hours each. *The Dan Sileo Show* occupies morning drive time, 6 to 9 a.m. Sileo, not necessarily a household name among sports fans nationwide, is famous in Florida for having been a football All-American with the Miami Hurricanes in the 1980s. As a professional, he played briefly with the Tampa Bay Buccaneers and then two teams outside the NFL, the Orlando Thunder of the defunct World League of American Football and the Las Vegas Sting of the Arena Football League. He has been a sports broadcaster longer than a football player, starting in San Francisco on KNBR 680 and "The Ticket" 1050. After stints in Tampa at WDAE 1250 and Los Angeles with Fox Sports Radio, he came back to Florida.

In The Team lineup, he is the wild man, talking more "smack" and risking more outrageous statements than any of the other show hosts. "Pin it right here on the *Dan Sileo Show*," he says regularly, in an original variation of the usual "stay tuned." When a caller asks, "What are you doing, Dan?" he likes to reply matter-of-factly, "Talking to you." He is lively, funny, and opinionated in talking about his beloved football. His listeners know that he calls the pigskin the "pill" or the "rock." Sileo's greatest strength is coming across as genuine and passionately committed to whatever position he takes.

A new listener might fix on Sileo's anti-intellectualism and, sometimes, even ignorance. One morning he was outraged at news that the city of Berlin wanted to host the summer Olympics in the same stadium where Hitler held the infamous Nazi Olympics in 1936 and fulminated for several minutes about the idea of Olympics in the stadium "built by slave labor from the concentration camps." Although the new listener might wonder where Sileo got the idea of concentration-camp labor being used to build the stadium—unlikely since labor performed by prisoners was punitive and not usually constructive in any sense of the word—a regular listener would dismiss that thought and focus on feeling that Sileo is on the side of the "good guys."

Sileo is determined to fight racism in sports but resents when race is invoked to excuse bad behavior. He blasts regularly, almost daily, college football and basketball coaches who overlook criminal acts by star players or recruits and has been vituperative against his alma mater Miami for accepting linebacker Willie Williams into the school and on the Hurricanes team despite his having been arrested a number of times. Whatever his rougher edges, Sileo's heart is in the right place.

The strength of The Team's morning show is the personality of Dan Sileo. That carries over into the uncommon access he has to all kinds of sports figures but especially those in the world of football. As the Tampa Bay Buccaneers opened their two-week training camp in August 2004 at Disney's Wide World of Sports Complex, Sileo was there, broadcasting live the entire first week and counting General Manager Bruce Allen, Coach Jon Gruden, and assistant coaches and players among the guests. It is not only a matter of access. Because Sileo knows football inside out and knows the Bucs, the Raiders, and, seemingly, most other teams from years of participation and coverage, he's able to extract from the guests information about rebuilding a football team or improving the offense at a level that most sports broadcasters don't achieve.

Sileo's skills include breaking and making news. He broke the story about veteran receiver Tim Brown being let go by the Oakland Raiders and led the attempt—possibly inspired by Brown himself—to have Brown's contract picked up by the Bucs. Earlier in 2004, after UCF's football coach Mike Kruczek was let go, Sileo proposed that UCF sign a top level coach and floated George O'Leary's name as a trial balloon. Insiders gossip that O'Leary himself suggested it to Sileo. It might also have been UCF Athletic Director Steve Orsini who worked with O'Leary at Georgia Tech. Regardless, Sileo's listeners certainly felt like insiders when that trial balloon landed safely and O'Leary was hired by UCF.

As a foil and straight man to Sileo, program engineer Simon—if he has a last name, listeners don't know it—is low-key, a calming counterpoint to Sileo's hot mode which he himself often attributes to his Italian heritage. Simon talks slowly and evenly and doesn't get excited, contrasting with Sileo who is excited most of the time. In addition to being a nice guy, Simon is a hockey expert, often talking about the sport. Primarily, Simon is there to ground Sileo, screen calls, and provide heavy-metal music and other 1980s hits as bumpers (music played before and after commercial breaks).

As is not always the case in sports-talk radio, callers are an important part of the program. Sileo has many devoted fans in Orlando and Tampa who call regularly and greet him as their "Hurricane Brother" and other terms of affection. He often gets calls from former listeners who don't hear him regularly because he or they have moved, but who enjoy talking to him or expressing an opinion about a sports event or scandal. Most callers are concerned about Florida's college football teams, especially the Hurricanes and Gators. With the Orlando Magic winning only 21 games in 2003-2004, fans had much to be outraged about, and the trade of Tracy McGrady to the Houston Rockets after the season was the cap to the franchise's worst year. Although Magic supporters were upset for months, and Sileo was among them, the level of emotion seemed much more restrained than it is for even minor football news. After fifteen seasons, the Magic's roots in Orlando don't go nearly as deep as the Hurricanes and the Gators—even though neither is actually a home team.

After 9 a.m., The Team carries one hour of "Keep 'N Score [sic] with Sentinel Sports," sports talk moderated by *Orlando Sentinel* sports editor Lynn Hoppes starring columnists Jerry Greene and Mike Bianchi who are sometimes replaced or supplemented with other members of the newspaper's sports staff. The relationship between the *Sentinel* group and the station's hosts is supportive and complementary. Jerry Greene who trades on being less than svelte and is very funny about sports in his column "From the Cheap Seats," is a weekly participant on *Coach & Company* and also pops up occasionally on *The Finish Line.* However, the program is paid for by the *Sentinel* and not produced by The Team, so it is, for all practical purposes, an infomercial.

From late morning through afternoon, two nationally syndicated sports-talk programs, the *Fox Morning Extravaganza,* 10 a.m. to noon, and *The Jim Rome Show,* noon to 3 p.m., fill the air time. For The Team, these are the less lucrative parts of the day. Most local advertisers want to be in on morning-drive time or afternoon-drive/dinner time. So *The Dan Sileo Show, Coach & Company,* and the first hour of *The Finish Line* are where the station charges the highest advertising rates.

Coach & Company, the program that takes over at 3 p.m., reflects the personality of Marc Daniels, program director for The Team and one of the best-known voices in Central Florida as a result of his play-by-play work and hosting of the show. At thirty-nine, he has been the station's program director for nine years and in radio sports since he was fifteen. What he has never been is a "coach." The nickname came along somehow during more than twenty-two years of working in radio and has stuck. Daniels says he can't explain it.[5]

The nickname fits Daniels if "coach" is understood to mean someone who is knowledgeable and generally convinced that he's always right about any sports topic. That's how he comes across during *Coach & Company,* sharing information with his sidekicks, "Stunning" Steve Egan, and producer Craig Bullock. Egan, who also does the news breaks on the half-hour and hour comes across as an amiable, nonargumentative partner for Daniels; he is laid-back where

Daniels is insistent. Bullock is the utility player who takes a greater or lesser part in the program depending on whether he's needed.

In addition to hosting *Coach & Company,* Daniels has been the voice of the UCF football, basketball, and baseball programs for ten years, traveling with the teams and doing play-by-play for their games, most of which The Team broadcasts. When UCF plays away games, Daniels typically does his program on Thursday afternoon, travels with the team Friday, broadcasts the game Saturday, and travels back home Sunday. During the Arena Football League season over the summer, he broadcasts the Orlando Predators matches, a task he's been doing for more than thirteen years. Come fall, it's once again time for college sports. At The Team, Daniels is an acknowledged workaholic.

In play-by-play work, Daniels seems competent and fair in evaluating the players on both sides. Of course, he has total access to coaches and players from UCF and their opponents; his broadcasts are enlivened by interviews before, during, and after most games. However, since he is an employee of UCF, it is likely that as a sports-talk host on *Coach & Company,* he may tend to be more restrained in expressing a negative opinion about UCF sports than someone unconnected with the school. This is not an issue when things are going well. It can at least give the appearance of being a problem when UCF sports are under a cloud.

That's what happened in the November 2003 when the school's starting quarterback and other players were found to have missed classes they claimed to be attending. Coach Mike Kruczek dismissed the quarterback, who was expelled from the university. Other players were also expelled or suspended for the season. These events were a major topic on *Coach & Company,* and on the other call-in programs on The Team for weeks.

The question for regular listeners of *Coach & Company* was how long had Daniels been aware that there were serious discipline problems with elite athletes at UCF and that Coach Kruczek was unable to control some of them? At all levels of sports, play-by-play announcers have to reckon with the displeasure of their employers when they tilt too much toward independent journalism and stray from their mission to promote the team. Some have been fired for being too critical—or being good journalists. On the other hand, it's likely that most of Daniels' audience understands his dual role and is happy with the work he's doing.

Coach & Company is a generally entertaining three hours. Daniels, who insists on his point of view with callers and associates, like Sileo but without Sileo's rambunctious good humor, has a good deal of information to share because his understanding of all sports is extensive. During professional basketball season, former NBA coach Matty Guokas comes on once a week to share his expertise—especially about the Magic but also about other happenings in the NBA—with Daniels and callers. During baseball season, Minnesota Twins pitching great Frank Viola does the same thing for the pennant races. Daniels loves the New York Yankees, and Viola, who was a Yankee opponent for his entire baseball career, has a healthy interest in the other teams that contrasts nicely with Daniels' partisanship.

Being a Yankee fan is one of the constants among The Team hosts. Dan Sileo and the "Shot Doctor"—a golf expert whose real name is a secret for some unknown reason—from *The Finish Line* are also devoted to George Steinbrenner's men in pinstripes. The partisanship—which is good-humored rather than fanatical—is further proof of Orlando being home to many people whose sports loyalties are still in other places. Florida has two professional baseball teams, the two-time World Series champion Florida Marlins in Miami and the Tampa Bay Devil Rays, but neither is nearly as much of a sports-talk radio topic among hosts and callers in Orlando as the New York Yankees. The lack of interest in professional baseball close to home is perhaps another part of the general lack of interest in baseball in Florida, according to Clear Channel Regional Vice President of Programming Central/North Florida Chris Kampmeier. It must be added that Miami and Tampa Bay are not Orlando, and once again the teams are not in Orlando.

Clear Channel collects the highest ad rates on The Team for placement during the first hour of *The Finish Line* from 6 to 7 p.m. The host is Jerry O'Neill, a veteran broadcaster with a history in St. Louis and several Florida markets, who is paired with the Shot Doctor, who plays the fool to O'Neill's smart guy. O'Neill is assertive, dominant, and argumentative with his partner, but surprisingly gentle with the callers. In one of the promotional spots for the show, O'Neill says, "We tell you what *we* think. We don't tell *you* what to think." That approach to listeners sets *The Finish Line* apart from the other programs on The Team—and many other sports-talk programs. Perhaps because the first hour of the show is broadcast during most people's dinner time in central Florida, O'Neill says in his official biography, "If you call in to the show, it's as if you've just joined our table."[6] While most listeners probably react most intensely—love him or hate him—to Dan Sileo and consider Marc Daniels a source of information, they may feel most at home over dinner with Jerry O'Neill and the Shot Doctor.

O'Neill and his mysterious partner take their program outside the studio once a week, often on Friday evening, to a local restaurant or sports bar. They announce where they will be several days in advance to build the live audience so that many of the people at the venue have come specifically to greet them and participate in the show. Obviously popular, both men interact well with the mostly male audience, who seem genuinely happy to be there; joking and laughter are always heard in the background and encouraged by the hosts.

The warm feelings for Jerry O'Neill and the Shot Doctor may be related to their ongoing banter. O'Neill is the expert with greater background in sports lore. The Shot Doctor plays silly and is regularly reprimanded and set straight by O'Neill on everything from sports topics to any others that come up. The one thing O'Neill doesn't make fun of is the Shot Doctor's golf wisdom. His tips of the week are extensively promoted by the station and also appear on the Web site (www.740theteam.com). However, "Shot's" golf game is another story. That's a fair target for O'Neill's wisecracks.

If sports-talk radio is ultimately as much about entertainment as it is about information, then it isn't enough simply to provide a lineup of call-in sports programs to keep and develop an audience of faithful listeners, 3 percent of whom will occasionally dial their favorite host, according to Daniels. The Team stars divide into some archetypal family patterns. Sileo is the black sheep uncle or brother who's been a bad boy but whose heart is in the right place. Daniels is the nerdy, know-it-all brother who's always right. Jerry O'Neill and the Shot Doctor in their bickering are the typical married couple, reminiscent of Ralph and Alice Kramden arguing nonstop about everything though fond of each other deep down, Daniels said.

Every Friday morning at 10:15 when the *Sentinel* people have left the studio after "Keep 'N Score," The Team hosts sit down and tape a feature called "Open Mike." It runs for about forty-five minutes on

Friday afternoon as the last segment of *Coach & Company.* As the name suggests, "Open Mike" is a free-for-all on the sports news of the day, and anything else anyone wants to bring up.

In April 2004, one of the topics related to race. University of Central Florida President John Hitt and Board of Trustees Chairman Dick Nunnis—the former president of Disney World—attended a UCF board meeting wearing outsize Afro wigs in honor of player Dexter Lyons who favors an enormous Afro hairstyle like the one often seen on Detroit Pistons' star forward Ben Wallace. Some UCF fans had been coming to games in Dexterlike Afros for months, but Hitt's appearance caused a firestorm of criticism and allegations of racism. Hitt and Nunnis immediately apologized, and the topic played on sports radio for a few days.

In talking about this incident, The Team hosts agreed that the critics were overreacting because no racism had been intended. Someone mentioned that Dexter Lyons thinks the Afro wigs are a compliment to him and was honored that President Hitt had joined in wearing one. Supporting that, O'Neill said he considered it his job to show passion, to try to make a difference, "to take people from being passive to active" about racism or whatever other issue he talked about. Sileo added: "I like to talk about race. I don't want to push anyone, but I want to talk to as many people as I can to give an interpretation that makes sense." In keeping with the The Team's low-keyed approach, after a commercial break, taping resumed, and the conversation went on to other topics.[7]

On the weekends, The Team intersperses Fox Sports radio programming with a mix of local infomercial programs such as *The Boatwrench Show, Car Time with Jay Zembower,* and *Cycle Rider Radio Network.* The only program The Team produces during the weekend is *The Pat Williams Show,* Sunday mornings from 7 to 8 a.m. It is also the only intellectually challenging program in The Team lineup. Williams is a Renaissance man who brought the Magic franchise to central Florida. That followed twelve years as general manager of the Philadelphia 76ers, including the team that won the NBA title in 1983. He holds a doctoral degree, is a topnotch motivational speaker, and has written more than twenty books.

The Pat Williams Show is much more serious than most of what is broadcast on The Team. Williams' program has a simple format: during the hour, he does two in-depth interviews, each with the author of a new book related to sports. Because he has thirty minutes for each interview, a long time in radio broadcasting, and doesn't worry about being intelligible to the lowest common denominator of listener, he is able to ask the questions, listen intently to the answers, and follow up on points that need explanation. In this program, there is little sports slang, no jokes, and no attention to entertainment. The listener may find the interviews interesting or not, but that is up to them.

Williams is a self-effacing interviewer; he doesn't use the interviews to highlight his own knowledge, nor does he compete with or show up his guest. As a result, the interviews are fascinating and unique in the Orlando radio market. Program director Daniels is very proud of *The Pat Williams Show* and recommends it highly. Asked why it airs at a time when few people would be likely to hear the program, Daniels explained somewhat ruefully that Sunday at 7 a.m. was the only time the station could guarantee the program would not be pre-empted by live sports broadcasts.

As the home of UCF sports, and with Daniels serving as both the station's program director and the voice of UCF football, basketball, and baseball, the closeness of the relationship between station and university is evident. When UCF plays a weekday evening game in any of these sports, *The Finish Line* is often shortened or entirely pre-empted while *Coach & Company* functions as a lead-in or pregame show. Saturday games preempt the Fox Sports programs.

The station's major professional sports affiliation is with the Tampa Bay Buccaneers. It carries all of the Bucs' games, taking them directly from WQYK in Tampa, but is not involved in producing the broadcasts. On occasion, 740 will feature other live professional sports from Fox or even ESPN, according to availability and scheduling.

Given its commitment to local sports, one might expect that The Team would broadcast the Orlando Magic, but that is not the case. The Magic organization produces its own radio transmissions and makes them available to the Magic network throughout Florida. In Orlando, the Magic are carried by WDBO, the all-news talk-radio station owned by Cox Broadcasting that serves as the flagship station for the Magic network. That leaves The Team with an awkward situation someone cleverly turned into a provocative promotional opportunity. The Team uses the tag line, "We're the station of the Magic fan," leaving WDBO, which calls itself "the home of the Orlando Magic," presumably the station of the Magic corporate establishment.

COMPETITION FOR "THE TEAM":
WORL, "THE FAN"

January 1, 2005, was the tenth anniversary of sports-talk radio in Orlando. For most of that time, The Team has had a monopoly on the sports-talk format in Central Florida. Competition came in mid-2004 when WORL 660 converted from news talk to sports talk, renaming itself "The Fan." Using some material from Sporting News Radio and partnering with Fort Lauderdale-based WFLL, 1400 The Fan, the new Orlando sports-talk station got most of its programming from WFLL. The only daily program originating in Orlando on The Fan was *Gary Cohl and Friends* from 5 to 7 p.m. weekdays. Cohl has been a well-known sports personality in central Florida, and has a lot of credibility with fans. In addition, WORL held the rights to broadcast Miami Dolphins, Florida Marlins, and Florida State games.[8] But it wasn't enough. By early 2006, WORL had changed formats again, this time shifting to business news, although retaining some evening sports programming from Sports News Radio and broadcasts of Florida Marlins games.[9]

The advent of The Fan was expected to push The Team to ramp up its promotions to connect with the community and reach out to existing listeners and potential new ones. Even before the competition from The Fan, The Team personalities made between 400 and 500 public appearances annually. They run three golf tournaments for charity during the year, which listeners are invited to join to play with one or more of the radio hosts. In addition to broadcasting from the Buccaneers' training camp, at least one program comes live from the annual Bay Hill tournament created by Arnold Palmer and part of the PGA tour. Other venues are used as targets of opportunity present themselves.

To reach its overwhelmingly male audience, The Team runs commercials on WESH Channel 2, the NBC-affiliate television station; WKMG Channel 6, the CBS affiliate; the all-news Channel 13, owned and operated by the *Orlando Sentinel* and Bright House; and print ads in the *Sentinel*. Station executives see the biggest potential for growth among minorities, especially African Americans and Hispanics. Today audiences include approximately 15 percent African Americans; 19 percent Hispanics; and 3 percent Asians, according to Daniels. At the time of this writing, none of these groups is represented among the program hosts, nor are women, who are more and more becoming an audience for sports.

Interestingly, 1400 The Fan features a weekly program that airs Fridays from 6 to 8 p.m. called *Chicks on Sports* that 660 The Fan in Orlando also carries. The blurb on the Web site promises "two beautiful women [who] toss around the hottest sports issues."[10] Fox Sports and ESPN already showcase a few women sportscasters who know their subject and represent a big step forward from the models and actresses that used to get assignments without necessarily knowing anything about sports. Trends tend to arrive later in Orlando, which is more conservative than some larger cities. It may be that the time of the female sports anchor—as distinguished from "chicks"—on local sports talk radio is approaching.

Compared to what can be heard regularly on the national *Tony Bruno Show,* for example, Orlando sports-talk radio is restrained where conversation about women is concerned. This is not accidental. Program director Marc Daniels said locker room talk is not his style. He further explained his feeling that "some things are not suitable for kids." Jerry O'Neill and the Shot Doctor also maintain decorum and stay away from jock talk. On The Team, Sileo is the only host who calls women "chicks," but he is not offensive about it and probably only hardened feminists would object because he is otherwise generous in his references to women. Indeed, he was very supportive of the woman who brought allegations of rape against Los Angeles Lakers' star guard Kobe Bryant.

However, The Team Web site, which highlights its programs and hosts, has a new feature, the "Babe of the Day," supplied by *Stare* magazine, showing a different semiclad beautiful woman in a provocative pose each day. That seems an unnecessary nod to locker-room attitudes because so far it is not supported by the station's other marketing and promotional activities. Maybe someone is waiting to see how the listeners react.

In general the Web site (www.740theteam.com) is a useful portal for sports news of any type with links at the top of the home page for the NBA, PGA, MLB, and so on, each of which has a dropdown menu linking to specific teams, scores, station features, and other information. It also features major stories of the day, upcoming special appearances by the hosts, and tournaments and contests for the listeners.

Discussion

In the 1990s, many stations jumped on the sports-talk bandwagon after the success of WFAN in New York and a few other pioneers. Later there was retrenchment as some of the stations converted back to other formats. In the twenty-first century, however, a new expansion of sports-talk radio may be occurring. It might be related to how Americans perceive the general state of the world. The trauma of 9/11 and the subsequent war on terrorism have once again created a situation in which many people find the news of the day unpleasant. They want to escape reminders of what troubles them, from terrorism to taxes.

In this atmosphere, sports, which are easily understandable and have clear rules, tend to become more necessary to more people. People want the entertainment that sports provide. Talking about sports and listening to other people—knowledgeable or not—talk about sports is entertaining. It's news, but not the kind of news that seems impossible to absorb or leads to feelings of hopelessness. Whatever the content of the sports news, it seems more manageable than current events, more approachable, and easier to fix, reform, replay, or improve in whatever way might seem necessary.

If the people who now live in Florida—almost all of them coming at some point from somewhere else—came because they were escaping from the cold, high taxes, personal insecurity, job loss, or other kinds of personal bad news, it makes sense that in Florida they would continue to want to escape from the bad news. At least some of the fans of sports-talk radio in Orlando probably have some of these feelings that draw them to make the friendly hosts at The Team part of their lives.

There may be places in the United States where local sports-talk radio is edgy, nervous, and problematic, but Orlando is not one of them. It is hard to imagine there would be much of an audience in central Florida for that kind of approach.

NOTES

1. Hille, Bob. "Best sports in city: More than feeling." *The Sporting News*. August 9, 2004, pp. 20-28.

2. Kampmeier, Chris, Regional Director of Programming, Central/North Florida, and Orlando Director of Programming, Clear Channel Radio. Interview by author. March 16, 2004. All comments from Kampmeier come from this interview.

3. Confirmed by a Florida friend who considered it quite normal behavior for a college football fan and alumnus.

4. Daniels, Mark, WQTM Program Director. Interview by author. November 11, 2004. All comments from Daniels come from this interview.

5. "740 The Team, Orlando's Sports Station." Accessed March 20, 2006. Available at http://740theteam.com/main.html.

6. Ibid.

7. *Coach & Company.* WQTM, Orlando, Florida. April 2, 2004.

8. "Foster Sports, Inc., a Subsidiary of Care Concepts I Inc., to Expand Sports Radio Presence to Central Florida." Press release. Accessed April 12, 2006. Available at http://www.findarticles.com/p/articles/mi_m0EIN/is_2004_April_29/ai_n 6004648#continue.

9. "Money Watch Radio Network." Accessed March 20, 2006. Available at http://www.660worl.com.

10. "Fox Sports Radio, 1400 AM." Accessed March 20, 2006. Available at http://www.1400wfll.com.

Chapter 5

KOZN, "The Zone," Omaha, Nebraska: "Unsportsmanlike Conduct"

J. H. Lipschultz
M. L. Hilt

Omaha's KOZN 1620 AM is known as "The Zone." The radio station is one of more than seventy in Nebraska, Minnesota, Iowa, Kansas, and South Dakota owned by Waitt Media—the twenty-third largest U.S. radio company. Since launching 1620 The Zone and its local afternoon sports-talk show *Unsportsmanlike Conduct,* the station has filled a void in local talk radio.

The Zone began as a sports-talk station on 1180 AM, which had been a news-talk station. In 1996, the station began to focus on sports programming. SportsRadio 1180 KOIL was born. The station carried SportsFan Radio Network programming weekdays, a local sports-talk show in the afternoon, and ESPN Radio, which was a weekend service at the time. Two years later, Mitchell Broadcasting applied for and was granted a new frequency, 1620 AM. Sports talk moved up the dial from 1180 AM to 1620 AM. KAZP 1620 AM went on the air in 1998, about the same time ESPN Radio expanded to a full week of programming. The owners changed the name of the station to "1620 The Zone" and changed the call letters to KOZN in 2002.

They developed a new afternoon show called *Unsportsmanlike Conduct with Kevin Kugler and Bob Bruce.* Bob Bruce was replaced by Mike'l Severe on the afternoon show.

The Omaha, Nebraska, radio market lacks major-league professional sports of its own. In an interview with the authors, KOZN Program Director Neil Nelkin said there is much interest in sports in general:

Sports-Talk Radio in America
© 2006 by The Haworth Press, Inc. All rights reserved.
doi:10.1300/5335_06

Omahans select teams to follow as fans and become very loyal. We've seen this with our broadcasts of Chicago Cubs baseball. There were many who thought that if there were any local loyalty to a Major League Baseball team, it would be the Kansas City Royals. I think this feeling was based on the proximity of Kansas City to the Omaha market and the fact that the Royals Triple-A minor league team has been based here for many years. We had carried Kansas City Royals baseball for a number of years without much success, either in ratings or revenue.

Our research indicated strong fan support for the Minnesota Twins, the St. Louis Cardinals and the Chicago Cubs. We carried about 120 Cubs games during the 2003 season and found advertiser and listener acceptance was very positive. This year we increased our schedule to the full 162 Cubs games and have seen even better results.[1]

Beyond the Cubs games, sporadic pro-sports interest may be found in the Royals (aired in Omaha on KOMJ), the Colorado Rockies, and the Minnesota Twins, as well as the NFL's Kansas City Chiefs, Chicago Bears, and Dallas Cowboys.

"The target demo for us is men, eighteen plus," Nelkin said.

We generally appeal to a broad spectrum of male listeners, but our best numbers are usually men, twenty-five to forty-nine. We have seen significant growth in this demographic. . . . The station is usually in the top three for our weekday talk shows, and has been ranked number-one frequently during our local afternoon talk show.

The most significant focus in the state is on the Nebraska Cornhusker football program, and local sports bars fuel the interest.

The *Omaha World-Herald* reported that Omahans spend more per capita at bars than similar mid-sized cities. A social-club president concluded: "It's a sports town; it's a Husker town. . . . It's a major drinking town. That's what everybody knows to do on the weekend."[2]

Sports talk in Omaha occurs within the larger context of talk radio in a state dominated by intense fan interest following back-to-back University of Nebraska national football championships in the mid-1990s. The success seemed to fuel expanded coverage on local television sportscasts (e.g., *The Big Red Report*) and radio. Husker media coverage in the market is ongoing throughout the year.

COLLEGE SPORTS IN A NON-PRO-SPORTS TOWN

It would be difficult to overemphasize the dominance of Nebraska football in this part of the country. Husker T-shirts, caps, and jackets produce a sea of Big Red on and off the field. Stop at a local grocery store or mall, and it would be unusual to not see someone sporting Husker gear.

Beyond Husker football, basketball, and baseball, the College World Series (held at Omaha's Rosenblatt Stadium every June), Creighton University Bluejay basketball (Creighton is located in Omaha), and University of Nebraska at Omaha hockey get some coverage throughout the year—particularly outside of the football season and the football spring-practice period. Beyond the KOZN programming, Omaha's news-talk shows often talk sports when Husker football is in season. This chapter will examine 1620 The Zone's content for how local sports is framed by the hosts and callers.

FRAMING AND SPORTS-TALK RADIO

Local sports-talk radio is part of mass media, which constitute much of what is accepted as the culture at any given time or in any specific place. Sports talk offers the opportunity to influence, for example, ticket sales. The messages, in short, are embedded with social-cultural meanings, which help define interest in local sports teams. Framing of sports involves definition, shared norms, themes, and meanings: "In essence, by organizing complex . . . topics around distinctive arguments and themes while concurrently downplaying others, journalists help shape an issue's deeper meanings and implications for the public."[3] The arena of local sports-talk radio can be driven by controversy and conflict.

Framing sports through talk may be understood from a cultural perspective. Carey (1992) linked culture to common information and "unity."[4] Sports may bring a community together through the intoxication of success and winning. Culture focuses on media *representa-*

tions or "significant symbolic forms,"[5] and "expressive artifacts—words, images, and objects that [bear] meanings."[6] Sports, then, are a matter of human language in which "myth, ritual, . . . story, narrative, chronicle" help strengthen social bonds.[7] Nowhere is this more obvious than in Nebraska: the Husker football team is a dominant "identity" for the state, and 1620 The Zone can build "virtual communities" through the show and its Web site.[8]

By framing events, local sports-talk radio may define enemies,[9] suggest the parameters of debate, dialogue, and discussion,[10] and even engage the community in thinking about important issues, such as racial policy.[11] If *we* are "the Husker Nation," as some in Nebraska suggest, then *they* must be the Oklahoma Sooners or the Texas Longhorns. Debate about who should lead a football team as quarterback, for example, may sometimes pit student athletes of different races against each other. Although sports may function as diversionary entertainment,[12] the framing may reflect deeper societal concerns, divisions, and aspirations.[13]

On 1620 The Zone, the program schedule is dominated by ESPN Radio shows. *Unsportsmanlike Conduct* is the only locally produced daily sports-talk show on the station (see Table 5.1).

CONTENT: UNSPORTSMANLIKE CONDUCT

At KOZN, a 7,100-watt station, Kevin Kugler co-hosts a 3 to 6 p.m. local sports talk show with Mike'l Severe. Kugler is sports director at the station and was the 2003 Nebraska Sportscaster of the Year. He was the radio voice for the Omaha Racers (a former Continental

TABLE 5.1. Typical 1620 "The Zone" program schedule.

Time	Program
Midnight	*Todd Wright All Night*
5 a.m.	*Mike and Mike in the Morning*
9 a.m.	*Colin Cowherd*
Noon	*Dan Patrick*
3 p.m.	*Unsportsmanlike Conduct*
6 p.m.	*ESPN Game Night*

FIGURE 5.1. KOZN, Omaha, Nebraska, afternoon-drive hosts: (left to right) Kevin Kugler and Mike'l Severe.

Basketball Association franchise), and continued as the voice for University of Nebraska at Omaha Mavericks Division II basketball and football games. Kugler also hosted *Big Red Wrap-Up* weekly on Nebraska Educational TV. Mike'l was hired in 2004 and also works as a morning reporter at a local television station.

Nebraska Football: A Year-Round Topic

At the end of the 2003 football season, despite a winning record, Nebraska Head Football Coach Frank Solich was fired. Defensive Coordinator Bo Pelini, who came to the Huskers from the Green Bay Packers, coached the team to a postseason bowl game victory. Some considered him the front-runner to be the new head coach. Instead, Oakland Raiders Head Coach Bill Callahan took the job after an extended search and the media frenzy that surrounded it. 1620 The

Zone discussed the fact that Pelini would likely leave the program rather than stay as defensive coordinator, as in this recorded excerpt:

KEVIN: Look, I understand that there's going to be that sentiment. . . . Say Bo Pelini went down, packed up his office, and left. You have to understand though that Bo Pelini is a very prideful guy. He is a guy that felt like he was going to be or could be the head coach at Nebraska, and he thought that he did a good enough job shepherding his team through a very choppy sea for the last month . . .

BOB: He was passed over. He was essentially told along with [assistant coach] Turner Gill: "You weren't good enough for this job . . . "[14]

1620 The Zone regularly carries live weekly NU football press conferences. Following the announcement of the hiring of Callahan

FIGURE 5.2. Exterior of KOZN, Omaha, Nebraska.

by Athletic Director Steve Pederson, The Zone tackled the controversy over Pederson implying during the press conference that Solich had been afraid to play for a national championship:

CALLER: He just couldn't let it go . . .

KEVIN: I was a little disappointed by that, too. That was one of the things he was looking for . . . somebody who wasn't afraid to play for a national title.

CALLER: . . . I think that Pederson could have just let it lie. He didn't have to make that comment and label Solich as a fearful coach. To me that's character assassination.[15]

Overall, despite spending a lot of time throughout the year on Nebraska football, callers are given relatively little time when compared to the time given to host banter and expert analysis from sports writers. Players and coaches also are sometimes interviewed during the show, which again cuts into the time available for caller talk.

Winter Sports: Creighton and Nebraska Basketball

The highlight of the 2003-2004 basketball season in Nebraska was a National Invitational Tournament play-in game between Nebraska and Creighton at Omaha's new Qwest Center arena. Nebraska had a record of 16-12, while Creighton was 20-8.

KEVIN: I understand that Creighton is likely disappointed with the appearance in the NIT after being in the NCAA for five straight seasons. I understand that, but I don't think that either team has a tremendous amount to play for in the NIT. I mean it's going to be a fun atmosphere tonight at the Qwest Center. I'm looking forward to being there, and I'm looking forward to watching the game between these two rivals. . . . Other than bragging rights in the state, it's not going to be any big deal. . . .[16]

One of the features of this day was allowing fans from each team to offer a brief "rant" about the local rivalry. Nebraska won the game in a close contest but was eliminated from the tourney in a later round.

College World Series: A Nebraska Baseball Focus

In recent years, the College World Series (CWS) has become *the* sporting event of the year in Omaha. Since the 1950s, the CWS has been played at Rosenblatt Stadium. Over the ten days of games, more than a quarter-million fans pay to attend. The Zone was the flagship station on the Westwood One Radio Network, and the station surrounded games with live chat from the ballpark. Before the 2004 series began, The Zone spent many days talking about CWS play. Initially, there was much interest in whether the Nebraska Cornhuskers or Creighton Bluejays would be among the final eight teams making it Omaha. Once the local teams were eliminated from play, attention turned toward the other favorites—Big 12 powerhouse Texas, which was the number-one seed, and traditional CWS teams from Florida, California, and Louisiana:

KEVIN. The excitement has begun. The build-up has begun. . . . It's a great event, and it's always fun to be out at Rosenblatt Stadium. . . . Great match-up Friday night: Texas, Arkansas. Fantastic match-up. Can't wait to see Dave Van Horn [former NU baseball coach]. How he's reacted to be the crowd . . .

MIKE'L: Not surprisingly, Texas the early favorite. I saw a poll today . . . thirty-six percent said Texas.

KEVIN: I would agree. You look at Arkansas and Arizona, and you wonder how these two teams are here because they don't have the big stars. You don't look at these guys and go, "Oh wow, they're loaded," like you do a Texas. Like you do, perhaps, an LSU.[17]

National and Regional Sports Events

Unlike sports-talk radio in nearby Kansas City, Omaha sports talk regularly devotes segments to national stories of the day. Perhaps because Omaha has a lack of its own major-league professional sports, ongoing general coverage of NASCAR, NFL football, the NBA playoffs, and the major-league baseball season (particularly the Cubs) is extensive.

Some coverage is devoted to Omaha's indoor-football team (the "Beef"), although discussion of the team is not taken very seriously. The Omaha Royals minor-league baseball team also is mentioned,

FIGURE 5.3. KOZN logo.

particularly in that dead period between the CWS and the start of the Husker football season. On days when not much is new with the local college or local teams, pro sports take center stage. Because the station carries many Chicago Cubs games, the Cubs tend to be a summertime focus.

A relatively small number of listeners call into the show on a daily basis, and they also post on the station's Web site message board. This listener liked the sports-talk format, but not as much as live sports:

> I think it is great to have baseball and other live sports on radio. I like sports talk shows more than regular talk, but listening to live broadcasts is even better. You have the Cubs on Omaha 1620 and the Royals on Lincoln 1480, NCAA Basketball tournament games, etc. Hear it as it happens instead of guys just chatting about it. These are sports stations and I want sports, not just people talking about it.[18]

Caller comments are strictly limited in terms of time and content, and they tend to be used as catalysts for host opinions.

CONCLUSIONS AND INTERPRETATIONS

The Zone's brand of sports talk radio is host-driven with little reliance on audience participation. Callers are featured in segments, such as "The Rant" and trivia contests, but most discussion of daily topics is between co-hosts and experts.

Omaha's lack of a major-league sports franchise results in a narrow list of topics for discussion—Nebraska football throughout the year, local sports when in season, and major national stories. At the same time, the hosts often go off on tangents, such as the weather, road construction, and their Web site's "Babe of the Week" photograph.[19]

When the hosts focus on the local-sports scene, they do not hesitate to take a critical stance. Far from being blind-faith boosters of the Nebraska Cornhuskers football team, the hosts are quick to challenge decisions made by the athletic director and coaches. Even so, when the Huskers or any local team are winning, the hosts jump on the bandwagon and celebrate success.

The Zone is an interesting example of local sports-talk radio in a market devoid of major professional sports teams. Minor-league teams, such as the Omaha Royals baseball team and the Omaha Beef indoor football team, are taken less seriously, if discussed at all. Major college sports teams, then, are the bread and butter of *Unsportsmanlike Conduct.*

APPENDIX: AN INTERVIEW WITH NEIL NELKIN, PROGRAM DIRECTOR, "THE ZONE"

Why is local sports-talk radio important in the Omaha market?

There are passionate, knowledgeable sports fans in the Omaha market that want to talk sports and want to participate in discussions about sports. . . . Obviously Nebraska Cornhusker football is the dominant franchise, but there is a pretty good following for Creighton basketball and baseball, Nebraska-Omaha football, basketball, and hockey, and River City Lancers minor-league hockey. Sports-talk radio gives them a place to discuss their teams, and like any discussion about sports, there will be differences of opinion and arguments. When you add hosts who are opinionated and have feelings about sports, it can generate debate and controversy, and keep the conversation interesting.

We don't limit the discussions to just local sports because the major national sports get as much, and more exposure here, with the proliferation of ESPN's channels, Fox's regional channels, and the amount of sports available on cable and satellite. . . .

We believe that sports fans and the sports-talk listeners, while not always the same group, appreciate the outlet that gives them an opportunity to express themselves, listen to others express themselves, and participate in the discussion. Above all, it has to be interesting, entertaining, and have an ability to get the listener involved, even if they never call in.

Sports-talk radio, especially on a local level, gives advertisers the means to reach a very active, aggressive, and demographically valuable audience that they may not be able to effectively reach any other way.

Are there plans to expand local sports-talk programming?

We are always looking for the right mix of local programming, syndicated programming and play-by-play. Finding and developing a local talent is a time-consuming and expensive process with no guarantees that it will work. Every former jock or sports fan thinks they can be the perfect host, but it's not always true. It takes time and technique to develop a bond with an audience. It's much more than just talking sports with your buddies.

If we believe we have the right host or hosts who can deliver a strong local presence, we'll expand our local-programming schedule. I will generally prefer local programming to syndicated programming, while still recognizing that having the strongest national brand, ESPN, and some of the best national talent, like Dan Patrick, sure doesn't hurt.

*How important in Omaha is the focus on Nebraska football
versus other local teams and sports?*

Nebraska football cannot be overemphasized in this area. We can talk about pro sports, Iowa sports (we are just across the river from Iowa after all) or any other sports, but Husker football is the king. It has the most fans, the most interest, the most speculation and sometimes the most controversy. It has been called Nebraska's unofficial state religion, and that is not far from the truth. We cover the Huskers year round, but our coverage becomes much more intense from August preseason through the annual spring game.

We also have the advantage of not being the Husker broadcast affiliate. That allows us to be much more objective regarding the Husker program and not have to fear any reaction or reprisals from athletic-department officials.

We can criticize the program when it's needed, and we don't have to screen out callers who may be critical of the program. Our commitment to Husker football coverage is extensive in terms of personnel and resources. We do cover the other local sports and local teams, but nothing compares to Husker football.

Has the relationship with ESPN been a good one? Why or why not?

Our relationship with ESPN dates to the earliest days of ESPN Radio and has been good both for us as the local affiliate and for them as the network. We've grown up together, and it is still a dynamic, evolving relationship. ESPN is the biggest, most recognized brand in sports. The brand validates who we are and what we do. We never have to explain the radio station when we say we are ESPN Radio. It is instant credibility with listeners, advertisers, and guests on our shows. Without the ESPN brand, it would have taken much longer for the radio station to establish itself in the marketplace and would have required much more in promotional activity and expenditures.

When the hosts take an aggressive stance, how have the audience and advertisers responded, if at all?

We encourage our hosts to be aggressive and opinionated, but we require that they have the facts, do their homework, and know what they're talking about. The audience responds when they are engaged, and the results usually bring out the best in the hosts and the callers.

Our hosts know how to use callers to contribute to the entertainment and information value of the shows. They also know how to deliver a monologue that will develop a topic and keep it in front of listeners. Callers are not always necessary or even helpful when some topics are being discussed. The host needs to know how and when to integrate callers into the discussion to generate the passion and excitement to bring the listeners into the radio. Perhaps more important, the host needs to know when to end a call.

Even when callers are angry or hostile, the host can use them to further the discussion. If all callers always agreed with the hosts, there would be no show. Advertisers can be sensitive to some topics, and sometimes disagree with a host's position. Most have learned that they are buying a means to reach the audience and that simply by advertising on a particular program, they are not endorsing the views of the host. It has sometimes been an educational process to explain this to an advertiser.

It is a great opportunity when an advertiser tells us that a customer has come to his business to complain that he advertises in one of our shows and the customer actively disagrees with the host and will not patronize the advertiser unless he drops his ads.

This allows us to open a dialogue with the advertiser and explain the value of the program, and the host. We are a very foreground medium. The ads are in the foreground. Listeners hear what we say. We get them actively involved in the program content. The ads in that environment are also in the foreground, and are generally more effective than if they were placed in a more passive environment.

Is the advertising community enthusiastic about the target market of this show? Does this format appear to be very profitable?

It has taken time and effort to educate the advertising community to the value of the sports-talk audience. Many media buyers simply use adults, twelve plus, as their criteria when making a buying decision. It may be easier for the buyer, but it is certainly not the best use of a client's advertising budget. By targeting specific demographics, we can deliver a much more efficient schedule for an advertiser, reaching the audience most likely to respond to the message.

We have seen many advertising success stories, and we use these as referrals for new or prospective clients. When buyers have used us for the right advertiser, used the right creative, and run an effective schedule, we can almost always deliver the expected results. This generates client loyalty and advertiser renewals. When we deliver for the advertiser, enthusiasm follows.

The sports-talk format is a good business decision for our station. We are the market leader in the format and deliver a very high-profile, aggressive, foreground broadcast product. In the long term, if we continue to post sales revenue increases, and maintain responsible control of our costs and operating expenses, we can expect the format to remain profitable.

Sports-talk formats generally deliver good profits for many stations. This format traditionally scores higher power ratios than many others, and delivers a demographically desirable audience with higher than average levels of education and career achievement. We also see much higher than average levels of disposable income among our sports-talk listeners.

For many years, sports-talk WFAN in New York was the top revenue-billing station in the country, even though it was hardly ever in the top five rankers in its market. The format seems to be strengthening and developing long-term growth. We continue to be optimistic that sports talk and play-by-play will continue to generate revenue shares in excess of ratings shares.

(Nelkin has worked in broadcasting for more than forty years, and he has been in the Omaha market since 1993.)[20]

NOTES

1. Nelkin, Neil. Interview by author, July 2, 2004.

2. Laue, Christine. "Does Cupid live here? Omaha doesn't have a reputation as a dating hotbed, but it's not devoid of opportunity." *Omaha World-Herald,* E-1, May 2, 2004.

3. Shah, Dhavan V., Mark D. Watts, David Domke & David P. Fan. "News framing and cueing of issue regimes: Explaining Clinton's approval in spite of scandal." *Public Opinion Quarterly 66,*(3), Fall 2002: 339-370.

4. Carey, James W. *Communication As Culture: Essays on Media and Society.* New York: Routledge, 1992.

5. Ibid., p. 8.

6. Ibid., p. 30.

7. Ibid., p. 37.

8. Barnes, Susan B. *Computer-Mediated Communication: Human-to-Human Communication Across the Internet.* Boston: Allyn & Bacon/Longman, 2003.

9. Lenart, Silvo and Harry R. Targ. "Framing the enemy: *New York Times* coverage of Cuba in the 1980s." *Peace & Change 17*(3), July 1992: 341-362.

10. Kruse, Corwin R. "The movement and the media: Framing the debate over animal experimentation." *Political Communication 18*(1), 2001: 67-87; Simon, Adam and Michael Xenos. "Media framing and effective deliberation." *Political Communication, 17*(4), October 2000: 363-376.

11. Kellstedt, Paul M. "Media framing and the dynamics of racial policy preferences." *American Journal of Political Science 44*(2), April 2000: 239-255.

12. Graber, Doris A. *Mass Media & American Politics,* Sixth Edition. Washington, DC: CQ Press, 2002.

13. Endres, Kathleen L. "'Help-wanted female': *Editor & Publisher* frames a civil rights issue." *Journalism & Mass Communication Quarterly 81*(1), Spring 2004: 7-21.

14. KOZN recording. Lincoln, Nebraska. January 9, 2004.

15. Ibid.

16. KOZN recording. Lincoln, Nebraska. March 16, 2004.

17. KOZN recording. Lincoln, Nebraska. June 14, 2004.

18. KOZN Message Board. Accessed June 15, 2004. Available at www.1620thezone.com.

19. KOZN Web page. Accessed June 15, 2004. Available at www.1620thezone.com.

20. Nelkin interview.

Chapter 6

KJR, Seattle: "It's Our Job to Provide the Biggest Menu"

Troy Oppie

INTRODUCTION

I still remember January 2, 1992. The radio under my pillow was on when I woke up, but instead of rock 'n' roll jock Gary Lockwood, I was hearing two new local hosts talking about college football and the Seattle Sonics. I was only partly shocked, as the station had carried Supersonics basketball for a number of years already and had steadily been building their sports-talk lineup through the midday until all that remained of the original KJR was Gary Lockwood in the mornings. But I was slightly angry, too; where was I going to get my "Police Blotter," "News From Abroad" or "Oceans of Beautiful Music?" Most important, who was going to replace the "Lock-Jock" as the radio host most hated by my mother?

KJR fended off angry callers for weeks; some even got on the air under the guise they were calling to talk sports. Even with the very vocal opposition, Program Director John D. Dresel (who had only been program director for a month at the time of the change) and owner Barry Ackerley stuck with the new format, a change that would ultimately tip the balance of power on Seattle's AM radio scene.

This chapter is a look inside Seattle's sports-talk radio station, 950 KJR-AM, where I served for a time as an intern. We'll examine the history of KJR and how the station balanced its programming around other stations' sports broadcasts. We'll also look at the station today, from my experience as a long-time listener and intern, to interviews

Sports-Talk Radio in America
© 2006 by The Haworth Press, Inc. All rights reserved.
doi:10.1300/5335_07

with other media, listeners, and KJR staff. Finally, a glance at the future of KJR: Can the station survive the sports broadcasting bidding wars to come?

PART ONE: ROOTS

KJR radio actually began in Seattle's Ravenna neighborhood at 1000 AM on the dial in 1922. A flour mogul, Oliver David Fisher, bought the rights to KJR in 1926, and paired KJR with KOMO 950 AM creating Seattle's first duopoly. Upon the FCC's antiduopoly ruling in 1944, Fisher elected to sell KJR and keep KOMO, but the frequencies were flipped so KOMO could receive a nighttime power increase. The power increase was essential to Fisher because of KIRO radio's new 50-kilowatt broadcast, which was the first 50-kilowatt tower west of the Mississippi River. In the Northwest, those three stations are referred to as the big three; KOMO's format of the time was news and variety shows, KJR was more music and live entertainment programming, KIRO was building its audience with news talk and popular music, and KOMO had been the dominant station during Seattle radio's infancy.

KJR's first programming venture outside of Fisher was contemporary music, balanced with cultural programming such as comedy shows, radio theatre, and some news. In 1954 KJR was playing music from the new technology of the time known as "records," even experimenting with "rock 'n' roll" for a short time before dismissing the music as a fad. The format was officially known as "middle-of-the-road" programming, and the station was about to get a big surprise.

In 1959, KJR hired Pat O'Day, a DJ who blended rock 'n' roll with a seemingly endless cast of zany on-air characters. His shows immediately "captured the imagination of Seattle's teenagers," said an interviewee in the *Seattle Rocket,* a local rock publication. O'Day's popularity spread quickly, and more attention was paid to the Seattle music scene during the O'Day years than would be until the grunge movement of the 1990s.

KJR was a radio juggernaut in Seattle, owning a 37 percent rating at one time in the 1960s. O'Day was promoted to program director, and KJR dominated Seattle's airwaves until the late 1970s.

A series of ownership changes through the 1980s led to a revolving chair behind the station manager's desk, sagging ratings, and eventually a format change in 1988 from Top 40 to Classic Hits.

The station was the rights holder for Seattle Supersonics basketball, a partnership that was a direct result of then-owner Barry Ackerley also owning the Supersonics. As the Sonics began the return to their prime through the early 1990s, the evening sports-talk programs became increasingly popular. Sports shows were added in afternoon dayparts as well, and KJR benefited from a University of Washington national championship football season that fueled the phone lines with rabid Husky fans.[1]

Experimental Stages

Before 1987, sports-talk radio did not exist. New York's WFAN pioneered the sports-talk format. Still, in its infancy, sports-talk radio was still a giant experiment said Rich Moore, KJR program director who's been with KJR since he interned there in 1992.

"It was in experimental stages, but the whole premise was that a sports station should be purely credible. You report, talk about facts and you have to play that game," Moore said.[2]

Local stations, both wary and unable to staff local shows twenty-four hours a day, were aided by national programs such as *Sports Byline USA,* and shortly thereafter ESPN Radio, The Sports Fan Radio Network, and Fox Sports Radio. KJR had used *Sports Byline USA* to supplement its programming for many years before the completion of the format change and introduction of ESPN Radio to the Northwest.

Moore continued, "Back then, it was purely sports-talk, purely [a] credible source, and there wasn't much of what we see now, of the entertainment factor."

In Seattle, Nanci Donnellan proved to be the grandest and most successful of sports-radio experiments.

The Fabulous Sports Babe

Then-Program Director Rick Scott, who now operates a national sport-talk radio consultant firm out of Bellevue, Washington, discovered Donnellan on Tampa Bay's WTKN hosting an afternoon sports-talk show. Scott pursued Donnellan relentlessly, feeling that her personality was a perfect fit to bring KJR into the spotlight of talk radio in Seattle.

"This is a task very few people would want to take on in Seattle," Scott told Donnellan while courting her from across the country. "Because when you take on this role, everybody in going to hate you in this town."

Regardless of love or hate, they listened. The "Fabulous Sports Babe" proclaimed herself KJR's "lead dog," and bigger than Kurt Cobain or Bill Gates. She also hated Seattle, calling it a "fucked-up backwater town," filled with the "dumbest people in the world," in her tell-all book *The Babe in Boyland*.

Donnellan's attitude was exactly what KJR needed to draw people to the radio, and ratings tripled from what they had been at the time of the format change. She wasn't afraid to tell callers just how dumb they were, and made her name living on the edge of reason with her listeners. People would tune in just for the carnage each day. In all my interviews, on and off the record, I have not encountered a single person who genuinely enjoyed listening to the Fabulous Sports Babe on KJR. But they certainly listened, based on the same premise that people slow down to look at an accident in the opposite direction on the freeway: possible disaster and assured entertainment.[3]

"The reason why the entertainment aspect really came into the fold is because the initial foundation of what sports radio became had a following," said Moore. "But in order to get that following up to the level in which the stations can compete both in ratings and revenue, we had to attack a demographic that demanded the entertainment as well."

Moore credited several things, including the birth of ESPN Radio, for bringing many more resources and talent to the table and creating a public need to build on the sports radio station that did exist, but didn't necessarily carry sports talk as the majority of their programming.

Locally, Moore credited Donnellan for being the first real personality behind the sports-talk microphone, and putting KJR and Seattle itself on the map.

"She had a shtick, a strong, in-your-face attitude and came here not really knowing anything about the west coast or Seattle. [Having her here] built us a following, outside of what we were getting from play-by-play and sports news," Moore said.

That shtick prompted many upset listeners, as well as upset KJR sales associates who were finding it harder to sell the station that carried such an outlandish host during the middle of the day.

Donnellan credits Rick Scott for putting his foot down against the station management and salespeople, literally throwing himself in front of the studio door to keep the people out. Scott stands six feet, six inches tall, but his faith and Donnellan's ratings were enough to drive away the internal detractors after the first few months.

A few years down the road, things turned ugly when ESPN Radio came calling with a national contract offer and KJR tried to stick to their guns on their contract with Donnellan. The battle that ensued on-air as well as behind closed doors was very spiteful, and resulted in Donnellan leaving Seattle on her way to a national radio talk show on ESPN and eventually a television simulcast of that radio show on ESPN2.

Donnellan was eventually released by ESPN after the telecast of her show bombed, and she was picked up by the Sports Fan Radio Network, who released her in 2001. Her battle with cancer has kept her in retirement in Florida. Her book effectively burned most of bridges she had at ESPN, and no one knows whether she will return to a job in radio.[4]

Her effect was lasting, however, and set the tone for shows to come, in Seattle and elsewhere. Meanwhile, as personalities lit the coals beneath listeners, off-the-air developments helped expand the amount of what Program Director Moore called "our base listeners."

Wheeling and Dealing the Broadcast Rights

In 1992, KJR only held broadcast rights for the Seattle Supersonics. KOMO-AM 1000 was a contemporary-music station with UW football and basketball on weekends and evenings, and KIRO Newsradio 710 was all news and talk with Seahawks football and Mariners baseball. Part of the transition to a twenty-four-hour sports-talk station was the addition of the ESPN Radio network, which filled overnights, weekends, and covered special events like Monday Night Football and the NCAA basketball tournament.

Moore says there was a feeling of static success until 2002, when the University of Washington's broadcast rights were bought by Action Sports Media (ASM), a group owned by Microsoft pioneer Paul Allen. ASM then placed the Husky broadcasts on KJR.

The Action Sports Media buyout of the University of Washington's broadcast rights set in motion a series of events that changed the sound and ratings pyramid of Seattle's AM radio.

"The radio stations were all owned by companies that weren't selling [to other owners], and were committed to what they were doing," Moore said. "When everyone is consistent on that path, everyone kind of protects each other and goes on that path with their own product; there wasn't competition."

The result was a high concentration of sports coverage on weekends and evenings, but little direct tie-in with those broadcasts during the week on KJR because KJR didn't have the rights to the play-by-play of those teams.

ASM cited the availability of programming outside of game day as a specific reason it chose KJR over the incumbent KOMO for Husky football and basketball broadcasts.

Said Rick Furr, ASM general manager:

> On Saturdays, you had this huge audience for Husky football, and then there was a complete drop-off during the week. One of the things KJR brings to the table more than anybody else in town is to promote the Huskies during the week.[5]

The University of Washington football program is the backbone of sports in Seattle. Consistently until this year, 72,000 fans bustled through the gates of Husky Stadium for each home game. A few hundred thousand more listen to the games on the radio, and the loss of UW's broadcast rights, even to a nonsports station such as KOMO, was a major blow to its audience.

KOMO reacted swiftly, outbidding KIRO radio the very next year for the Seattle Mariners broadcast rights with a contract rumored to be the largest in all of baseball. Neither side released monetary figures, but the deal was approximated at $10 million per year, for six years. The acquisition of the Mariners prompted a complete promotional rebirth of KOMO, and the format was changed from news-talk with a mix of local and national hosts to a twenty-four-hour news-traffic-weather format anchored by 162 (or more) Mariner games per year.[6]

The difference between the two types of purchases is which side was supporting which. KJR's programming is supporting UW athletics with the availability of more airtime. KOMO has banked on Mariner baseball to draw fans into its regular news coverage, which can be risky, but isn't a new or uncommon idea.

When NFL television rights were granted to the highest bidder, Rupert Murdoch's Fox Network outbid CBS for the broadcast rights for NFC football games. Fox bet on its football broadcasts to draw viewers into its other programming by using a combination of in-game promotional spots, tie-ins, and direct-follow programming carefully planned to draw the game audience into the immediate next show.

Warsaw Sports Marketing Center Director Rick Burton said:

> Rupert Murdoch overpaid by $100 million to get the rights, and he knew that he would lose money on football. But he also thought it would make his network legitimate, and that may be the same kind of situation here.[7]

Burton's use of the word "legitimate" is ironic, because the sports-talk industry is moving away from the idea of a twenty-four-hour legitimate sports-news program schedule. The entertainment factor is what drives the ratings, but Moore said there still has to be some kind of legitimate sports-news base to keep the sound of the station grounded, and those base listeners tuned in.

> We pursued the UW contract for years, because we knew it would be a big boost to our audience to have both the "honks" (as rabid UW fans are known in Seattle) and the folks who just tune in for the games listening to KJR. We took the same approach to the Mariners contract, but were outbid early in the game.

A station can survive without the broadcast rights for the majority of teams in its market; KJR proved that, but did it pioneering a new sound in Seattle radio. As the sports-talk format matures, the line between entertainment and legitimate sports information has become blurred by promotions and dayparts that often stray from the topic of sports. Where that line is and why it works in Seattle will be discussed next.

PART TWO: SPORTS RADIO 950, K-J-R!

Paying Tuition to Work in Radio

Gary Lockwood used to start his show at 5:30 a.m. with, "Is anyone awake out there?" I often felt the same as I drove into work during my internship with KJR's morning-drive show, *Mitch in the Morning.*

A quick history lesson on Mitch Levy, the host of the show: He was not the first choice when he was hired as a midday *(Mitch in the Midday)* host out of a small talk station in Florida. The original host's first show was in the fall of 1995 and he promptly ripped the Sonics, the coaching staff, and the upper management of the team.

In 1995, Barry Ackerley still owned the Sonics, and had recently bought back into the ownership group of New Century Media, which purchased KJR and a few other Seattle stations from Ackerley a few years prior.

As the story goes, the Sonics/KJR ownership group was listening to that host's first show, and his plane ticket out of town had been purchased for him before he was off the air his first day at work.

Mitch Levy was offered the job and began his shows in the 10 a.m. to 2 p.m. slot before moving to the morning-drive program a few months later.

In 2001, I found myself staring through the glass at one of the sharpest, funniest hosts I'd ever heard on radio. On my sixth day as intern, the morning producer informed me that he had put in his two week's notice thirteen days earlier and the next day would be his last. Due to the host's ill temper off the air and the lack of an operating budget (or so I was told), I was asked to temporarily fill some of the duties in place of the morning-show producer. Needless to say, that was an amazing opportunity, and I hope I made the most of it. As an intern, I found one gets hung up on more often than not. But I had a lot of respect being shown to me by the program director and other producers and learned some tricks of the trade.

The Sound of the Station

There is no direct competition for KJR; Seattle is one of only a few major cities without a second full-time sports-talk station. This means that the program director needs to look outside the format to find the other radio stations pulling the target audience away from

KJR. KIRO dominates the overall ratings, but KJR is competing directly with them and NPR, as well as shows featuring Howard Stern, Tom Leykis (a local shock-jock, who is also nationally syndicated), and the classic-rock format. The mix of those groups breaks down as such: news folks (KIRO and NPR) are looking primarily for sports news and information. The rest fall into the category of entertainment mixed in with sports.

Ultimately, the competition dictates the sound of the station as it differs from daypart to daypart. KJR's morning show is a collection of entertainment segments and sports interviews and crosstalk between the host and the co-host or other show crew. *Mitch in the Morning* is responsible for the KJR "Sports Babes" calendar, as well as "The Bigger Dance," an NCAA tournament-type contest that pits female celebrities against each other on the basis of looks and sexuality. That isn't something you'll find in the afternoons, said Moore.

> Because in the mornings, where we're competing in our [demographic] with Stern and Leykis, and those types of programs, there's going to be more guy talk than in the afternoons, where we're talking more to the blue-collar sports fans, the guys driving around in their trucks.

In fact, you could say KJR's lineup gets quieter as the day progresses, before rebounding with the last local show of the evening.

The 10 a.m. to 2 p.m. slot belongs to Dave Mahler, known as "Softy." Mahler is your typical loudmouth sports fan who has a few too many at the game and may or may not end up being escorted from the stadium before the night is over. Mahler follows the tradition of Donnellan, in that his show is based around his hard-hitting, in-your-face attitude with callers and listeners alike. Where he differs is his unwavering support for the local teams, through thick and thin. Mahler is quick to criticize the local teams, in fact he couldn't keep an audience if he didn't, but his show is a loud, brash discussion of Seattle sports.

Dave Grosby, aka "The Groz" is an older, quieter, more polished version of Dave Mahler. Grosby has been at KJR since the early 1990s, and returned to KJR after a brief stint at KIRO in the late 1990s. Grosby is always well prepared for his show, which hits sports news hard and public-interest news when necessary. The past three years he has teamed with late-afternoon host Mike Gastineau for a segment called, *Groz with Gas.*

Both Grosby and Gastineau are professional hosts who talk sports and take calls from a very devoted audience largely made up of those aforementioned KIRO and NPR-type listeners. But the hour devoted to *Groz with Gas* is a complete turnaround from the norm. Anything goes, from guy talk, to oddball news, to sports and back again. They don't take calls during that hour, and conversations are often interrupted by fits of laughter from the hosts. That segment was expanded to two hours without success (ratings actually dropped) and is currently filling the 3 to 4 p.m. hour on KJR.

David Locke hosts *Locked on Sports* from 7 p.m. to midnight. Locke is a very heady individual who also anchors Sonics, UW football, UW basketball, and Mariners postgame shows. *Locked on Sports* regains the in-your-face attitude that KJR loses to an extent with Grosby and Gastineau. Locke hosts a very intense show, five hours typically heavy with stats and up-front sports talk. The intensity of *Locked on Sports* has proven to be its greatest asset, as well as its most criticized feature, said Program Director Moore.

"We really try to have something for everyone in our lineup," he said.

Who Is the Audience?

We keep coming back to the idea of two groups of listeners—the base sports-information listeners and the entertainment listeners. As you might expect, one of those groups is significantly and consistently younger than the other.

As a result of more entertainment-based sports programming, meaning hosts with strong personalities talking about sports as well as guy talk, KJR's audience has gotten progressively younger.

In 1992, the audience was largely in the thirty-five to fifty-four demographic. Today, KJR's listenership has evened out. The heaviest group falls in the males twenty-five to thirty-four range, trailed closely by both males, forty-five to fifty-four and males, thirty-five to forty-four. By contrast, KIRO's profile lists the same raw number of listeners in the males twenty-five to thirty-four category, but that grouping of listeners only makes up about 5 percent of KIRO's audience, whereas it's almost 20 percent of KJR's audience.[8]

Pouring over Arbitron ratings, the biggest surprise I got was where KJR ranked among high-income listeners. That isn't that surprising, said both Program Director Moore and former KJR Sales Associate Rich Horner.

"That part of the audience made it easy to sell air-time on the station," said Horner. "[As sales associates] we could directly target high-end dealers for cars, appliances, electronics, things males with spending decisions and spending power are going to be buying, instead of going through an advertising agency."[9]

Moore said this is directly correlated to the influx of sports and sporting events in popular society.

> It's this income-earner that can afford the cost of season tickets, that can afford the time to go to the games and become involved. As these events and stadiums have become much bigger productions housed in much more comfortable and posh surroundings, it's going to draw a larger base audience that is partially attending for the spectacle in addition to the fans who are just interested in the meat and potatoes of the game itself.

What does this mean? In Seattle, that base audience of sports-information listeners might be smaller than other cities our size but it is going to listen. The rest of the listeners are likely more interested in what's going outside of sports than talking at length about why the Seahawks' wide receivers are dropping 60 percent of their passes.

Sports Fans in "Hooterville"

Nanci Donnellan ("the Fabulous Sports Babe") verbally assaulted Seattle sports fans from her first day in the city she called "Hooterville." Seattleites are "tree-hugging, coffee-sipping, Birkenstock-wearing idiots," she said.[10] If you were to compare Seattle fans to the sports fans of New York, Philadelphia, Los Angeles, and Oakland, that is a possibility. But it may just be true that there is more going on in Seattle, said Fox Sports Net Northwest television anchor Angie Mentink.

"People have more to do out here, there's more options for sporty entertainment," said Mentink. "They might go hiking, or boating, or something else that is a personal sport instead of tuning in to find out how the team they partially follow did in the game that weekend."[11]

When you combine that available resource with generations of losing teams, it's not any wonder that as Seattle sports teams go, so goes KJR.

"Seattle doesn't have any real history," said Moore. "The days of the Sonics championship are gone, the Seahawks have never gone farther than the second round of the playoffs (1984), and we're kind of living the whole Mariners rollercoaster ride that's been going since 1995."

Sports radio's audience grew significantly in two periods, from 1994 to 1995 with the introduction of the Fabulous Sports Babe and the Sonics record-setting season and playoff collapse, and again from 1998 to 2001 based on hot-button issues of discussion: UW football, the Mariner's hot and cold alternating seasons, finally a big-name coach and owner behind the Seahawks, two new stadiums on the way, and a Sonics team that was struggling to find its identity in a dominating NBA Western Conference.

Through that entire rollercoaster ride that any city undoubtedly goes through with its own sports teams, fans found other things to do. There simply weren't enough hard-core sports fans in Seattle to keep teams healthy during extended stretches of sub-.500 seasons, and Seattle almost lost the Mariners to Tampa Bay and the Seahawks to Los Angeles because of that hot-and-cold support provided by fans up here.

Industry analysts have said from afar that KOMO radio banked its entire future on the success of the Mariner broadcasts. Not only did the Mariners have a dismal season this past year, but KOMO was unable to hold Mariner listeners beyond baseball season. For the past two years, KOMO's ratings have spiked around Mariner season, approaching KIRO's ratings, but have always fallen off in the winter Arbitron ratings period. That is further proof not only that a sports broadcasting contract cannot solely rebuild a struggling station, but that the majority of Seattle sports fans are quick to turn the radio off on a team that is not winning games.

The opposite of Mariners ratings has been shown recently in the Sonics radio ratings. The team had very low expectations to start the 2004-2005 season, but quickly jumped to the top of the standings. Radio and TV ratings climbed each week of the basketball season, but a downturn in the team's fortunes would no doubt reverse the trend.

Connecting with the "Non-Base" Listener

Moore's philosophy in programming KJR is based on combining the two types of sports-talk stations, the credible all-sports stations and the "guy-talk" stations.

"Why are we both?" Moore asked rhetorically. "Because we have no competition. It's our job to provide the listener with the biggest menu to our demographic [in order] to build the biggest cume we can, [so that] sales benefits."

The *Mitch in the Morning* show does the best job connecting with guys who enjoy sports but aren't necessarily sports junkies. Mitch Levy's attack is to prepare with both interesting national sports news, topical local sports news, and entertainment news from around the world. The show takes tangents based on funny or sexy stories pulled from the Internet during the middle of the show, and these tangents have been allowed to dominate the entire show from time to time.

Levy, while in control of his show, is very good about letting a topic run a show if that topic is worthy. Obviously, a tense sports issue will dominate conversation, as did the firing of University of Washington football coach Rick Neuheisel for example. But, every once in a while, a single conversation sparks a show's worth of dialogue or even its own reoccurring segment.

For example, a former traffic reporter (a service provided to Seattle radio by a third party called Metro Networks) with a very sexy voice attracted Levy's attention and was the subject and participant of many on-air conversations involving male-female relations and sex. Eventually, a segment was produced weekly called "Pizza 'n' Porn," in which the former traffic reporter, Tracy Taylor, would report on a pornographic video she had watched the night before as well as the quality of a pizza delivered by the segment's sponsor.

I remember fielding calls during that segment, most of them from the core audience screaming in my ear about the lack of sports content on the morning show. A side note to those calls is that while many said they were fed up and would never listen to *Mitch in the Morning* again, most called to complain routinely.

Segments such as "Pizza 'n' Porn" are typical for Levy's show; he likes to push the envelope, and has such a razor-sharp wit that very little sneaks by him. Levy refused my repeated requests for an interview on this project. As a listener myself, I thought the show suffered without a trained producer; I simply did not have the power to get the big-name guests Levy was used to having. But there was something different every day that he brought to the show to keep it interesting and moving its entire four hours. No one is better at that in Seattle than Mitch Levy.

KJR was one of the pioneers of "guy talk" in Seattle radio. As the station grew out of the experimental stages of sports-radio infancy, the direction changed to accommodate the need for a more diverse audience, one that was not solely interested in sports, but one that could be held by sports talk mixed in with general guy talk as well. Part Three of this chapter examines where sports radio in Seattle might be headed.

PART THREE: THE FUTURE

All the interview subjects I spoke with said there is no cap on the number of people we can attract to sports radio. The sports potential is too great; no other subject, save for political radio in a presidential election year, can go between the extreme highs and lows of sports. Sports is something people can be passionate about without being too serious, said FSN's Angie Mentink, and that helps build the audience at times of high sports interest, and can also hurt ratings during periods of low sports interest.

Moore admitted fine-tuning remains to be completed on the "guy talk" half of the format. Recent incidents of indecency in the media have prompted every station to pay more attention to their product than in the past.

"I think it will contain guy talk, I don't think guy talk will go away, but it definitely will contain it," Moore said of harsher FCC penalties to offending stations and their owners. But he also called such curtailing a good thing at KJR.

"It will level off where it needs to level off to maintain its credibility and we can still have good success, because there's plenty of other ways out there for us to have good success because [this is] now an accepted format."

In addition, Moore bet that a "zero-tolerance" policy adopted by the FCC will help sports-talk radio because the talent at KJR can work around sports to present it in an entertaining way.

"[If] you put that same rule to Howard Stern, Leykis, and the rest, Howard Stern says 'I'm quitting' [Stern made a much-publicized switch to satellite radio in early 2006]. They have no options."

A trend that will help prolong and grow the sports-talk audience is the age of its main demographic. Sports talk is getting younger, while competing formats are getting older. Moore hopes that sports talk can hold those younger listeners as they grow up to ages not currently listening to sports-talk now, all while continually grabbing the younger listeners. Because KJR can be both a credible and an entertaining sports station by using its talent wisely and maintaining team broadcast contracts, Moore sees that growth to be a possibility for KJR.

> What's really going to change in this industry will be the technology, how we get the product to the listeners. If we can keep up with the Joneses, in a sense; radio on satellite, radio on cell phones, the Internet, we'll be able to grow and flourish within this format as much as we have in our first twelve years.

CONCLUSION

As technology grows in ways no one can predict, KJR will adapt itself around that technology and relate it to the format. The mix of credible sports talk and guy talk will not go away, but will be refined as the ratings and society dictate. But Moore feels KJR has found a good, successful mix of information and presentation to carry them well into the future. Will it matter who owns the broadcast rights for Seattle's sports teams? Neither Moore nor Mentink think so.

"There's only so many sports games, you've still got to have engaging personalities behind the [microphone] the other twenty hours of the day," said Mentink.

The Fabulous Sports Babe still might not think so, but KJR has found a home and a following in "Hooterville."

NOTES

1. "KJR History" (document online). Seattle: KJR Radio Memories, 2001. Accessed July 26, 2004. Available at www.kjrseattle.com; "KJR History" (document online). Seattle: Puget Sound Radio Broadcasters Association, 2002. Accessed July 26, 2004. Available at www.psrba.org.

2. Moore, Rich. Interviews by author. Tape recording. May 2, 2004, and September 29, 2004. Unless otherwise indicated, all comments from Moore are taken from these interviews.

3. Donnellan, Nanci and Neal Karlen. *The Babe in Boyland.* New York: Harper Collins, 1996.

4. Ibid.

5. Wither, Bud. "KJR seals deal as UW's flagship station." *Seattle Times,* C-1, March 5, 2002.

6. Scott, Alwyn and Martin McOmber. "What's the Future of KOMO-TV." *Seattle Times,* B-10, November 12, 2002.

7. Condatta, Bob. "Mariners mean more than money to KOMO." *Seattle Times,* C-1, May 15, 2003.

8. Newham, Blaine. "KJR switch a dial down to 'guy talk' for UW," C-1, May 5, 2002.

9. Horner, Rich. Interview by author. Tape recording. July 20, 2004. Unless otherwise indicated, all comments from Moore are taken from this interview.

10. Donnellan and Karlen, pp. 43, 79.

11. Mentink, Angie. Interview by author. Tape recording. February 19, 2004. Unless otherwise indicated, all comments from Mentink are taken from this interview.

Chapter 7

WIP, Philadelphia:
"The Station with the Big Mouth
and Even Bigger Heart"

Douglas Pils

When covering an event, whether it's a game or a city council meeting, journalists are taught to look for conflict. Two sides at odds with each other make a compelling story and conflict attracts the attention of other like-minded people to root for their side of the argument, thereby extending the story's life. WIP in Philadelphia has been giving some of the United States' most rabid sports fans the perfect avenue to put such thoughts on the airwaves since December 7, 1987, when the city's oldest radio station became the nation's second all-sports, all-the-time station following New York's WFAN.

However, WIP started giving listeners more than just sports talk and a place to rail on Philadelphia Phillies' general manager Ed Wade. (WIP's Web site asked visitors to vote on whether Wade should be fired as the Phillies slid out of the 2004 playoff picture.) The station goes beyond the box score, because ratings are built on the entertainment dollar. Sports-talk radio has become another form of entertainment, vying for consumers' time just like television, the movies, and going to the mall.

WIP helped pioneer radio in the City of Brotherly Love and its kitschy brand of sports talk, which frequently strays into areas requiring a rating system similar to the motion-picture industry, and spawned copycats across the nation. For a town waiting for a major sports championship since the Philadelphia 76ers won the 1983 NBA crown, WIP hosts and callers can get venomous and downright mean

Sports-Talk Radio in America
© 2006 by The Haworth Press, Inc. All rights reserved.
doi:10.1300/5335_08

when they do talk sports. However, WIP trademarks include the Wing Bowl, a chicken-wing eating contest held since 1993, and the Miss WIP contest since 1996, in which the winner needs little more than various physical talents.

WIP may lean toward the salacious, but it also helps the community with its Radiothon, a benefit held for the twelfth year in 2005. The station runs a thirty-seven-hour on-air auction, in which listeners can bid on sports-related items and the proceeds help the Eagles Youth Partnership and City Year. The station promotes the event by saying it comes "from the station with the big mouth and even bigger heart!"

* * *

The station, whose call letters originally stood for "Wireless in Philadelphia," hit the airwaves on March 17, 1922, about the same time as WFI, WGL, and WOO, and it was owned by the Gimbel Brothers Department Store.[1] The name "WIP" was drawn from a hat when the store became the licensee in 1922.[2] The station was in the brothers' store, and a children's show hosted by "Uncle WIP" was one of its most popular.[3]

Little is childish about WIP's broadcasts now, unless you count detractors calling the station's broadcasters and listeners little boys. Former Philadelphia Phillies manager Jim Fregosi was caught calling them a lot worse in the early 1990s. Fregosi was talking about WIP in the presence of a reporter from *The Philadelphia Inquirer,* who then reported that Fregosi said that the station's only listeners were men from South Philadelphia who had sex with family members and that the people who worked at the station were just like the men from South Philadelphia. Fregosi's Phillies were the defending National League champions at the time, but the team slipped to 54-61 and fourth in the East Division during the strike-shortened season. He undoubtedly heard plenty of grief from fans and from hosts. Fregosi said:

> I don't deny saying it. But I must reinforce that by no means does it reflect my true feelings concerning our fans. I'm embarrassed, and I'm embarrassed for my family. I've spent 35 years in this game, and for someone to try to tear that down, it's a shame. . . . I didn't think I had to be careful in my own office.[4]

WIP's mantra reads "entertainment first, sports second," but it was clearly starting to have an impact on the sports figures in its hometown. Fregosi lasted two more seasons in Philadelphia before being let go in 1996, when the Phillies finished below .500 for the fifth time in six seasons in his tenure.

In the spring of 1987, WIP was sold to Spectacor, which also owned the Philadelphia Flyers and the Spectrum arena, and in November that year it became all sports, except for morning drive. Steve Martorano hosted that show, a general talk show, but he often discussed sports. Martorano was with WIP as a midday host until summer 2005.[5]

The all-sports format at WIP started in 1987 with veteran local sportscasters such as Tom Brookshire, Bill Campbell, Joe Pellegrino, and Howard Eskin, who left the station during the 1990s only to return. (Eskin, who started hosting WIP's first sports show in September 1986 from 5 to 6 p.m., currently mans the 3 to 7 p.m. afternoon drivetime slot.)[6] These broadcasters had a reputation for hosting serious discussions about the local sports teams—the Phillies (baseball), the Eagles (football), the Flyers (hockey), and the 76ers (basketball). The mantra has almost always been to talk about the four professional teams and nothing else.

Dipping down to talk about college teams could alienate listeners not interested in certain schools. If you start talking about Penn State, then fans of Pittsburgh, Notre Dame, or Virginia are changing the channel. The station even shies away from talking about the "Big Five," Philadelphia college basketball teams St. Joseph's, Temple, LaSalle, Pennsylvania, and Villanova. The schools used to stage triple-headers at the Palestra in Philadelphia, but talking about one school over the other might turn off listeners.

In the early 1990s, the serious sports talkers were gradually replaced with guys who sounded more like fans than experts. This move created the genre of "guy talk," in which callers and hosts ignored sports for extended segments and started discussing women and other topics normally reserved for the local bar. This began when former *Philadelphia Inquirer* columnist Angelo Cataldi joined the morning show with Brookshire in November 1990.[7]

Former station manager Tom Bigby, who arrived in 1988 as a consultant and was named program director in 1989, encouraged his hosts to look for more ways to entertain the listeners. He put two sportswriters and a drivetime "personality" with no sports background together and let them talk about anything they wanted. "We're like a morning zoo for adults," Bigby said. It worked and WIP's ratings became the highest in the country for an all-sports station.[8]

Whether you like it or hate it, WIP's brand of sports-talk radio set the standard that stations around the nation emulated. Bigby made no apologies for his approach. "You have to be entertaining. It's radio first, sports second," he said. Bigby's theory forced other stations to adopt or copy the format because it lured advertisers who sought the male audience between ages twenty-five and forty-nine. The all-sports format attracted a wider audience base than all-news content.[9]

Chuck Cooperstein worked sixteen months at WIP in 1992-1993 before returning to the Dallas-Fort Worth market where he has been since 1984 with the exception of his short stint in Philadelphia. Cooperstein, known for his knowledge of a wide range of sports and for being a straight shooter, didn't fit Bigby's entertainment mold. Cooperstein's first trip to the Palestra for a Big Five showdown left him in awe of the spectacle and he thought he had perfect fodder for the next day's show. Cooperstein said Bigby marched down the hall and told him he wouldn't recommend focusing on local college basketball. Cooperstein, a play-by-play commentator for CBS football and basketball radio broadcasts, had a reputation as a serious journalist, so he fought Bigby's suggestions.

"I give Tom Bigby a lot of credit," said Cooperstein, who worked at KTCK 1310 AM, "The Ticket," a WIP clone, upon his return to Dallas, and now he's a local broadcaster on Dallas's ESPN radio station, KESN. "He created a format, a niche, and that niche created an opportunity for someone to make money. I've always said that Tom is one of the brightest guys in radio, but he was very difficult to work for."[10]

Like Cooperstein, many people found working for Bigby a difficult, if not impossible challenge. In early 2003, the WIP *Morning Show* lost funnyman Joe Conklin over reported conflicts with Bigby. Midday host Mike Missanelli left at the same time, and the duo showed up running a morning show at WMMR 93.3 FM in Philadelphia.[11]

Cataldi also called Bigby a tough boss. "He saw something in me that I didn't see in myself," Cataldi said. "Most of my success was due to him. . . . He's the hardest boss I ever had—extremely difficult on a day-to-day basis—but I respect him."[12]

Stations that tried to rely on sports experts talking about the intricacies of the hit-and-run or the trajectory of a fifteen-yard deep-out route didn't have staying power. Appealing to men's baser instincts of sex and locker-room humor opened the door to advertising revenue spent to attract diehard listeners. "It has moved so far away from being just a forum for highly analytical men who want to know who was on third base in some game in 1937," said Michael Packer, a talk-radio consultant in Detroit. "It's kind of the rock-and-roll of talk radio. It deals with a lot of issues, ethics and values that have an impact on people in everyday life."[13]

WIP's early success attracted Infinity Broadcasting, now CBS Radio, to buy the station for $13 million from Spectacor.[14] CBS Radio has since grown to own 179 radio stations in the nation's top fifty markets. CBS Radio stations carry games for at least twenty-nine teams in the MLB, NFL, NBA, and NHL, including the New York Yankees, New York Mets, Chicago White Sox, New England Patriots, New York Giants, Chicago Bears, and the Detroit Red Wings.[15]

WIP has contracts to carry games for the Philadelphia Flyers and the Philadelphia 76ers. However, the root of WIP's success goes back to how well it entertains its listeners, not how well it talks about sports.

Bigby said:

> If you do sports talk, it won't survive. If you do sports entertainment, the possibilities are endless. There was an off-season when the station let itself be information-driven. [But] you don't reach the younger demographics by informing, you reach them by entertaining.[16]

* * *

WIP currently owns the rights to the Flyers and Sixers games and it had the Eagles for twenty-three years until the NFL team switched in 1992 to another station, WYSP 94.1 FM. The duality of being the flagship station of the Flyers' and Sixers' home games and the station where radio hosts criticize those teams has not always been smooth.

No case represents that more than *Eric Lindros and the Flyers v. WIP,* a defamation suit against the station for something one of its broadcasters said. On February 28, 1997, Craig Carton, a WIP reporter, said on air that Lindros missed a game that month because he was hung over after drinking too much the night before. He said the team listed Lindros out with a sore back he suffered two nights earlier to cover up for his hangover. The report outraged Lindros and the Flyers filed a suit on March 5, 1997.[17]

Lindros dropped the suit after the Infinity Broadcasting Corp. of Philadelphia issued the hockey player an apology and made a contribution to the Children's Miracle Network. Lindros said he was happy a bad situation turned positive and he also made a contribution to the charity. In the letter of apology, Infinity said:

> The entire management of WIP regrets this unfortunate incident and wishes to apologize to Eric Lindros, the Flyers and their fans for the broadcast. After an investigation of the facts . . . WIP executive management has concluded that the sole reason Eric did not play   was because of his injured back and not for any other reason.[18]

Cooperstein had been out of Philly for five years when the suit was dropped, but he knew WIP didn't mind the furor it created with the Lindros comments and his lawsuit.

"It's like, 'Love me, hate me, don't ignore me,'" Cooperstein said in 1997. "They've basically gone to the lowest common denominator. And they're a highly profitable radio station. We can argue until the cows come home whether the price they paid is worth it."[19]

WIP hosts have run into their fair share of bad publicity, if there is such a thing in sports-talk radio, for on-air comments. One of the more recent incidents shows how media consolidation can at least give the perception that we are not as free as we once were to speak openly about all things corporate.

In July 2003, Infinity Broadcasting suspended Cataldi for two days without pay after he used a Nazi term while complaining about the Philadelphia Eagles' policy of banning outside food from their new stadium. Team president Joe Banner said the ban was necessary for security at Lincoln Financial Field. That decision angered fans that were used to taking food into Veterans Stadium, where the Eagles played before building the new facility.

On July 15, Cataldi responded by saying on air that if the team picked the extra security guards, he expected them to be wearing swastikas, a symbol of Nazi Germany during World War II. Banner and team owner Jeffrey Lurie are Jewish, so the comment didn't go unnoticed. Cataldi's bosses suspended the host without asking him to apologize or meeting with him. "Recognizing the nature of sports-talk radio and opinions and emotions it creates, I was shocked that, without notice and without due process, Angelo was suspended," said Cataldi's agent at the time, Steve Mountain.[20]

Cataldi considered resigning over the matter, but he returned to work two days later, expressing frustration over his suspension and with his employer for not standing by his constitutional rights to freedom of speech:

> Infinity Broadcasting chose to suspend me for two days earlier this week because of comments I made about the policies of the Philadelphia Eagles and rules they have imposed in their new stadium. Infinity officials said a comment I made suggesting the Eagles' new rules are so strict that "their security people should wear swastikas" violated the company's policy against personal attacks.
>
> Do I wish I had used a different analogy? Yes, I do. The last thing I was trying to accomplish was to alienate anyone of the Jewish faith, or of any faith for that matter. But the truth is, I didn't. There were no calls of complaint to this station—not one. I didn't even receive a single e-mail complaining about the unfortunate characterization. My co-workers never even mentioned it after I had made the remark. *I was suspended anyway . . .* I don't believe what I said was an attack against anything but the policies of the Philadelphia Eagles. It had nothing to do with any individual on the Eagles. I was angry at the rules. So were thousands of others.

Cataldi criticized the station management, saying it had the "absolute responsibility" to protect its hosts' rights to say exactly what they feel.[21]

Mike Missanelli, who left WIP to host a morning show at WMMR 93.3 FM, wrote a guest column in a Philadelphia newspaper supporting Cataldi, his former co-worker. Missanelli said money and corporate ownership have changed sports-talk radio. He said Philadelphia teams now hold a "financial hammer" over hosts' heads, and station management no longer backs them up. Missanelli cited that change as the reason he left WIP to co-host the morning show on WMMR. He pointed to the chain of ownership involving the NFL's television contract and WIP as motivation for Cataldi's suspension. WIP is owned by CBS, which has a television contract with the NFL. "Bottom line? A necessary editorial voice was silenced by corporate weasels," Missanelli wrote.[22]

In the column, Missanelli, who later returned to WIP but was fired in March 2006, also recounted a reprimand he received at WIP for poking fun at Lurie and Banner, who met at a youth camp growing up. He said on air that Banner didn't seem like a crazy guy and that the wildest thing he probably had ever done was to pour water down on Lurie from the top bunk while he was sleeping. At the time, the Eagles were renegotiating their broadcast contract with WYSP and, according to Missanelli, the team intimated that maybe it should look into taking the contract to another station.

A week later, Infinity (now CBS) signed the new contract with the Eagles and Missanelli received a written reprimand that said further personal attacks on the team would cause him to be fired. Missanelli fulminated that while the letter cautioned against verbal attacks on the Philadelphia Eagles, 76ers, and Flyers, it left out the Phillies. He surmised that it was because the Phillies had no business dealings with WIP or its owners. Missanelli wrote that the Flyers had inserted a clause in their contract with WIP specifically disallowing verbal blasts against the team. He said he and other hosts knew nothing of the clause, which, he said, amounted to allowing the Flyers to define what was and was not a "personal attack."[23]

The clause in the Flyers contract came about, in part, because of the Lindros ordeal. Cataldi and other hosts said it represented an attempt by the station to muzzle them and an effort by the Flyers to seek control of the way they covered the team. "I am offended that the Flyers feel they can set the rules on how WIP does talk radio," Cataldi said. "I am not about to allow them to dictate how their rules apply to me."[24]

In 2002, Eskin promised to "bury" New Jersey municipal prosecutor Michael Greenblatt in 2002 after a speeding ticket trial. Eskin was ticketed for driving 100 mph in a 40 mph zone in Voorhees, New Jersey, telling police he was late for a Flyers news conference. Eskin could have received fifteen days in jail, but his New Jersey driving privileges were revoked for sixty days instead. Eskin claimed that Greenblatt was "showboating" during a drawn-out explanation of the radio show host's offense.[25]

In 2000, Eskin got himself and WIP in trouble with the Miss America Pageant when he said the beauty contest was fixed. Eskin told listeners on August 22, 2001, that judges "already know who's going to win before they get into the weekend." Eskin eventually said he was joking and didn't think anyone would take him seriously, but the Miss America Organization filed a slander suit against the host and Infinity. The lawsuit said Eskin's comments damaged the pageant's reputation and could hinder the organization's fund-raising for scholarships.

The two sides settled the lawsuit after Infinity and Eskin issued an apology and Eskin agreed to apologize on air. Eskin's written apology was:

> I regret having made those comments, which are untrue, and I apologize for doing so. I intended those comments to be a joke and I did not have any facts to support them. I do not know of any reason to question the honesty and integrity of the judging of the Miss America Pageant.[26]

One of the station's biggest pranks didn't result in a lawsuit or suspension, but in the court of public opinion, it's something that will never be forgotten and, in the mind of one football player, never forgiven. In 1999, Cataldi and many in Philadelphia wanted new Eagles coach Andy Reid to select Heisman Trophy winner Ricky Williams from Texas with the second pick in the NFL draft. Reid, who had helped develop Brett Favre into a NFL Pro Bowl quarterback as a Green Bay assistant, had other ideas. He wanted a quarterback to build his team around and he selected Syracuse quarterback Donovan McNabb after the Cleveland Browns took Kentucky quarterback Tim Couch with the top pick.

Cataldi expected this, so he bused thirty loudmouth Philadelphia fans to New York for the draft to boo anyone not named Ricky Williams. As McNabb was shaking hands with NFL Commissioner Paul Tagliabue, the boos that started when the quarterback's name was announced were still roaring. The "Dirty 30," as they have come to be known, couldn't have been more wrong.

McNabb and Reid have restored Philadelphia as one of the NFL's top teams, advancing to the National Football Conference championship game in 2001, 2002, 2003, and 2004, and th the Super Bowl in 2005. McNabb passed for 16,926 yards and 118 touchdowns in his first six seasons and rushed for 2,459 yards and twenty touchdowns. One of his many defining moments in those six seasons was completing a fourth-and-26 pass in the 2003 playoffs against Green Bay to put Philadelphia in the NFC title game against Carolina.

Cataldi said everyone wanted Williams because he set the NCAA rushing record and fans hoped he would become the next Jim Brown, Cleveland's Hall of Fame running back from the 1960s. The New Orleans Saints took Williams at number 5, but no one compares him to Brown. Williams' defining moment came weeks before the beginning of the 2004 season when he retired from the Miami Dolphins, reportedly to escape a suspension for a possible third failed drug test. Williams announced his decision so late, Miami didn't have time to find a capable replacement before the start of training camp. The enigmatic Williams rushed for 6,345 yards and forty-one touchdowns in those same five years, but he never carried his team like McNabb.[27]

Cataldi has acknowledged several times that the decision to carry thirty people to New York to boo McNabb defies logic. "We know we made fools of ourselves," Cataldi said. "In fifty years on this earth, it has to be the dumbest thing I've ever done."[28]

Cataldi has apologized to McNabb on his television show and repeatedly admitted the promotion was a mistake. Rhea Hughes, his morning show co-host, has called it the greatest promotion WIP has produced, but Cataldi will never see it that way. "There's got to be something better I can contribute than to boo the greatest player to put on the Eagles uniform," Cataldi said.[29]

While the station has committed some social infractions with comments and pranks, it also has served the community. In May 2000, a man sent Hughes an e-mail threatening to shatter 76ers star Allen Iverson's kneecaps and dismember his daughter's body. Hughes alerted the team, who contacted authorities. Jay W. Charles, a retired high school teacher from Leola, Pennsylvania, was sentenced to three years of federal probation and a $5,000 fine in November 2000 for sending the threatening e-mail.[30]

In 1992, Cataldi, Al Morganti, and then morning co-host Tony Bruno launched a ballot-stuffing campaign to get Phillies catcher

Darren Daulton and first baseman John Kruk on the National League All-Star team. Fans bombarded the station with extra ballots: one listener sent two cases of 5,000 ballots that he picked up in Milwaukee and he mailed them air express. "I don't know what he spent to mail them," Cataldi said. "Some people would just mail in one ballot. We ended up getting them from 12 different ballparks."

Daulton trailed Benito Santiago by almost 390,000 votes, but he wound up surpassing the San Diego catcher and starting his first All-Star game. Kruk made it to the game as a reserve, selected by the National League manager, and the fans voted the first baseman a starter in 1993.[31]

In January 1990, Cataldi and WIP launched a "Wilt in Philadelphia" campaign in an effort to build support for the 76ers to retire Wilt Chamberlain's No. 13 jersey. The NBA Hall-of-Famer had a long feud with his former team because he said he had been promised part ownership by former co-owner Ike Richman, but Richman died before a deal could be struck. On March 18, 1991, an emotional Chamberlain had his No. 13 raised to the Philadelphia rafters eighteen years after he retired.[32]

* * *

The WIP Morning Show consists of Cataldi, Al Morganti, Rhea Hughes, and Keith Jones. Cataldi has been its star since 1990 with his comedic timing and commentary. Morganti covered the Flyers for ten years for the *Inquirer* and he's known nationally for his hockey coverage on ESPN. Hughes is a former WIP Eagles reporter and Jones played hockey for the Flyers.

In addition to Eskin and those on *The Morning Show,* other WIP hosts include:

- Anthony Gargano, who was born in South Philadelphia and is another former writer, having worked for the *New York Post* and the *Philadelphia Inquirer.*
- Glen Macnow handles some of 7 to 11 p.m. shifts and he's another former *Philadelphia Inquirer* reporter. *Philadelphia* magazine named him the city's best sportswriter in 1993.
- Big Daddy Graham takes on some of the overnight shifts. Another Philadelphia native, Graham also dabbles as a musician and a comedian.[33]

Cataldi, Morganti, Hughes, Eskin, and Macnow have all been at WIP for more than ten years.

Cataldi and Graham each have their own Web sites separate of WIP's at www.angelocataldi.com and www.bigdaddygraham.com. Both write columns about anything they choose, from reports on their vacations to opinions on Eagles camp. Graham also uses his site to promote his music CDs, books, and upcoming comedy shows.

Although known for his biting commentary, Cataldi can still turn the magnifying glass on himself and come up with insight that reaches his listeners on a human level. He calls his online columns "Angelo's Rants," but they're not all a madman's ravings. On July 23, 2004, his mother-in-law, Carol Autenrieth, passed away after a battle with ovarian cancer. Cataldi was asked to deliver her eulogy because he said "no one else could hope to get through it without breaking down," and then he "ranted" about it in his column.

> By the time a person reaches 53 years old, he's supposed to have already learned most of the important lessons of life. Over the past few days, however, I've learned something brand new about my job and about myself. I learned why sports is so important to people, and especially to me. Sports is a departure from reality. I don't like reality very much. I like reality less now than ever before. . . . I did the best I could in the five-minute tribute, though it was an impossible task. How do you capture the spirit of 80 well-lived years in five minutes? What no one knows—what even my own wife doesn't know—is that I had to edit my own speech because I cried every time I got to a certain part while I was rehearsing it.

After Mrs. Autenrieth died, Cataldi said he thought: "How could I ever relate to the fantasy world of sports after a real experience like this one? By the next morning, it was no longer an issue. By 6:15 a.m., I was ranting and raving. . . ."[34]

Cataldi operates his Web site as a nonprofit, turning over any money generated to three charities—the Children's Miracle Network, the Gift of Life, and the Children's Hospital of Philadelphia. Gail Cataldi, his wife, chose the three to honor Colin Baker, the son of family friends, who had two lung transplants before he died in 2002. Through July 2004, Cataldi's site had raised $8,053. Part of that money comes from businesses touted as "Angelo's All-Star Picks."

The companies contribute money and that gets their logo posted on Cataldi's site.[35]

Cataldi even gives his listeners "Angelo's Book Club," with short reviews of about twenty books. It hasn't risen to such heights as Oprah Winfrey's book club, but at least it partially destroys the notion that all those who listen to WIP have somehow lost their brain and ability to think.

* * *

WIP spent fifteen years in studios on 5th Street in Center City until it moved in August 2004 to new studios with updated technology in Bala Cynwyd, a suburb of Philadelphia. Cataldi heralded the move as leaving behind the ancient world of 8-track tape and leaping forward with new computers and an improved radio signal. The new studio is about three times bigger than the old one, which, for the final year WIP was there, didn't have cable television. The hosts and employees celebrated leaving their old home by throwing unwanted computers, typewriters, and anything else they could find off the four-story building. Microphones carried the demolition live on air, delighting listeners with some good clean destruction.

> I have no idea why we became the orphan child of Infinity Broadcasting. I'm just thrilled that we've finally found a home that should allow us to prosper against an increasingly competitive field of morning-radio shows in Philadelphia. Will our show sound any different now that we've updated our technology? Absolutely. Though we are on the AM band, our signal should be clearer, our voices more distinct (but no more professional, unfortunately).[36]

Cataldi and other hosts who live outside of Philadelphia should also enjoy the move because it helps their pocketbook. Without having to pay Philadelphia's 3.7716 percent commuter wage tax, among the highest in the nation, Cataldi, who lives in Mount Laurel, will save approximately $37,716 on his reported $1 million salary.[37]

The new office at least puts WIP back on an even playing field technologically with ESPN Radio's station, WPHY 920 AM, which bills itself as "Philadelphia's Real Sports Station." WIP still has a stranglehold on its target audience of males age twenty-five to forty-nine, but in August 2004, the ESPN station started running a series of print advertisements that WIP was losing listeners. The ads cited a decrease from 21,500 to 18,900 among persons twelve and older Monday through Sunday from 6 a.m. to midnight and from 38,700 to 32,400 Monday through Friday from 6 a.m. to 10 a.m. from spring 2003 to spring 2004.[38]

Despite its attempt to show WIP losing some strength, ESPN sales manager Josh Gertzog acknowledged that his station will never attract the number of listeners WIP does. "They have 10 to 15 times as many listeners as us," he said. "We don't have the greatest signal, but we have a great product. The Wing Bowl isn't sports. The Miss WIP Pageant isn't sports. We provide a great product with nationally known hosts and a local show in the afternoon."

However, one local show in the afternoon for a station whose home is across state lines in New Jersey doesn't cut it with Philadelphia's demanding fans. WIP gives them access to talk about Philly teams twenty-four hours a day. Cataldi scoffed at the ESPN station's attempt to show WIP's strength weakening. "I've been here for fifteen years and know that Philadelphia only cares about Philadelphia," he said. "ESPN is barely a blip on the screen. I challenge them to check our ratings in January after football season. Anyone can select a two- to three-month period and extract numbers."[39]

Competition aside, Missanelli sees the freedom sports talk once gave its listeners in Philadelphia slipping from the early days of WIP. Once, he wrote, Philadelphia sports talk had been the "voice of the fan. . . .Today, sports-talk radio in Philly is the deer in headlights, trying to avoid getting shot down by corporate bullets."[40]

Bigby, the man who helped create the sports-talk genre, has moved on and doesn't like talking about what he did at WIP. First, he still works for CBS Radio as the operations manager for WYSP in Philadelphia, and second, he considers any decisions he made along the way proprietary and doesn't want anyone stealing his methods.

When Bigby left, Macnow wanted to make sure the former station manager and Cataldi shared credit for building WIP. "Tom and Angelo are the two people responsible for WIP's success," he said. Despite disagreement with many of Bigby's methods, Macnow added, "I can't argue with the track record."[41]

Bigby said his methods work for him and that CBS Radio must like them because he's still with the company. "Fifteen years is a long time to be at one station. I'm proud . . . that we created something new and different," said Bigby.[42]

NOTES

1. Mishkind, Barry. "Philadelphia Section." The Broadcast Archive. Available at www.oldradio.com/archives/stations/philly.htm. Accessed July 31, 2004; WIP-610 Philadelphia Web site. Available at www.610wip.com/about/. Accessed July 31, 2004.

2. "The saga of call letters: from KAAA to WZZZ." *Broadcasting 107,* 67: August 6, 1984.

3. Wilkinson, Gerry. "Uncle WIP." Broadcast Pioneers of Philadelphia. Available at www.geocities.com/broadcastpioneers/unclewip.html. Accessed July 31, 2004.

4. National Sports News. "Names in the game." The Associated Press. May 17, 1994.

5. George, Jim. "Philly AM radio history." Pirate Jim's Radio Site. Available at www.angelfire.com/nj2/piratejim/phillyamhistory.html. Accessed August 15, 2004.

6. Ibid.

7. Ibid.

8. Edelson, Mat. "Radio plays; sport talk." *Sport 83*(6), 8: June 1992.

9. Craig, Jack. "All-sports banks on show biz." *The Boston Globe,* p. 78, May 10, 1991.

10. Cooperstein, Chuck. Interview by author. Dictation. August 18, 2004. All comments by Cooperstein come from this interview unless otherwise noted.

11. Bykofsky, Stu. "Shakeup at WIP includes arrival of new 'hands-on' boss." www.philly.com, April 25, 2003.

12. Klein, Michael. "Tom Bigby is leaving WIP-AM." *Philadelphia Inquirer,* p. D02. July 8, 2004.

13. Abbott, Jim. "Jock talk: Enter the sports jungle, discover the minds of men." *Orlando Sentinel Tribune,* B-1, June 19, 1999.

14. Viles, Peter. "Infinity goes shopping in Philadelphia; buys all-sports WIP-AM for $13 million; raises speculation about Don Imus syndication." *Broadcasting 122*(41): 38. October 5, 1992.

15. CBS Radio Web site. Available at www.cbsradio.com/about/index.php. Accessed March 28, 2006.

16. Stark, Phyllis. "Sports-talk format scores with fans; focus on entertainment seen as key." *Billboard,* p. 16. February 2, 1991.

17. Bonfatti, John F. "Lindros, radio station agree to settlement in libel suit." The Associated Press. April 2, 1998.

18. Bonfatti.

19. Kinney, David. "Philly sports-talk radio station may have crossed the line." The Associated Press. July 14, 1997.

20. State and Regional Wire. "Broadcaster suspended over remark during rant over Eagles' food ban." The Associated Press. July 22, 2003.

21. Cataldi, Angelo. "Text of Angelo Cataldi's statement." July 25, 2003. Available at www.philly.com/mld/dailynews/sports/6383214.htm. Accessed August 21, 2004.

22. Missanelli, Mike. "Why sports talk is for the birds." www.philly.com.

23. Missanelli.

24. Philly Talk Radio Online. June 23, 2000. Available at phillytalkradioonline .com/whats_newz_page4.html. Accessed August 24, 2004.

25. State and Regional Wire. "Judge revokes Jersey driving privilege for 60 days." The Associated Press. August 14, 2002.

26. Domestic News. "Radio host apologizes for calling Miss America Pageant 'fixed.'" The Associated Press. May 7, 2001.

27. Salguero, Armando. "It's official: Williams out for the season." *Miami Herald,* p. 3D. August 3, 2004.

28. Nolan, Jim. "Yo, Donovan, sorry about draft day." *Philadelphia Daily News,* Local, p. 4. January 23, 2002.

29. Sielski, Michael. "McNabb rises above draft shanigans." www.phillyburbs .com. December 16, 2003.

30. Sports News. "Central Pa. man gets probation, fine for threatening Iverson." The Associated Press. November 22, 2000.

31. Owen, Mike. "Ballot-stuffing." The Associated Press. July 3, 1992.

32. Sports News. "Chamberlain jersey retirement." The Associated Press. February 22, 1990.

33. WIP-610 Philadelphia Web site. Available at www.610wip.com/about/. Accessed July 31, 2004.

34. Cataldi, Angelo. "Angelo's rants." Available at www.angelocataldi.com/ old_rants.html. Accessed August 1, 2004.

35. Cataldi, Angelo. "Angelo's charity." Available at www.angelocataldi.com/ angelos_charity.html. Accessed August 14, 2004.

36. Cataldi, Angelo. "Angelo's new crib." Available at www.angelocataldi.com/ old_rants.html. Accessed August 21, 2004.

37. Klein, Michael. "Watts up." *Philadelphia Inquirer.* Available at www .timesleader.com/mld/inquirer/2003/10/22/news/local/7079/8236409.htm. Accessed August 21, 2004.

38. Nachman, Laura. "Negative advertising." August 6, 2004. Available at www.phillyburbs.com/pb-dyn/news/220-08062004-343856.html. Accessed August 14, 2004.

39. Ibid.

40. Missanelli.

41. Nachman, Laura. "WIP exec leaves mark on station." July 9, 2004. Available at www.phillyburbs.com/pb-dyn/news/220-07092004-328915.html. Accessed August 14, 2004.

42. Ibid.

Chapter 8

WGR and WNSA, Buffalo: Sports-*Talk Radio* versus *Sports*-Talk Radio—Competition Within the Sports-Talk Format

William Raffel

Although some of the largest markets in the United States have two sports-talk radio stations, the same cannot be said of most other cities. Buffalo, New York, was an exception when WGR (550 AM) became a full-time sports-talk station on January 31, 2000, followed by WNSA (107.7 FM) on October 2 of that year. The battle ended on April 30, 2004, when Entercom Communications, owner of WGR, purchased WNSA from Adelphia Communications in bankruptcy court. WNSA's personalities were released as preparations were made to launch a light album-oriented rock format on the frequency.

The same forces that brought about the competition ultimately led to its demise: free-market economics, the consolidation of ownership, and the deregulation of broadcasting. Both stations competed by serving a different niche of the market, with WGR emphasizing the techniques of modern commercial talk radio—including a tendency toward "guy talk"—and WNSA focusing on strictly the discussion of sports. In the end, WGR won the war but now is starting to use some of WNSA's promotional strategies to build a larger audience for itself. This chapter will describe the evolution of sports-talk broadcasting within Buffalo, the dynamics of the competition, and ultimately its demise.

Thanks to Tom Byrne and Mark Scott for reviewing drafts of this chapter.

EXHIBIT 8.1. WGR/WNSA: Significant developments.

Spring 2001	Buffalo Sabres make second round of Stanley Cup playoffs. Ratings rise for WNSA in morning and afternoons.
Spring 2002	Tom Bauerle leaves as WGR morning host. Kevin Sylvester joins Bulldog.
Summer 2002	Mike Schopp leaves as WNSA afternoon host for the same slot at WGR. The Coach remains for football seasons only. Howard Simon moves to afternoons at WNSA with Rick Maloney hosting the morning show.
Winter 2003	The Coach co-hosts his final shows on WGR.
Fall 2003	Bulldog moves to afternoons on WGR alongside Schopp. Bob Gaughan joins Kevin Sylvester in the morning. Jim Brinson takes over mornings at WNSA following cutbacks at Adelphia.
Fall 2004	Howard Simon hired by WGR. Jeremy White named co-host. Sylvester and Gaughan dismissed.

Source. Pergament, Alan. "Empire cuts third of staff." *Buffalo News,* D-3, August 19, 2003.

BUFFALO SPORTS ON THE RADIO

Buffalo is loved by its residents but is often mocked by outsiders as a rust-belt city with nonstop blizzards during the winter. Four consecutive Super Bowl losses by the Buffalo Bills during the early 1990s did not help that image. The city's other major team, the Buffalo Sabres of the National Hockey League, lost twice in the Stanley Cup finals. Minor-league teams include the Buffalo Bisons of the AAA International League plus the Buffalo Bandits indoor-lacrosse team. An NBA franchise, the Buffalo Braves, was once located here but left town amid the economic declines of the 1970s. Although the Buffalo metropolitan area has declined in population, the area continues to benefit from the quality of life associated with a larger metropolitan area, including professional sports.

Fans in Buffalo are passionate about their teams in some unique ways. Andy Roth, the current program director of WGR, came to Buffalo from positions in New York City, Chicago, and Philadelphia.

Since the average commute to work is only twenty-one minutes in Buffalo,[1] this leaves more free time for sports and other interests:

> The sports fans here understand sports better than anyplace else I've been. And I think it's because they appreciate it. They appreciate the Bills. They appreciate the Sabres for what they are, which is entertainment. People still view sports as entertainment and not business here. And I think that's great. And I also think people really love the fact that on Sundays, it's Bills night. And they do it as a community.[2]

For a sports-talk station, the lack of major-league baseball and basketball can pose a challenge. From the beginning of the Bills training camp in July through the end of the Sabres season in May or June, the teams are fodder for a considerable amount of programming. But what happens in the off-season? The problem is not as big for WGR hosts who often drift away from sports and are sometimes criticized for it. WGR host Kevin Sylvester said:

> The e-mails sent here, "Where's the Bills and Sabres talk?" You tell me today what the hell to talk about. "They cut the offensive lineman." "Oooh, what are they going to do without this guy who they cut in May? Ooooohhhh." What was there to talk about? We already did this show on the Sabres. What does Calgary have that the Sabres don't have? There's only so much you can talk about.[3]

At WNSA, Howard Simon preferred to stick with local topics but had to be more creative at the end of the Sabres season:

> You'll find different ways to bring up Bills issues. You always go to that topic of, "Who is your favorite all-time Bill?" And "What's your first sports memory?" That's when you pull out the generic topics that you don't use from July through the end of the hockey season. . . ." Pete Rose . . . should he be in the Hall of Fame?" We'll have NHL work stoppage stuff. There's always stuff. . . . What's the worst Bills team of all time? What's the greatest Sabres team of all time?[4]

FIGURE 8.1. Howard Simon, WGR, Buffalo, New York.

Although fans in Buffalo attend games of the lesser teams, such teams do not generate the passion or phone calls as do the Bills and Sabres. In fact, Buffalo Bisons games are broadcast on WWKB, a sister station of WGR, and Roth has no interest in moving them to WGR.

Sports have been a major part of Buffalo radio for many years. In the 1970s, three of Buffalo's full-service AM stations,WBEN, WGR, and WKBW (now WWKB) blended talk shows and broadcasts of games with news and music. By the late 1980s, WBEN was the dominant station, with broadcasts of the Bills, Sabres, and Bisons.[5] The competition diminished on June 18, 1988, when WKBW changed its call letters to WWKB, ceased local programming, and started broadcasting the first of several satellite formats.[6]

Around the same time, WGR began phasing out music and launching an edgier talk format after Taft Communcations sold it to the newly formed Rich Communications Corporation, owned by the family known for Coffee Rich creamer and which also owned the Buffalo Bisons.[7] This management change also led the station to outbid WBEN for broadcast rights and to gradually become the dominant sports station.

In September 1991, Art Wander began hosting an evening sports-talk show opposite the long-popular evening sports on WBEN.[8] Amid sagging afternoon ratings and Wander's popularity, the station fired its afternoon-drive personalities in January 1994, moved Wander to afternoon drive, and for evenings, hired a former defensive line coach for Buffalo Bills, Chuck Dickerson, who became well-known as "the Coach." Dickerson lost his coaching job three days after the 1992 Super Bowl[9] because of some comments about the opposing Washington Redskins.

According to Dickerson, Redskins tackle Joe Jacoby was "a Neanderthal—he slobbers a lot; he probably kicks dogs in his neighborhood." And he analyzed tackle Jim Lachey this way: "The thing we've noticed about him more than anything from watching the tapes of them is that he has bad breath. Players will fall down without him even touching them."[10]

The comments backfired as the Redskins' coaches showed players Dickerson's remarks, and several credited him with providing extra motivation to defeat the Bills. However, the incident did demonstrate that he would make an entertaining radio host.

Six months later, Dickerson and Wander traded places, and Dickerson remained in afternoon drive for the next eight years. Colleagues praised his knowledge of sports, football in particular. Kevin Sylvester, a former morning host at WGR, credits Dickerson with giving the station a strong sports image, leading to the all-sports talk format:

> Chuck was THE guy and the undisputed guy for sports talk in Buffalo, and there never will be another. I'm not going to be Chuck Dickerson no matter how long I do the job or how popular I become. I'm not going to be Chuck Dickerson because he was the king. And he always will be the king.

Dickerson's personality was so strong that his competitors found themselves becoming the "anti-Coach" as a way of differentiating themselves, a role Sylvester himself played on rival AM talker WBEN. When Mike Schopp competed with the Coach on WNSA, he called his show "Sports Talk for Smart People," a dig at Dickerson and WGR as a whole. Ironically, Schopp later found himself co-hosting WGR's afternoon-drive time with Dickerson:

He was pretty savvy as to how to make a show, a show. And that probably shouldn't have surprised me, but it did a little bit. He felt strongly that it was okay to make people angry. If he had to make people angry, he would do that—whatever he would do to make the show, to arouse the show.[11]

In a column that would prove ironic, Alan Pergament, television and sports broadcasting columnist for the *Buffalo News,* initially called Dickerson, "A reasonable, well-informed man who doesn't exaggerate for entertainment's sake."[12] Within a year, Pergament started writing negative reviews, at one point calling him, "a *New York Post* kind of guy, who would rather inflame than inform."[13] He described how Dickerson called a Bills lineman "a piece of pus," and an attorney for the Buffalo Bills a "Nazi," as a recording of Nazis chanting "Sieg Heil" played in the background.[14] Critiques of the Coach would become a regular part of Pergament's columns over the years, but WGR staffers contend Pergament prefers an older style of sports talk no longer viable in the marketplace.

The Coach's theatrics also prompted some listeners to spin their dials, including one former WGR morning sports-anchor:

When Chuck first came here, I loved the guy because I'm a big football guy. And I loved his opinion and stuff like that. But as time evolved and maybe it was because of the way he evolved as a personality, he loved the combative stuff that I heard. And I everyday would tune in, "Let's see what Chuck's talking about." But the minute he started yelling at folks, I'd have to go somewhere else because I just don't dig the yelling.

Even though WGR has mellowed since the Coach's departure in 2003, his approach to sports-talk continues to define the station in the minds of many listeners.

ECONOMICS AND THE BIRTH OF FULL-TIME SPORTS TALK

WGR and WNSA developed as a result of economic forces, particularly the elimination of many ownership restrictions. When duopolies* were permitted in 1994, ownership of Buffalo radio stations consolidated faster than in other cities, so much that Buffalo was called "a model of duopoly's explosion."

Owners do not like their various stations to compete with each other, so they strategically try to attract demographically unique audiences to each one. Rich Communications had sold WGR to Key-market Broadcasting, which in turn sold the stations to Sinclair Broadcasting.[15] With the passage of the Telecommunications Act of 1996, WGR became horizontally integrated[16] with three other AM stations, including WBEN and WWKB, along with two FM stations.[17]

Both WGR and WBEN continued broadcasting a mix of news and sports, differentiated through target audiences and dayparts. WGR attracted a younger audience than WBEN, and both stations mixed their programming so as not to compete with each other.[18] With the exception of morning drive, news shows on WBEN were opposite sports shows on WGR, and vice versa. WWKB had tried many satellite networks, ultimately becoming an all-sports station with *One-on-One Sports*. However, all of this programming was national in scope with no local origination.

In July 1999, Entercom Communications Corporation of Philadelphia reached an agreement with Sinclair to purchase its radio holdings in Buffalo. The deal closed on December 15, amid rumors of programming changes.[19] One month later, Entercom announced that all news and general talk programming would move to WBEN, while WGR became all sports. The popular *Jim Rome Show* moved from WWKB to WGR, but the rest of *One-on-One Sports,* was dropped to eliminate any competition with WGR.[20] A number of leading sports figures in Buffalo were invited to move their shows from WBEN to WGR but declined, including the coach of the Buffalo Sabres Lindy Ruff along with three current and former sports writers for *The Buffalo News,* all of whom objected to WGR's more sensational talk format. WGR affiliated with the ESPN radio network for overnight and weekend programming.

In direct contrast, WNSA was born as a result of vertical integration, the desire of John Rigas to profit from all radio and television

---

*Duopolies allowed one company to own two AM and two FM stations in the same market. Under prior FCC regulations, an owner was limited to one station on each band per market.

broadcasts of Buffalo Sabres hockey. Rigas was the founder, chairman, and CEO of Adelphia Communications, the owner of the cable systems serving Buffalo and its suburbs. Rigas purchased a one-third ownership interest of the Sabres in January 1994 from the team's primary owners, the Knox family, at a cost of $15 million.

As a franchise located in one of the smallest cities in the NHL, the Sabres had been losing money for years and were struggling to meet the payroll.[21] Adelphia had a contract to carry Sabres games on its Empire Sports Network, seen on cable systems throughout the state. Rigas helped the team meet more payrolls with additional investments during the late 1990s, until accumulating a majority interest in 1998 and becoming the team's chairman.[22]

Originally, it appeared as though Rigas had invested his own money, but when the team filed for Chapter 11 bankruptcy, $130 million was listed as a debt to Adelphia.[23] This co-mingling of personal and corporate funds ultimately led to Rigas' conviction on federal fraud and racketeering charges.

The Sabres had been broadcast on WGR throughout the early 1990s before moving in 1997 to an FM oldies station, WHTT. This was partially out of a desire not to be associated with the constant criticism on WGR and to have a working partnership with Mercury Communications. Mercury owned the top-rated FM stations appealing to men, and the stations were expected to publicize the team on their morning shows.[24] However, to maximize his investment, Rigas wanted the Sabres radio broadcasts on a station controlled by Adelphia, to complement the television coverage.

Adelphia purchased one of the last independent and locally owned stations in Buffalo, WNUC (107.7 FM) for $6 million, dropped its new country format, and on October 1, 2000, relaunched it as WNSA, "Western New York's Sports Authority."[25] (The slogan was dropped following a trademark infringement lawsuit from "The Sports Authority" sporting-goods chain.[26]) The station had changed hands many times over the years, as its signal was stronger in rural areas than in parts of metropolitan Buffalo. Adelphia planned to run the station from the same facility as Empire and quickly built a radio studio. WNSA's best-known host, Howard Simon, recalls they did not even have a production studio for awhile. The station initially planned to have local hosts for morning drive, then between noon and midnight, with Fox Sports Radio filling the remaining time. WNSA later dropped Fox for *One-on-One Sports,* which later became Sporting News Radio, as it was a better match for the station's local programming.

WNSA's first days were filled with uncertainty over program hosts. Mike Schopp was hired from a Rochester station for afternoon drive, while Tom Campbell, a former morning host on Buffalo's other country FM station was selected for mornings. Immediately before WNSA's debut, Campbell accepted a position in Memphis, Tennessee.[27] Following some interim hosts, Adelphia moved Howard Simon from Empire over to radio, as he had formerly been the sports director of WBEN. Simon tired of mornings and eventually shifted to afternoons when Mike Schopp hopped over to WGR, as Adelphia began having financial problems. Economics cast a strong shadow over WNSA's final two years, with the station enjoying some good ratings while staffers feared its ultimate demise.

THE NATURE OF THE COMPETITION

Amid questions of whether the Buffalo market could sustain two competing sports-talk stations, WGR and WNSA competed by taking two completely different approaches, with WGR relying more on personalities, opinions, and some nonsports topics, while WNSA favored longer, in-depth, factual discussions of sports. WNSA's hosts certainly hoped to attract callers, but its format was not as driven by them, and they were not afraid to keep callers on hold for a much longer time than WGR.

Behind the Scenes at WGR

Friday, May 28, 2004, was the last work day before Memorial Day weekend, but things were not slowing down at all for the morning crew of WGR.[28] At 9 a.m., it was time for the "Stone Cold Lock," when callers share their betting picks for the weekend. Gambling is a popular pastime around the station, thanks in part to former morning co-host Bob Gaughan, who turned his personal interest into a popular hour of programming with Kevin Sylvester. This feature follows "Ticked Off Thursdays," in which callers are invited to vent their frustrations. As an intern busily screened calls, producer and board operator Greg Bauch looked over a book that would be a topic for the following Tuesday, *How to "Pick Up" Beautiful Women.*[29]

WGR does not limit itself to sports during any of its locally produced dayparts, but especially during morning drive. The day's non-sports topic heading into this Memorial Day weekend was honoring veterans with callers paying tribute to individuals who had served in the military. WGR staffers say they are replicating what happens in sports bars. People do not sit down and start mentioning their favorite teams right away. They might touch on lighter subjects first and work their way up to a conversation about sports:

> [Sylvester:] People want to laugh more in the morning. They also want something they can take to work to tell their buddy or people next to them around the same age, "Did you hear this joke?" "Did you hear what these guys said when they were ripping on this guy? It was pretty funny."

> [Gaughan:] We used to just talk sports, and then we realized, "Hey that person probably has a 401K or something like that." So we might do a money segment. That's not sports, but that guy, I guarantee you that we're aiming for, that 35-year-old guy, has a 401K, and that would fit into what that person does.

> [Sylvester:] If you think about how people watch games now on television or go to games, they're distracted by other things. Unless it's your team playing, there are so many times where you're flipping the channels, and you get stuck on *Behind the Music* and you're watching some of that on Steely Dan or you're watching Boa vs. Python. . . . And you come back to sports in a little bit. I think we do a lot of that. A typical guy sits down and watches TV at night will watch some game, flip to another game, then watch the hot chick on a different channel.

Andy Roth, WGR's program director, considers this blend of sports talk with other issues important for making listeners feel more at home with the station, and he encourages hosts to blend in some interesting happenings from their own lives into the discussion.

Traffic and weather reports round out the morning show, along with three "20/20" sports updates per hour.* *The Buffalo News* installed new printing presses and started runs of its Sunrise Edition earlier to avoid circulation delays. Consequently, many sports scores have not been reported.

WGR hosts take pride in expressing their own opinions and not changing them for broadcast. Although they admitted sometimes wording their opinions more strongly to spark listener interest, Gaughan made no apologies for being who he is:

> I get hot and heavy with you, and you're taking a side that you really don't believe in, it's going to come across on the radio. And I will waste you on that subject. I will just destroy you. Because deep in your heart, you don't really believe what you're saying. Try and do that for three hours. Try to take a side on something you really don't believe in for three hours. . . .

For example, many stations in town were talking positively about John Stephens, a local high-school student who was a contestant on Fox Television's *American Idol,* but WGR's morning team was mocking his singing. Sylvester said they brought it up because guys were being forced to watch the show by their girlfriends.

Special attention is paid to the way topics are selected and worded so listeners are motivated to call. In the early days of sports talk, the host took the role of expert for callers to ask questions. Because of the popularity of ESPN and sports Web sites, that model is considered outdated at WGR, as described by the station's afternoon hosts.

> [Chris Parker:] It is all about what we have to say about something, not just the issue. There's gotta be something we can sink our teeth into and really get into that is going to get people buzzing about it, to want to talk about it and react to it. . . . You just can't pick out Martina Navratilova. "That's great. She played. That's wonderful. 803-0550." No one's going to call. There's got to be more there than that. Whereas I think you may have ten years ago been able to have that conversation. "Isn't it wonderful that she . . ." And people would be like, "Yeah, you

---

*Morning drive on WNSA was also more structured than the afternoon and relied much less on phone calls than the afternoon show.

know, I remember when she played . . ." and have a totally different sort of conversation than you would have now.

[Mike Schopp:] Nowadays we might take a story like that, considering she's forty-seven and won in forty-six minutes, and yesterday, I compared it to shooting your age in golf. We might have some kind of conversation about old athletes and amazing things they do. Or different athletic feats. The conversation needs to broaden nowadays because there's just so many other ways that sports fans can find out or think about or talk about Martina Navratilova winning if that's what they're inclined to do. They have other ways of satisfying their needs in that area than just us.

As program director, Roth is constantly listening to the station and working with hosts to improve their topic selection.

Behind the Scenes at WNSA

President Bush came to Buffalo on April 20, 2004, to promote the USA Patriot Act but mentioned the Buffalo Bills in his opening remarks. "First, I am glad to be at the home of the mighty Buffalo Bills. [Applause] I traveled today with Congressman Quinn and Congressman Reynolds, two fine members of the United States Congress from this area, who assured me this is the year. [Laughter]."[30] This line prompted Howard Simon to recall covering Ronald Reagan when working at an Elmira, New York, radio station in 1984. Tom Gali, Simon's producer, searched the Web for other audio snippets from the president, and produced a mock interview of Simon asking the president about the Bills' chances for success in the current season.

The sketch opened the show at 2 p.m., during a day that would largely be devoted to the Bills' selections during the upcoming NFL draft, along with NHL playoffs, and a discussion of who would be the next manager of the Yankees. The first hour was rather sparse with callers, so Gali would often drop in sound effects or even contribute an occasional comment or opinion. But the pace picked up once the *SimonCast*—a telecast of Simon's show on the Empire Sports Network—began at 3 p.m.

Shortly before the top of the hour, Simon flipped an ordinary light switch behind his audio console to turn on TV lights. Three overhead remote-controlled cameras looked down on him and Ricky Jay, the afternoon "Sports Ticker" anchor. Although he had moved around the studio a bit during the first hour, Simon now sat in a chair and remained fairly still throughout the following three hours. He did not look directly into the cameras and maintained the program as a radio show, remembering that he was being watched:

> I've gotta make sure I don't do something that looks stupid. I can't react to a caller or make faces, and sometimes when it's radio-only if I get a real stupid caller, I can look at Tommy and make some kind of stupid face or pretend like I'm really annoyed. . . . I mean Tommy and I still try to approach it as a radio show. If we have sound bites, we'll still run sound bites. We can't run taped interviews. I couldn't run the George Bush bit now because I'm standing here on television. You lose the theatre of it all.

Some regular viewers report that Simon does occasionally make faces, but television does bring in more out-of-town calls: New York City, Arizona, and California today. Plus since WNSA's signal is strong to the east of Buffalo, many people from Rochester and outlying towns also participated.

The format of the show reflects Simon's development as a radio personality. Formerly uncomfortable offering his opinions, Simon now does with ease, though he still prefers interviewing guests:

> It's good for me, because I'm learning about stories and other cities, and other experts. You know, draft experts and things that I don't normally know about. And I would hope it's interesting for somebody listening rather than just hearing me for four hours. And it keeps me on my toes. It provides a nice break. . . . Then in a couple segments, go back to taking calls and e-mails. And you get a guest in. And it keeps me fresh actually.

One particular afternoon, he chatted with a baseball reporter from Sporting News Radio, the author of a guide to the upcoming NFL draft, plus a couple college football players up for grabs: Sean Ryan, a tight end who is a native of Buffalo, and Lee Evans, a wide receiver who was ultimately selected by the Buffalo Bills. Although Simon has a sense of humor, his interviewing approach is friendly, and non-confrontational.

When asked about the programming philosophy of WNSA, Simon did not have a prepared answer. The station had not had a program director for awhile due to budget cutbacks, but Bob Koshinski, the former head of the now-defunct Empire Sports Network, occasionally made suggestions. No one ever explained a direction for WNSA to Simon, because it was commonly understood to be similar to Empire. Although he did admit to occasionally yelling at rude callers, he preferred not to, so long as differences of opinion were not expressed in a personal way. Other personalities on WNSA included Jim Brinson, the morning host, and "Zig" during the evenings.

Program Differentiation

In order to have a unique niche within the Buffalo market, WGR and WNSA each differentiated their on-air sounds within the sports-talk format. WGR emphasized the techniques of contemporary talk radio, sometimes at the expense of sports programming. In direct contrast, WNSA emphasized sports, sometimes at the expense of the modern talk-radio style. Mike Schopp moved from WNSA in June 2002 to WGR amid Adelphia's financial problems and a desire to accept some fill-in shifts at ESPN radio that WNSA had prohibited. To him, this contrast served both stations well.

> We did compete with them [WNSA], but my mindset [on WGR] was to appeal to men who were listening to music stations or to other talk shows. And without sounding like I'm taking sports fans for granted because I don't, I feel like sports fans will listen to the sports station, generally, unless they have a serious objection, which we think we don't offer a reason for. And it's about getting the guys who are listening to other shows or listening to Led Zeppelin for the forty millionth time to try something else. That's the way I see the field. And that's been the way I saw the field before WNSA went away. They were a part of the landscape, but they weren't the only part of it.

People at WGR and WNSA say they did not listen to the competing station all that much because they were each committed to their own style. Simon also feared hearing WGR hosts belittle his station, which would needlessly upset him.

One reflection of this difference was the way callers were treated on the air. While Dickerson could be combative, nowadays WGR hosts insist they never intentionally try to anger callers. But calls on WGR are sometimes short, whereas WNSA took pride in letting listeners have longer conversations. According to former WNSA producer Tom Gali:

> Some hosts will be just, "Make your thought. Good. You're gone. On to the next call." Well you know what, it's sports talk. It's not sports statement and leave. Talk to the host, and that's what we do. And that's what we do a little bit different than [W]GR. They let them make their opinion. Okay, they're gone. We let them express themselves a little bit. So I think it makes more interesting radio here.

But with those longer discussions, callers often had to wait for long periods before going on the air. On the day of my visit, one caller had been on hold for thirty-seven minutes, another for twenty-nine, and a third for twenty-eight. At WGR, when the lines are full, hosts try to move through as many calls as possible. Andy Roth said:

> They need to get to all of them or else they won't be as popular. It's not that we tell people, "No you have a magic time that you're on the air. You can only be on the air for two minutes." But if there's five callers on the air waiting to go and they want to get their point in and we have ten minutes to go in the show, yeah, you know what, we're going to rush through you because we only have ten minutes to go.

In its earliest days as a sports-talk station, WGR's "guy talk" was hard-edged, especially during morning drive. Current afternoon host Chris "The Bulldog" Parker was originally paired with Tom Bauerle, WGR's morning drive host under its former news/talk format who admittedly was not a big sports fan. Parker moved from an evening sports-talk show on WBEN.

Together, Bauerle and the Bulldog talked sports mixed with a heavy dose of locker-room subjects. They conducted a survey of male callers about "testicular accidents," or what it feels like to be kicked in that area of the anatomy. The hosts used a street vulgarity ("prick") repeatedly, which prompted nearly a half-dozen complaints to the newspaper and numerous others to WGR, station sources said. The list goes on, especially with gross-out humor at the expense of women.

"The program has degenerated into 'Beavis and Butthead,'" wrote one listener in a letter to *The Buffalo News.* "The conversation strays all over the place with sports at times getting lost amid the clutter and inanity."[31]

The morning team's choice of language ultimately led to an indecency complaint before the FCC. WGR had distributed urinal splash guards with NHL logos to local bars and restaurants, and on May 8, 2000, Bauerle and Bulldog urged fans to "piss" on them. Michael P. Palko, a listener, complained about that and their repeated use of "prick."[32]

A majority of FCC commissioners ultimately agreed the language was not indecent because the words represented either slang expressions of frustration or a vulgar insult. Had they found a sexual meaning, that its purpose was to pander or titillate or was used for shock value, the outcome would have been different. Writing in dissent, commissioner Gloria Tristani noted that because urination is not considered fit for public viewing, the indecency complaint should have been upheld.[33]

When Bauerle was reassigned to host a general talk show on sister station WBEN,[34] Kevin Sylvester was rehired* to join Parker. The morning show is no longer R-rated, but Parker made no apologies for what it once was:

> I'm doing this show that's maybe not family hour anymore, right. And people didn't like that. I have a house. I have a wife. I have a mortgage. What am I supposed to do? . . . They want me to do this job. I can't say, "No, I want to go back and do my evening show." They really want me to work in the morning. Professionally, I would have been an idiot not to work in the mornings because it's a better time slot than what I had in the

---

*Sylvester had co-hosted a show between 10 a.m. and noon with Bob Gaughan but had left WGR to become sports director of a station in Charlotte, North Carolina. Parker has since been paired with Mike Schopp in the afternoon, while Sylvester and Gaughan were moved to mornings until November 4, 2004.

evenings. So I just had to do the job. There were things that we did that I probably five years prior would never thought I'd be doing. But I don't have any regrets about any of it. I don't necessarily love the way it's perceived now, but I had fun.

The biggest criticism of WNSA was that its connection with the Buffalo Sabres resulted in overly favorable coverage. Mike DeGeorge, a former anchor for the Empire Sports Network, resigned after management decided to increase Sabres coverage possibly at the expense of the Bills.[35] Simon said that DeGeorge made some good points but that management never set specific guidelines for what could and could not be discussed on radio or television:

> Look, I wasn't going to go on the air and demand John Rigas sell the team because he was an incompetent owner. I could get on the air and say they should have signed [Sabres star] Michael Pecca and they were low balling him, which I did. But you knew there was a limit. I mean, the guy did sign our check. . . . The myth was, "Well, you can't say anything bad about the Sabres. The guy who owns you own the Sabres." That's not true. If they played bad, we'd say they'd played badly. And I said they blew the Pecca situation. If they made a bad trade or whatever, I could have said what I wanted to say.

But to WGR hosts, WNSA's programming was bland. Not only was there the potential conflict of interest, but WNSA's fact-based approach was not as dynamic as WGR's emphasis of opinion. WGR stood out by asking tough questions, which fit with its more combative image:

> [Bob Gaughan:] One of the things that came out [of focus groups] was people tuned in because they expect us to ask the tough questions. Somebody is going to bring up the tough issue. That's what they come to [W]GR for.

> [Kevin Sylvester:] I think if you like ice cream, we're rocky road and they're vanilla.

WGR was not without charges of bias either, as the Coach was known for talking trash about the Buffalo Bills, and especially his former boss Marv Levy, who had fired him.

Ratings Results

After their launches, both WNSA and WGR remained competitive with each other. Generally speaking, WGR had higher overall shares and better ratings in morning drive, with WNSA winning the afternoons. The overall size of the audience was larger in the afternoon as well.

Sports-talk radio was slow to catch on at first. WGR's switch to the all-sports format brought an immediate 40 percent reduction in its overall ratings, from a 4.7 percent share of the market down to 2.7. Within the targeted demographic of men between the ages of twenty-five to fifty-four, the number fell from 5.0 to 3.3.[36] When WNSA changed its format for the fall 2000 book, WGR's overall share stayed at 2.8, with WNSA earning an overall 1.4. WNSA's FM frequency historically had been low rated in Buffalo.[37] (See Figures 8.2 through 8.5.)

In spite of the intense competition between WGR and WNSA, neither station attracted a large following among its desired audience. Buffalo's AOR station routinely has overall shares ranging from 11.4 to 19.1 of men between twenty-five and fifty-four. The country station is usually number two followed by WBEN and two alternative rock stations appealing toward the younger range of the audience. WGR usually had anywhere from the nineth to the thirteenth largest share of the market with WNSA either directly behind or a bit further down. (See Figure 8.5.)

Nevertheless, WNSA's performance pleased Simon. Between the ESPN affiliation, Jim Rome, and WGR's larger staff, Simon said WNSA should have been crushed in the ratings. Still, he was a bit hesitant to take credit for the station's success:

> We don't have the resources, the manpower, the anything that [W]GR has had. And I think to be around three and a half years and to give them a real battle in the ratings really says a lot. Because there's a lot here we could be doing a whole lot better. And there's a lot I wish we could do. But we just don't have the man-

power to do it. And I don't know if that speaks volumes about how people like us, [or] if we're good. Or if it speaks volumes about people just don't like [W]GR so much, they'll listen to us. I'm not sure. But I'm pretty proud of what we've done here for the last three and a half years.

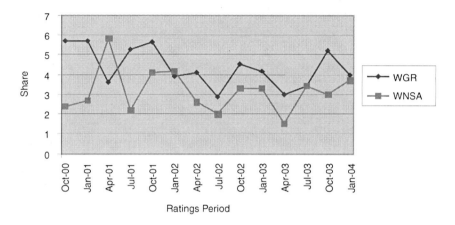

FIGURE 8.2. Monday through Sunday twenty-four-hour shares (men twenty-five to fifty-four).

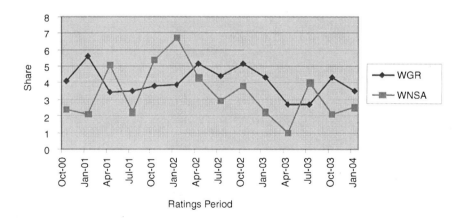

FIGURE 8.3. Morning-drive Metro Survey Area shares (men twenty-five to fifty-four).

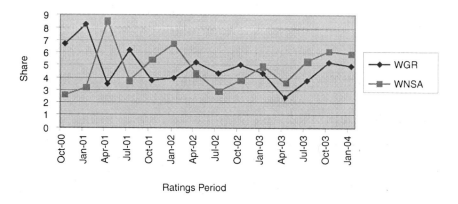

FIGURE 8.4. Afternoon-drive Metro Survey Area shares (men twenty-five to fifty-four).

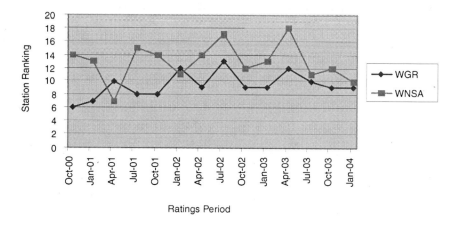

FIGURE 8.5. Market rankings (men twenty-five to fifty-four).

After first saying that Buffalo could sustain two sports-talk sta-tions,[38] two years later WGR's General Manager Greg Reid ex-pressed some doubts.[39] Mounting financial problems at Adelphia made it possible for Entercom to end the ratings war through a buyout.

The End of Major Competition

In spring 2002, allegations of corporate fraud were raised against John Rigas and his two sons for allegedly spending funds belonging to Adelphia Communications for their own use. They were indicted on twenty-three fraud and conspiracy charges, with John and son Timothy convicted on eighteen of them in federal court.[40] The Buffalo Sabres owed $130 million to Adelphia and the team was forced to declare bankruptcy on January 30, 2003, listing debts owed to Adelphia. The team was purchased by Thomas Galisano, a billionaire from Rochester, which placed the team under separate ownership from WNSA.[41]

The financial troubles marked the beginning of a slow death for WNSA that was drawn out over two years. On March 17, 2003, the SimonCast began, with Howard Simon's radio show being used to fill airtime on the Empire Sports Network.[42] Throughout this time, Simon was impressed with the professionalism of everyone at the station.

> We're not letting it get on the air. You can't tell that we're in danger of being unemployed. We do joke a lot around here, and I think that's how you deal with it. The guys are in pretty decent spirits. People don't really walk around here feeling sorry for each other and moping at everything. They're doing okay. I've been surprised by that.

When the station was up for sale in bankruptcy court, Entercom offered $9 million, but the bid was subject to higher offers. If accepted, it was common knowledge that Entercom would drop the sports format and eliminate the competition with WGR. On April 20, 2004, the day I visited WNSA, there was some last-minute hope. Citadel Communications, owner of five other Buffalo stations, had submitted a rival bid.[43] Citadel broadcasts Buffalo Bills games on its AOR station, and there was hope that the sports format could continue. However, Entercom countered with a bid of $10.5 million dollars, which was accepted by the bankruptcy court. WNSA hosts said farewell on April 29, 2004, before a staff meeting at which their employment was terminated.

Simon posted a brief farewell message on Two Bills Drive, an Internet fan site for the Buffalo Bills, which was flooded with messages thanking him and wishing him well. Many fans had hoped WGR would hire Simon, but Roth says the station was not interested in any of WNSA's personalities. Some messages also attacked WGR and its hosts, but this did not concern them. According to Schopp:

> I think people were excited about [competition] and loved having a choice, like they would in any aspect of life. And the subtraction of the station returns Buffalo to a situation where there is no such choice when it comes to sports radio. So in turn, they're likely to be disappointed about that. I don't think it runs too much deeper than the fact that they had likeable personalities, and people liked listening to the station. And anytime something you like is taken away from you, you're probably going to be upset.

Simon and Jim Brinson, WNSA's former morning host, did not disappear altogether. In early May 2004, they started their own after noon talk show on the Empire Sports Network produced by Neil McManus, former WNSA morning producer, and had to sell their own advertising. In mid-July, they started simulcasting the show on WLVL (1340 AM), a signal strongest in Niagara County and the northern suburbs of Buffalo but with more static toward the south.

The radio broadcasts had barely begun when Brinson announced he was leaving to become the new program director of WABZ, a sports-radio station in Little Rock, Arkansas, to do play-by-play for University of Arkansas football and basketball. Simon and McManus planned to continue the radio and cable venture. Although Simon told *The Buffalo News* that he would miss working with Brinson, his departure made the partnership more financially viable.[44]

WGR FIGHTS FOR A SECOND LOOK

WNSA disappeared as WGR was making some subtle changes of its own, not so much with its "guy talk" and treatment of sports, but with its relationship to listeners. The station continues to be defined in many minds by the Coach, even though he has not been on the station since the 2003 Super Bowl. During his last two years, he worked only during the Bills season, preferring to live in Florida the rest of the year. In October 2003, Darcy Regier and Lindy Ruff, the general manager and coach of the Buffalo Sabres, agreed to have shows on WGR once again. The signing was not received well at WNSA, still the Sabres' radio home. Bob Koshinski, General Manager of Empire and WNSA, told *The Buffalo News,* this showed WGR was mellowing:

> It is . . . uncommon in the business for the coach and general manager to be on a competing station. . . . I was surprised Regier agreed to do it considering the past history between the station and him. Over time, WGR has decided to do business the way we do business.[45]

WGR reacquired the rights to the Sabres games for the 2004-2005 season[46] and rejoined the New York Yankees network after WNSA carried the Yankees in 2003. WGR hosts insisted this would not affect their discussion of the Sabres.

Opinions differ at WGR over how much the station is changing. Morning host Bob Gaughan said there are no major differences, but the Bulldog said the station needs to develop a new image.

> I feel like there's a shadow there, and it's up to us to be good enough and strong enough and entertaining enough to redefine who we are as a station. I don't think that's unfair. I hope that's not too bold. But that's what I'm out to do. . . . I think we're out to be everything that Mike's indicated that Andy wants us to be, which is a station and a show that people will identify with as, "You're talking sports in Buffalo, we listen to those cats right there. Those are the guys."

Roth concedes that when listeners have a strong impression of a station, it can take a several years to change. It is hoped the Sabres will help build ratings for the morning show, as people fall asleep with the games on their clock radios and wake up to WGR when their alarms go off. WNSA had branded itself with the Sabres, and that helped the station's ratings.

Roth is also trying to reengage WGR with the community, in the same way Simon did at WNSA. For example, after saying that table tennis was not a sport, Simon was challenged to a match at a senior-citizens center by Mark Mogavero, a table-tennis champion at the National Senior Olympics. Simon admitted to being badly defeated in front of about forty senior citizens but considered this kind of promotion essential for building audiences:

> It's all about getting out and meeting people so they see who you are. Maybe they don't know about your station. But I go out and I do an appearance and, "He seemed like a nice guy. I'll go listen to their station. I didn't even know they were around." And maybe they get hooked on us after that. We're in existence because of people listening to us. If you don't respond to them and you take the, "I'm not going out to play table tennis. I don't have time for that," that's not a good thing. These are your listeners, so you should be responsive to them.

Roth is encouraging WGR program hosts to do similar things. Based upon the NFL draft combine, in which players have their health, playing abilities, and IQ examined, WGR held a "Host's Combine," in which personalities had to run to the bathroom or answer trick questions live on the air. While listening to evening hosts Brad Riter and Jeremy White, Roth had an idea that could involve the audience directly:

> Brad and Jeremy were talking about how no one plays baseball anymore, pick-up baseball. And I was going home that night, and I ran into Paradise & Casey. There's a little park. And there's this open green field there about the size of a football field. And fathers and their daughters were playing pick-up softball because they need to practice. They couldn't get a field because all the fields were in use. And I called them [Brad and Jeremy] up and said, "We can do this. We're going to get you guys to do your own pick-up softball game."

As part of reconnecting, Roth is encouraging WGR hosts to share more about their personal lives, and to even to involve WGR sports reporter Paul Hamilton in such conversations (journalistic ethics prohibit him from acting as a regular talk host). Roth is confident all these strategies will boost not only the station's ratings but its presence within the community.

These guys are starting to do that. And it's not that they were behind a brick wall, they didn't want to do it. When you're not affiliated with a team and you have this reputation, it's hard to
connect. And it takes a while really to reconnect with people.
Once we reconnect, everything is going to be really, really good.

Ironically, the very techniques that were used to entice callers
alienated a larger segment of listeners who would never call the station. These two groups are often distinct. WGR's sales staff sometimes encounter businesspeople who cannot believe the station has
affluent and educated listeners when they hear unsophisticated callers on the air. WGR's constant criticism of the local teams and guy
talk created such a strong impression in the community, the question
now is whether WGR can remold that image, in the face of continuing
afternoon competition. An alternative remains in the market for at
least part of the day. Future ratings will determine whether Entercom's $10.5 million investment to eliminate the full-time competi-
tion was worthwhile.

EPILOGUE

November 4, 2004, marked a major change for WGR.[47] The
morning team of Kevin Sylvester, Bob Gaughan, and Gary Pufpaff
were let go the previous day, and Howard Simon joined former evening co-host Jeremy White as WGR's new morning team. Simon said
he was surprised at how quickly the deal was reached, and he had little choice given the difficulty of working independently.[48] With advertising contracts tied to the Bills season about to expire and the continued uncertainty over the future of the Empire Sports Network,
Simon feared unemployment in the future. As with all WGR hosts,
Simon is discussing some nonsports topics, which he admits is challenging, but has been told not to do anything that would make him uncomfortable. Andy Roth said the reason for the change came down to
one word—"ratings."[49] While Roth said he liked what the former
morning team did, if the ratings are not good, his opinion does not
matter. He called the decision "mutual" between himself and senior
management but declined to discuss further rationales behind the
change.

The end result seems to be a marriage between WGR and WNSA. Simon and Schopp have returned to their former time slots from WNSA, working alongside hosts from WGR. But Roth attributes the schedule more to loyalty of Buffalonians to their favorite teams and personalities.

> People like what they like. They like the Bills of the early 90s and realize that no Bills team will ever be like it again. The people [who last in] the media in this town are also the ones they love. The best talents survive.

And with Simon's hiring, this time Entercom has bought out all of WGR's competition and practically eliminated all the competition for sports talk in Buffalo. This is perhaps the strongest statement that the era of the Coach has ended.

NOTES

1. All ratings information in this chapter comes from Abritron's Radio Market Reports for Buffalo-Niagara Falls.
2. Roth, Andy. Interview by author. Tape recording. May 28, 2004. Except where otherwise noted, all comments from Roth come from this interview.
3. Gaughan, Bob and Sylvester, Kevin. Interview by author. Tape recording. May 28, 2004. Except where otherwise noted, all comments by Gaughan or Sylvester come from this interview.
4. Simon, Howard and Gali, Tom. Interview by author. Tape recording. Observational material, including in-studio comments, comes from the author's visit to the WNSA studios, April 20, 2004.
5. Pergament, Alan. "Radio station deal yields rich lode of rumors." *Buffalo News,* B-2, February 21, 1987.
6. Donohue, Tom. "The end of WKBW's live assist music era." June 18, 1988. Online audio file. www.rockradioscrapbook.ca/goodbye.html. Accessed August 12, 2004.
7. Buckam, Tom. "The Rich family acquires WGR radio, WRLT-FM." *Buffalo News,* B-1, February 18, 1987.
8. "WGR AM 550." www.billdulmage.com/skeds/buffalo/wgr.html. Accessed August 16, 2004.
9. "Bills dismiss assistant." *New York Times,* B-13, January 30, 1992.
10. Berkow, Ira. "Coaches tango separately before their teams' super tangle." *New York Times,* B-3, January 26, 1992.
11. Parker, Chris "The Bulldog," and Schopp, Mike. Interview by author. Tape recording. June 22, 2004. Except where otherwise noted, all comments by Parker or Schopp come from this interview.

12. Pergament, Alan. "Dickerson gives fans 'reason' to listen: Folksy manner is pleasant contrast to Wander's raving." *Buffalo News,* C-1, June 25, 1994.

13. Pergament, Alan. "Face facts, Coach's handling of hasek rumor proves he's a joke." *Buffalo News,* B-2, May 8, 1999.

14. Pergament, Alan. "Dickerson's Nazi comment crosses bad taste border big time." *Buffalo News,* B-5, November 23, 1996.

15. Meyer, Brian. "Sinclair to sell six radio stations it owns here and 37 others." *Buffalo News,* A-1, July 27, 1999.

16. Drushel, Bruce E. "The Telecommunications Act of 1996 and radio market structure." *Journal of Media Economics 11*(3) (1998): 3-20.

17. Zier, Julie A. "Station sales encore in '94." *Broadcasting & Cable* (January 27, 1995): 32-35.

18. Violanti, Anthony. "Goodbye noon news. Hello more radio talk." *Buffalo News,* C-1, May 1996.

19. Violanti, Anthony. "New owner changes top management at local stations." *Buffalo News,* B-2, December 17, 1999.

20. Pergament, Alan. "WGR's move to all sports is all talk, no satisfaction." *Buffalo News,* B-1, February 5, 2000.

21. Collison, Kevin. "Key investor signs on with Sabres; Cable TV exec now largest single owner." *Buffalo News,* April 21, 1994, Local.

22. Collison, Kevin. "Nearing the goal: The tentative deal for the Rigas family to take total control of the Buffalo Sabres is a key element in the planned inner harbor development." *Buffalo News,* A-1, January 24, 2000.

23. Herbeck, Dan, and Pignataro, T.J. "Sabres file petition, call team bankrupt." *Buffalo News,* A-1, January 13, 2003.

24. Pergament, Alan. "Radio bad boys will lose their edge when Sabres come aboard." *Buffalo News,* B-2, August 16, 1997.

25. Pergament, Alan. "Bids due for WNSA; sports talk in danger." *Buffalo News,* C-1, November 12, 2003.

26. Linstedt, Sharon. "WNSA-FM is target of lawsuit; Florida retailer cites 'The Sports Authority Usage.'" *Buffalo News,* E-4, August 21, 2001.

27. Pergament, Alan. "Sports station has roster change before kickoff." *Buffalo News,* B-2, September 29, 2000.

28. Observational material and interview, including in-studio comments, comes from the author's visit to the WGR studios, May 28, 2004.

29. Eagan, John. *How to "Pick Up" Beautiful Women in Nightclubs or Any Other Place: Secrets Every Man Should Know.* Freehold, NJ: Secrets Publishing, 1993.

30. Bush, George W. "Information sharing, Patriot Act vital to Homeland Security." www.whitehouse.gov/news/releases/2004/04/20040420-2.html. Accessed April 20, 2004.

31. Violanti, Anthony. "Locker room humor turns WGR into a verbal trash bin." *Buffalo News,* D-1, May 10, 2000.

32. Federal Communications Commission, File No. EB-00-IH-0221, June 27, 2002. "In the Matter of Entercom Buffalo." www.fcc.gov/eb/Orders/2002/DA-02-1503A1.html. Accessed June 20, 2004.

33. Tristani, Gloria. February 28, 2001. "Press Statement of Commissioner Gloria Tristani." www.fcc.gov/Speeches/Tristani/Statements/2001/stgt119.html. Accessed June 20, 2004.

34. Violanti, Anthony. "Clip Smith is fired; Bauerle moving to talk show at WBEN." *Buffalo News*, D-5, January 31, 2002.

35. Pergament, Alan. "DeGeorge quits after Empire pumps up Sabres." *Buffalo News*, D-2, December 16, 2000.

36. Violanti, Anthony. "All sports format costs WGR in latest ratings." *Buffalo News*, Entertainment-2, July 28, 2000.

37. Pergament, Alan. "Sports radio execs see room for both stations on dial." *Buffalo News*, B-2, February 17, 2001.

38. Pergament, Alan. "Empire cuts third of staff." *Buffalo News*, D-3, August 19, 2003.

39. Pergament, Alan. "Weighty issues draw listeners away from sports talk." *Buffalo News*, D-2, January 25, 2003.

40. Zremski, Jerry. "Jury convicts John Rigas, son Timothy; second son acquitted of some counts; others pending/panel finds Mulcahey not guilty on all charges." *Buffalo News*, A-1, July 9, 2004.

41. Warner, Gene, Linstedt, Sharon, and Robinson, David. "Sabres saved: B. Thomas Golisano is excited about 'creating a new era' for the hockey club and promises to focus on the details to bring fans back to HSBC Arena." *Buffalo News*, A-1, March 15, 2003.

42. Pergament, Alan. "WNSA scoops up Yanks; Simon will be simulcast on Empire." *Buffalo News*, C-2, March 1, 2003.

43. Fink, James. "Entercom to buy WNSA for $10.5M." *Buffalo Business First*, April 23, 2004, www.bizjournals.com/buffalo/stories/2004/04/19/daily45.html. Accessed June 20, 2004.

44. Pergament, Alan. "Brinson's exit raises Simon's air supply." *Buffalo News*, B-2, July 31, 2004.

45. Pergament, Alan. "Return of Sabres brass to WGR surprises rival station." *Buffalo News*, D-2, October 11, 2003.

46. Ibid.

47. Fink, James. "Simon moves to mornings at WGR." *Business First of Buffalo*. Available at www.buffalo.bizjournals.com/buffalo/stories/2004/11/01/daily25.html. Accessed November 3, 2004.

48. Simon, Howard. Telephone interview by author. November 29, 2004.

49. Roth, Andy. Telephone interview by author. November 29, 2004.

Chapter 9

WHB, Kansas City:
"World's Happiest Broadcasters"

Max Utsler

You can often surmise a radio station will have an interesting history just by looking at the call letters. Take the case of WHB in Kansas City, Missouri.

It is one of the few stations with three call letters.

It is a rare "W" west of the Mississippi River, signifying a long history. Today, most stations west of the Mississippi carry a "K."

The old owners promoted WHB as the "World's Happiest Broadcasters."

And, yes, the folks who run WHB are among the "World's Happiest Broadcasters" these days. They have turned the station into a ratings-generating powerhouse, number 1 in men twenty-five to fifty-four in afternoon drive. They have earned the number 2 overall ranking in the crowded twenty-nine-station Kansas City market. They have become the flagship station for the Kansas City Royals. Arbitron has declared WHB the number 1 rated sports station in the country.[1]

And they managed to do all of that in a most unlikely way. WHB's story is the story of localism triumphing over expanding corporate radio ownership.

Back in the 1950s, with its 50,000-watt daytime signal, WHB was *the* "Top 40" station for listeners in four states. But as AM radio declined, WHB barely survived, playing musical chairs with non-musical formats. First, the owners tried a religious format, then a Spanish format, and finally a farm format. None worked.

By the mid-1990s, a Kansas City banker by the name of Jerry Green had grown tired of the banking business. He needed a new

Sports-Talk Radio in America
© 2006 by The Haworth Press, Inc. All rights reserved.
doi:10.1300/5335_10

FIGURE 9.1. WHB logo.

challenge. As a lifelong sports fan, he first attempted to buy the Kansas City Royals.

When that failed, he invested in something that was a far cry from a Major League Baseball team—KCTE, a 10,000-watt AM daytimer, with a signal that did not even blanket Kansas City. That was the beginning of Union Broadcasting.

So the tale of WHB is really a tale that starts with KCTE and how those two stations turned Union Broadcasting into a major player in Kansas City radio in the early 2000s. It is also a story of three men—Jerry Green, Chad Boeger, and Kevin Kietzman, all Kansas Citians—who managed to do what the so-called media experts in Kansas City said could not be done: they took on corporate radio and won.

THE EARLY DAYS OF WHB

John T. Schilling started WHB in 1922 after securing a loan from the Sweeney Automobile School. Schilling pioneered an early radio concept he called "The Invisible Theater." He raised money for the station by selling "seats." The seats did not exist at the station, but in the listeners' homes, the seats in front of the family radio. Even though the signal came into the home for free, the listeners were will-

FIGURE 9.2. Former Kansas City Chiefs quarterback and Hall of Famer Len Dawson is a frequent guest on WHB. He is flanked by afternoon-drive host Kevin Kietzman (left) and WHB president and general manager Chad Boeger.

FIGURE 9.3. WHB afternoon-drive host Kevin Kietzman (left) visits with Buck O'Neil, former star of the Kansas City Monarchs of the Negro Baseball League.

ing to send contributions to the station, much as public-radio listeners do today. It turned out to be a solid revenue source.[2]

However, the Invisible Theater could not generate enough funding to keep WHB out of financial difficulties. So in 1930 the Sweeney Automobile School sold the station to Cook Paint and Varnish, although Schilling continued to run the station.[3]

By the mid-1930s, live music made up a significant part of radio programming. WHB featured an up-and-coming artist by the name of William Basie, who later became famous by his nickname "Count." He entertained Midwest audiences with his distinctive "jump rhythm" music originating from some of Kansas City's finest nightspots.[4]

In 1943 WHB also served as a forerunner of what we now call "convergence." The station started a magazine called *Swing* as a means of advertising the station and its music programming. Each cover featured a different "Swing Girl."[5]

WHB applied for a television license in 1948, just as the FCC froze all new TV station construction. In 1953 WHB began a joint TV operation with KMBC. The station was affiliated with CBS. Cook Paint and Varnish soon bought KMBC-TV and KMBC-AM. By mid-1954, Cook had sold WHB radio to Mid-Continent Broadcasting, also known as the Storz Group.[6]

The Storz family had gained a certain amount of fame in the early 1950s by turning its Omaha station into a ratings juggernaut, partly due to stunts such as treasure hunts. Todd Storz brought the treasure hunt to WHB in 1955, captured the attention of Kansas Citians, and raised the ire of the local gendarmes, when four simultaneous traffic jams broke out as listeners converged on the Loose Park pond in an effort to find a turtle emblazoned with the WHB call letters.[7]

WHB's signature sound featured wild sound effects such as echo chambers and a very '50s-like set of jingles, but WHB also featured a new music programming theory—one Todd Storz came to call "Top Forty." Storz had noticed that restaurant customers kept playing the same dozen or so songs even when the jukebox featured five times as many choices. The waitresses would hear the same ten or twelve songs throughout the day, and then spend tip money to play those same songs again.[8] His philosophy happily coincided with the onset of rock 'n' roll. Who knows if Top Forty would have ever worked with a steady diet of Nat King Cole, Kate Smith, and Bing Crosby? But it did work with Bill Haley, Chuck Berry, and Elvis.

According to Kansas City radio pioneer Richard Fatherly, in certain dayparts WHB would pull in close to a 50 share.[9] The result was a station so popular, not to mention so economically powerful, that radio-station managers would book Kansas City hotel rooms just to come and listen to the station. Fatherly would serve as WHB program director from 1967 to 1969.[10]

The Rise of FM and the Fall of WHB

As the 1970s progressed, WHB and its Top 40 format found itself fighting the same foe as rock 'n' roll comrades such as KAAY in Little Rock, KXOK in St. Louis, and WLS in Chicago. FM was coming on strong and AM looked to be going the way of hula hoops, Nehru jackets, and 8-track players.

Over the next three decades, WHB changed hands several times and formats several additional times. But none captured the hearts (and ears) of Kansas City the way the "old" WHB had. The station still had the strong signal. But no one was listening.

KCTE: RADIO ON A SHOESTRING

Before you can really understand Sports Radio 810 WHB, you have to understand sports radio's roots in Kansas City—AM 1510, KCTE.

Chad Boeger graduated from the University of Kansas in 1995 with a degree in business administration. Like most new college grads, Boeger did not really know what he wanted to do for a career.

First he took a job with a small weekly newspaper where he managed the business, sold ads, and even delivered the papers. Less than a year later, at the age of twenty-four, he started his own business, a weekly tabloid called the *National Football Weekly.* Once again he immersed himself in every aspect of the business. Through the *National Football Weekly* he became friends with the Christian Vedder, general manager of KCTE Radio, a 10 kw daytimer sitting at 1510 on the AM dial.

KCTE had become Kansas City's first all-sports station in 1996 but had barely caused a ripple in the market. Little wonder, the station had only one full-time employee and carried all syndicated programming. Its lineup featured the now-defunct One-On-One Sports Network with personalities such as John "The Freak" Renshaw and Nanci Donnellan, aka, "The Fabulous Sports Babe."

Metropolitan Radio Group Inc., of Springfield, Missouri, owned KCTE. President Gary Acker had developed a reasonably successful business plan revolving around the idea of buying distressed properties, trimming costs, and reselling the stations for a profit. That was his plan for KCTE.

Vedder believed the only way 1510 could survive was by doing some local programming. So he asked Boeger to help him find the talent. Boeger had developed a considerable contact list through his sales work at the *National Football Weekly* but could not get anyone interested in developing a local sports talk show, at least not at the price the station could afford. Acker refused to come forward with any money. So Boeger agreed to do the show himself. He thought a talk show would be a good way to cross-promote his *National Football Weekly*. Boeger was converged before convergence was cool.

He called the show the *Sunrise Sports Team* and tapped local media figures such as television sports anchors Kevin Kietzman and Frank Boal and newspaper columnist Jason Whitlock as his sidekicks. All of them had well-paying, full-time jobs, so they could treat sports-talk radio more like a recreational activity than a career. Their bosses did not mind—it helped promote their regular gigs.

With Boeger at the helm, listenership was rising and the spot advertising rate was rising. Several months after the debut of the show, Acker, the absentee owner, arrived in Kansas City. As he walked through the door, he encountered Boeger.

"Who are you?" asked Acker.

"I'm Chad Boeger. I do your morning show."

"I didn't know we had a morning show. How much are we paying you?"

"Six-fifty an hour, thirteen dollars for a two-hour shift."

"Too much!" snapped Acker.

That initial meeting led Boeger to the conclusion his career would not flourish under the current arrangement. So he met with Acker and persuaded him to lease the station back to Boeger's newspaper under a local marketing agreement (LMA). Free of Acker's financial constraints, Boeger began selling KCTE as a combo with his football tabloid. The station began making headway.

To call the KCTE facility merely "bad" would be an insult to truly bad facilities. The building sat right in the middle of a lower-class neighborhood on the east side of Kansas City. The toilets sometimes did not work. The heat often did not work. The air conditioning never worked. The walls were lined with graffiti of the sort more likely found at a New York City subway stop than a radio station.

Termites found KCTE *the* rockin' place to hang out.

So it came as no particular surprise when the board "blew up" in November of 1997. It also came as no particular surprise when Acker dawdled about getting the board fixed. But it did come as a surprise when the *Kansas City Star* began receiving calls, hundreds of calls, asking what had happened to KCTE.

The station had been off the air for a month when one of Boeger's friends called to warn him that he planned to complain to the Federal Communications Commission about the dormant signal and unused license. Predictably, the FCC responded to the complaint and called a meeting. Two FCC officials, Gary Acker, his son Mark, on-air personality Mike "Z-Man" Zarrick, and Boeger met to discuss the station's future. After the FCC explained the seriousness of the problem, Acker offered to fire Boeger and revoke the LMA. One of the FCC officials, who lived in Kansas City, knew better: "Chad is the only reason you still have your license," he told Acker.

After that meeting Boeger concluded the only way to make KCTE work would be for him to buy it, but he also realized his $5,000 in savings would fall short of Acker's asking price. So he spent the next six months rounding up investors. At the same time three other groups of buyers emerged. While that drove up the price, it also reinforced Boeger's belief the station was a financially sound investment. He began talking to members of some of those rival groups and put together a partnership including Kietzman, former TV sports anchor Duke Frye, former Kansas City Royals Jeff Montgomery and Brian McRae, radio executive Brian Purdy, and the key player, Jerry Green.

Kietzman and Boeger arranged a meeting with Green who headed the most formidable opposing buyers' group.

Kietzman recalled they had only talked with Green for five minutes when he cut to the chase and said, "Are you guys telling me if I don't go with you you're not going to work for me?"[11]

That was exactly what Boeger and Kietzman meant. Boeger told Green he was ready to be the general manager and Kietzman reminded Green he had a pretty good job at Channel 4 and could stay there.

FIGURE 9.4. Former Major League Baseball player Brian McRae (left) and Chad Boeger are two members of the Union Broadcasting ownership group.

Kietzman recalled Green tapped his fingers on the table a couple of times and said, "Let's get together and do the deal."

"We both just sat there and tried to act cool, like we'd been in these meetings before," said Kietzman. "Remember, I was this guy that had been afraid to go to my news director at Channel 4 and ask for a thousand-dollar raise."

Green was born and raised in Kansas City where his dad started an auto dealership, Union Chevrolet, in 1928. When Green returned from college, he took over his father's business. Years later he sold that dealership and bought a Ford dealership. In 1960 he began on the ground floor of a new industry called car rental.[12]

"I was one of the first ten Budget franchises in the nation," said Green. Today, he has the largest Budget franchise in the nation, twenty-four stores in Kansas City, Wichita, Atlanta, Omaha, and Memphis.[13] In 1970 Green's holding company, Union Securities, bought an old bank and developed it under the name of Union Bank and added several branches. He sold that group, which gave him the time and money to look at doing something that had caught his interest—radio. He named his broadcast group, to no one's surprise, Union Broadcasting.

So with Green (and Green's "green") by his side, Boeger moved forward with the offer.

"It was the most nervous time of my life," said Boeger.

In mid-1998 Acker agreed to the deal, $925,000 for a station he had bought for $425,000 two years earlier. A tidy profit. And the word on the street was, "Boeger and his team had overpaid."

It was not the last time they would hear that charge.

Opportunity Knocks

Under Boeger's direction the station took off. KCTE moved into the top three in Kansas City for males twenty-five to fifty-four. Sales went up. The new board did not catch on fire. Other new equipment improved the sound and the consistency. But Boeger and his investors realized the limitations of a daytime-only signal. During the summer, when Royals baseball was in full swing, the station could be on the air until sunset, around 9 p.m. But in the late fall, when Kansas City's hearts and minds wrapped around the Chiefs, KCTE would sign off around 5 p.m.—right in the middle of afternoon drive.

"I'm driving home listening to Don Fortune," (a long-time Kansas City TV sports anchor who had made the move to KMBZ radio) said Kietzman. "He's got ratings. He's got a signal. He's got a multi-billion dollar company behind him. Boy, this is going to be hard."

For the next few months Union Broadcasting tried to get the FCC to allow it to switch KCTE to a twenty-four-hour signal. But a clear-channel signal out of Nashville stood in the way.

Meanwhile, Kansas City radio was headed in the same ownership direction as most major cities. Entercom, Sinclair, and Infinity had all entered the market. As a result only a handful of stations remained locally owned. Two of them were very successful but the others were barely worth the electric bill it took to run them.

But one prize stood out—WHB. Kanza Inc., headed by Michael Carter, owned and successfully operated four smaller market stations out of Carrolton, Missouri. Carter had bought the station from Shamrock Broadcasting in 1993 for $600,000.[14]

WHB was going nowhere fast with its farm format. So the Carters leaked the word the station might be for sale—but only to a local owner. Entercom, Sinclair, and Infinity were off limits.

In the spring of 1999 the negotiations began. By the end of the summer the two sides had struck a deal. At midnight on October 1, Union Broadcasting began operating Sports Radio 810 WHB under an LMA. For a short time they simulcast WHB programming on KCTE but soon changed KCTE to a talk format—Hot Talk 1510. On January 25, 2000, WHB officially became the second station in the Union Broadcasting group when the sale was completed.

The purchase price for historic WHB was $8 million. Once again Boeger, Green, and Union Broadcasting heard the cry, "You overpaid." The Carter purchase price seven years earlier would seem to reinforce that notion.

Green's response: "We overpay for everything."

"We felt like we could make a lot of money with this station even though we paid eight million dollars," said Boeger.

"Almost everything Green has ever touched has turned to gold," said Kietzman. "He always does it one simple way. He picks the right people. He puts them in charge. He doesn't meddle."

But Green points out the *terms* of the deal were much more important than the actual dollars of the deal. The investors put up $2 million. They took out a $2 loan million, and the Carter Group carried a note for $4 million over thirty years.

"That made the actual purchase price closer to five million dollars," said Green.

The overall market for radio stations in Kansas City took off at that point. Later in 2000, Susquehanna Radio paid a total of $120 million for two FM rockers (KCFX and KCMO-FM) and one AM talk station (KCMO-AM). Boeger said the estimated breakdown of that deal indicated the AM station going for something around $20 million.

Union Broadcasting also got a bonus in the deal, the result of an earlier negotiation between Carter and multistation conglomerate Entercom. Entercom's KCMO held the 810 spot on the AM dial. Since its inception in 1922, WHB had operated at 710 kHz. Entercom was looking for a stronger nighttime signal, one that would better suit KCMO's format. So they proposed a deal to Kanza.

The two stations would swap frequencies and dial position and Kanza would receive $1 million cash and a new transmitter. Mike Carter jumped on the offer and WHB moved its programming to the fifty-thousand watts of 810. A stronger daytime signal would help the farm format in place at the time. Nighttime was not an issue.

A year later, Entercom bought the Sinclair-owned Kansas City stations. But that purchase took them over the ownership limit set by the FCC so they had to divest. That is when they sold the three stations to Susquehanna for $120 million.

Little did Entercom know that seemingly innocent signal swap would turn out to be a key element in the competition between the corporate giant and the local ownership group.

THE COMPETITION HEATS UP

In 2000 Kansas City had twenty-seven commercial radio stations, a large number for a metro population of 1.8 million. By comparison, St. Louis with a metro population of 2.7 million had only twenty-nine stations. Dallas-Fort Worth, with a metro population of 5.1 million, had 40 stations.[15] So the WHB move to sports talk created intense competition in an already crowded market place. Entercom's KGME (1250 AM) had switched to all-sports format in the fall of 1999.[16]

Entercom's had another horse in the sports race. Its flagship AM station KMBZ (980 AM) called itself "News Radio 980 KMBZ," but the station also carried Kansas City Royals baseball, University of Kansas football and basketball, and occasional major sports events such as college-football bowl games, the NCAA Final Four, *Monday Night Football,* and baseball's World Series.

KMBZ also featured the long-running, afternoon-drive, sports-talk show hosted by Don Fortune. Previous hosts had included Conrad Dobler (a former St. Louis Cardinals football star), Al Eschbach, Kevin Wall, and John Doolittle.

Susquehanna bought KCFX, the Fox (101.1 FM), in 2000 from Entercom, which had bought it from Sinclair. The Fox programmed classic rock but had pioneered the idea of an FM station being the flagship for a National Football League team. In 1990 the Kansas City Chiefs made the daring step of moving to FM, a move that has worked out well for both sides.

In addition to the preseason and regular season games, KCFX broadcasts Chiefs-related evening programs three or four nights per week. The schedule included shows co-hosted by the coach, the general manager, and two or three different players.

Kansas City advertisers who wanted to reach the sports-oriented, twenty-five to fifty-four male audience had several enticing choices.

By this time, Boeger had assembled an impressive lineup of programs and program hosts on WHB. Talented and outspoken *Kansas City Star* columnist Jason Whitlock had been a frequent guest when Boeger hosted his own show. Whitlock had hit the Kansas City market like a tornado. A previously conservative and staid sports page had become a lightning rod for controversy. Whitlock quickly made a name for himself and began throwing his ample weight around. Whitlock moved into the national sports spotlight by becoming a semiregular guest on ESPN's Sunday talk show *The Sports Reporters,* featuring nationally known writers such as Mike Lupica, Bob Ryan, and Dick Schaap.

In other words, he made the perfect sports-talker, the right guy to host morning drive. The *Star* benefited as he mentioned his columns and his fame grew to rock-star proportions. WHB benefited because the newspaper drew attention to his sports gig. In addition, Whitlock, an African American, gave the black community a voice on what had previously been "all-white" air. Whitlock shared (a generous term) airtime with an assortment of sidekicks starting with Boeger himself and ranging from Steven St. John to "Magnificent Megan." But everyone knew why they called the show *Jason Whitlock's Neighborhood.*

Whitlock covered the 6 to 9 a.m. shift and then gave way to ESPN Radio and the *Tony Kornheiser Show.* But Kornheiser was the weak link in the schedule, so he was jettisoned for another local program, *Crunch Time.* This prompted Kornheiser to take WHB to task on his show for replacing him with "jock-sniffing radio guys."[17]

Frank Boal, another frequent guest from KCTE, headed the all-star lineup from 9 to 11 a.m. Boal, a TV sports anchor on WDAF (Fox 4) for more than twenty years, was well-known in the market, brought a journalistic approach to the show, and displayed prowess as an interviewer. Boal served as straight man for his two sidekicks, Tim Grunhard and Bill Maas, a pair of ex-Chiefs linemen. Maas also served as an analyst for NFL football on Fox. When the Chiefs were in season, Grunhard and Maas capitalized on their extensive NFL connections to bring guests of national stature to the show. When the topic was Royals baseball or Big 12 basketball, Boal carried the show.

WHB switched to syndicated programming at 11 a.m. with the *Jim Rome Show,* live from Los Angeles. Rome attracted a huge following in Kansas City as evidenced by the success of his much-ballyhooed "Tour Stop" appearance. Rome would later call it the second-best "Tour Stop" ever, even though Rome had never done one in such a relatively small market. Boeger and Kevin Kietzman had spent two years lobbying Rome to bring his show to Kansas City and another six months promoting it.

Kietzman took over at 2 p.m. for the crucial afternoon-drive slot with his program called *Between the Lines.* Kietzman, Boal's protégé at Fox 4 for ten years of nights and weekends, took a chance on KCTE and Chad Boeger. He quit Fox 4 and went to KCTE full-time.

"I wanted to compete," said Kietzman. "I had the feeling all along if we went and did radio that that would be more competitive than what I was doing."[17]

Union Broadcasting added Kietzman as a partner.

"I always thought somewhere in the back of my mind, someday I will own my own business," said Kietzman. "But I always thought maybe it will be a Taco Bell."

Kietzman brought a sound, news-oriented approach to his show with an emphasis on information gathering and interviewing as opposed to allowing callers to program the show.

That strong local lineup sandwiched around the *Rome Show* would later move WHB into the upper echelon of radio ratings in the market. The investors could start paying off some of that debt.

Movin' On Up

Soon after the acquisition of WHB, Union Broadcasting began to search for a new home. Boeger first looked for a building to lease. He wanted something in the centrally located area around I-435 and State Line Road, the street that separates Missouri and Kansas. He found what he thought would be suitable space, but the terms of the lease would not allow satellite dishes on the roof.

Enter Jeff Montgomery.

Montgomery had fashioned a stellar career as the Royals' top relief pitcher of the 1990s. When he retired, he kept his residence in suburban Leawood.

Montgomery had been one of the original investors in KCTE and later WHB. Now he decided to build a building and be a landlord.

He paid for 80 percent of a 16,000 square foot, two-story building. Union Broadcasting bought the other 20 percent. Green's son served as architect. Boeger designed the floor plan. The original plan provided for the radio station to take up the top floor and lease the bottom.

Good thing they did not find a lessee. The various elements of Union soon took up all but 2,000 square feet of the building.

One of the reasons the company needed that new space was that Boeger and friends had started a new company. Back in the early days of KCTE, the station had an almost nonexistent advertising budget. So it put its money and its message onto one billboard and into twenty different men's restrooms. It worked.

When KCTE's contract with the "indoor" advertising company came up for renewal, the company wanted to triple its rates. Boeger said he could not afford it. The advertising company wouldn't budge. So Boeger went to Green and asked if he could start a new company, Union Indoor. Within three years, Union Indoor had taken over the market. Union clients have their signs displayed about the urinals in major Kansas City venues such as Kauffman Stadium, Kemper Arena, Community America Ballpark, Verizon Amphitheater, and 110 bars and restaurants.

In July 2002, Union Broadcasting moved into its spacious new home, trading a 3,000 square foot caddy shack in Independence, Missouri, for a cushy clubhouse in Overland Park, Kansas, located in one of the most affluent counties in the country. The move further energized an already energized staff. Account executives loved bringing clients over to the new digs to listen in on a show or cook some barbecue on the deck that adjoins the studio.

The move also helped trigger some new promotions such as the "Turkey Bowl" and the "Big Boys Toy Show." The Turkey Bowl started as a good-natured, smack-talk fest (in Jim Rome vernacular) between Whitlock in the morning and Kietzman in the afternoon. It turned into a prime time Tuesday-night touch football game on the artificial turf at Rockhurst High School. Whitlock and Kietzman boasted of their football prowess. Whitlock had played football at Ball State as a lineman.

FIGURE 9.5. "Turkey Bowl" coach Kevin Kietzman (left) goes over the game plan with former Kansas City Royals relief pitcher Jeff Montgomery. Kietzman hosts the afternoon-drive program. Montgomery is one of the major investors in Union Broadcasting.

FIGURE 9.6. WHB owner Jerry Green (right) takes time out from a poker game at "The Big Boys Toy Show" to share a laugh with Kansas City Royals Hall of Famer George Brett.

It appeared the game would feature the crews from the two shows. But alas, neither show had enough players to form a team, so the two hosts began recruiting. And recruit they did. Whitlock's roster included: former NFL players Tony Blevins and Jeff George plus recently graduated KU quarterback Dylan Smith. Not to be outdone, Kietzman convinced former Missouri QB Corby Jones to come out and play. And to make sure he had enough depth at quarterback he added former K-Staters Lynn Dickey and Stan Weber. The rosters also included such local notables as the Royals' Joe Randa and Kansas City Wizards soccer goalie Tony Meola. The promotion for the game grew to epic proportions. So did the smack.

Admission to the game was either six cans of food for the Harvesters (a local food bank) or a new toy for Toys for Tots. The game and the preceding autography session drew something around 4,000 fans. At this writing, the game continues to draw a significant crowd. In 2004 the station gathered 61,000 pounds of food for Harvesters and filled three semi-trailers full of toys for Toys for Tots. For both organizations, it is their biggest single-day promotion, according to Boeger.

The Big Boys Toy Show is another brainchild of the station. The summer promotion features a trade show at the Overland Park Convention Center. "Toys" on display include big-boy "necessities" such as cars, boats, and motorcycles, plus sports equipment such as golf clubs and accessories and hunting and fishing gear. The show runs for three days and includes autograph sessions with celebrities and sports stars. Local celebs included baseballers George Brett, David Cone, Negro Leagues baseball ambassador Buck O'Neil and NFL Hall of Fame quarterback Len Dawson. Out-of-town celebs have included William "the Refrigerator" Perry, the Trim Spa models, and Heidi Fleiss, "the Hollywood Madam."

Not that KCTE had been without promotions in the past. Kietzman and his cohorts attracted national attention in spring 1999. Major League Baseball was entering into some acrimonious negotiations over a new collective bargaining agreement. The players were threatening to strike, and the owners were threatening a lockout. The WHB on-air staff had been riling up its listeners over the inequities in baseball's economic structure. So Kietzman hatched a plan. WHB purchased "Share the Wealth" T-shirts and started passing them out to its legion of soldiers. This would be Kansas City's way of saying the cur-

FIGURE 9.7. About 8,000 fans wore their WHB T-shirts to "Share the Wealth" night at Kauffman Stadium. They were protesting the inequities in Major League Baseball payrolls.

rent financial status of Major League Baseball was unfair to small-market teams such as the Royals and needed to be changed.

When the high-flying, free-spending Yankees came to town on April 30, Kietzman and his show's most ardent followers would buy $5 general admission tickets and march en masse to the left field general admission section, within shouting distance of the Yankees' leftfielder. After three innings, the entire group would march out of the stadium and spend the evening watching the rest of the game in the parking lot of the nearby Adams Mark Hotel. Kietzman figured he could get twenty-five or thirty people to go.

He was wrong—8,000 showed up.

"That changed everything," said Kietzman. "We knew we were big."

Kietzman also had a favorite football whipping boy, the Denver Broncos, or more specifically, John Elway. Thus was born, "Dump on the Donkeys" day.

The station had lassoed, or perhaps hired, War Paint, the Chiefs' *real* horse mascot, to join them in a Hooters' parking lot for what you might call a "Poop Rally." You see, the "Dump the Donkeys" idea centered around War Paint doing his business on a number of Bronco jerseys strewn across the parking lot. A large crowd gathered to see War Paint, and at each person's own risk, perhaps pet the handsome steed.

Elway's number 7 jersey dodged most of the nastiness that day while a much less famous number 32 bore the brunt of the discharge from War Paint's most recent trip to the lunch buffet.[18] Despite War Paint's valiant effort, two days later the Broncos defeated the Chiefs 20-6.

. . . and a Player to Be Named Later

WHB was cruising merrily along—at least on the surface. The station held the number 1 ranking in males twenty-five to fifty-four in Kansas City. From the fall book of 2001 through the winter book of 2004, WHB's share of the demographic ranged from 8.9 to 11.9. Arbitron called WHB the number 1 sports station in the country based on share, Boeger said. The employees were enjoying the new digs.

But Whitlock's contract would be up in December of 2002. He had been negotiating with WHB, but the buzz around Kansas City signaled Entercom would be making a big push to reel in a "big catch." The sizeable Whitlock matched that description both literally and figuratively.

Boeger knew of Whitlock's disdain for the early-morning hours. For that matter, the entire WHB listening audience knew of his disdain for the early-morning hours. Kietzman said he thought Whitlock and Bill Maas really wanted an afternoon slot.

Whitlock would later write in his *Kansas City Star* column:

> If I was going to continue in talk radio, I needed a time slot that would be more journalist-friendly and a radio employer with the resources, the savvy and the vision to take advantage of a unique opportunity to elevate sports-talk radio to an unprecedented height.[19]

Whitlock and Maas had also made known their interest in being part of the ownership group. They thought their tenure and stature had earned them seats in the boardroom even though they had not made a financial investment in the company.

"You should have seen the people who really ponied the money up in the beginning," said Kietzman.

WHB also learned another lesson during this process.

Station management understood that with Whitlock, the *Kansas City Star* came first, and with Maas, Fox Sports came first.

"You can't have as really important parts of what you're doing, people with second jobs," said Kietzman.

Whitlock had floated a few trial balloons through Jeffrey Flanagan's "Top of the Morning" column in the *Kansas City Star.* So it came as no surprise to Boeger when Whitlock announced he was heading to Entercom. It did come as a surprise to Boeger when Maas and Grunhard announced their defection to Entercom on the very same day as Whitlock, June 18, 2002.

"It hurt that they left, I took it personally," said Boeger. Maas and Grunhard were still under contract to WHB but left knowing they would have to honor a no-compete clause for several months.

Boeger had anticipated the Whitlock departure so he had been courting John "The Freak" Renshaw who was working in Los Angeles but was not under contract. They had already struck a deal with Renshaw, but he was not scheduled to start until mid-July.

"No one knew that except for Kevin," said Boeger.

Boeger called Renshaw and told him they needed him immediately. Renshaw said okay, so Kietzman filled in for Whitlock on Wednesday. Other staffers filled in on Thursday and Friday, and Renshaw started on Monday. Boeger looked like a genius.

"For the first couple of weeks he would come over and I would do his laundry," said Boeger. "We'd watch Royals games because he didn't have TV in his place. I'd fix him dinner." You won't find that job description for general manager in any management textbooks.

With three defections, WHB needed to do some damage control. So in a couple of months, the station added a couple of well-known Kansas Citians, Royals Hall of Famer George Brett and CBS sports broadcaster Kevin Harlan, to the payroll. Boeger also persuaded former KMBC-TV weekend sports anchor Dave Stewart to come on board. That gave him the pieces he needed to join Frank Boal on *Crunch Time* from 9 to 11 a.m.

WHB also needed a couple of reporters so the station raided the Entercom camp and hired Bob Fescoe and Nate Bukaty. They joined fellow University of Kansas alum Danny Clinkscale to create a strong, three-person reporting team. A month later WHB added the final piece to the puzzle by hiring Soren Petro. Petro had been the main afternoon sports-talk host on Entercom's KMBZ, but his contract was up and Entercom needed to make room for Whitlock and Maas.

"Once these guys defected, it was a programming war," said Boeger. "They wanted ESPN. They wanted Frank. They wanted Jim Rome. They wanted all of our Westwood One programming."

Boeger moved quickly to wrap up a deal with both ESPN and Westwood One. But they did not have a long-term deal with Rome.

"I was assured by the Rome people that there was no way in the world they would ever leave," said Boeger. But Entercom had some extra leverage. The Premier Network syndicates the Rome show. It also syndicates Dr. Laura Schlesinger and Rush Limbaugh. Entercom owns more than 100 stations in nineteen markets including eight in Kansas City.[20]

Many of those stations program Dr. Laura and Limbaugh, not to mention Rome. In September of 2003, WHB got the word Rome was moving to the *new* all-sports station in Kansas City, Entercom-owned 610 Sports, KCSP. So when KCSP premiered on September 10, 2003, Rome was sandwiched between Grunhard and newcomer Holden Cushner in the morning and Whitlock and Maas in the afternoon.

While WHB was disappointed in losing Rome, it had Soren Petro ready to move into that time slot.

"We had our best ratings ever the first Arbitron book after they left," said Boeger. In a recent ratings book, Petro beat Rome by nearly three share points, 7.1 to 4.3, and was number 3 in the market behind Rush Limbaugh and an FM rocker.[21]

The ratings in other dayparts were similar. In morning drive, Renshaw drew a 6.8 and second place in the market compared to a 3.2 and twelfth place for KCSP. But the afternoon drive slot was where WHB really flexed its muscles. Kietzman's show racked up first place among males twenty-four to fifty-five with a 9.9 rating. Whitlock and Maas showed up in a tie for twelfth place with a 3.3. Monday through Sunday, 6 a.m. to midnight, showed WHB in second place in the market with a 7.9 share. KCSP tied for twelfth with a 3.2.[22]

"It's been a pretty good butt whippin' for the first year," said Kietzman.

When the dust had cleared the Whitlock/Maas/Grunhard/Rome "trade" for Petro/Bukaty/Fescoe/Clinkscale looked a bit one-sided. But Boeger, Kietzman, vice president Todd Leabo, a very strong local supporting cast, Westwood One, and ESPN had also figured in the outcome.

As with most sports-talk radio, however, change was the rule rather than the exception. By the end of 2005, Renshaw had left WHB and was replaced by Bob Fescoe and Steven St. John on a show called *The Border Patrol,* a reference to the Missouri/Kansas rivalry. Also, Whitlock had left rival KCSP but continued his job as a columnist for the *Kansas City Star.* As of early 2006, Damon Amendolara handled the morning-drive show on KCSP while Marty Wall and Neal Jones hosted afternoon drive.

Playin' in the Big Leagues

Chad Boeger had spent most of 2003 involved in the game of musical talk show hosts, but he still found enough time to take on one more project—trying to wrestle the Kansas City Royals' radio rights away from Entercom. WHB's fierce competitors had held the rights for the past six years and had no intention of letting their cross-town rivals walk away with that prize. Susquehanna Broadcasting, which successfully carried the Chiefs on 101.1 FM (The Fox), KCFX-FM, also was expressing interest in carrying Royals baseball.

The Royals' marketing brass must have been ecstatic. The team was coming off of its first winning season in nearly a decade. The town was talking Royals baseball, and the three-station bidding war ensured the team would get top dollar for its product.

At first, Union Broadcasting was not going to bid for the rights.

"We had a bad experience the time before with people who are no longer there [with the Royals] who didn't play the game fairly," said Kietzman. "But Mark Gorris [Royals vice president of business operations] is a completely different animal."

Kietzman said the procedure for the new proposals was on the up-and-up, so Boeger and his cohorts put together a package. Part of that package was a promise to simulcast night games on 97.3 FM, KZPL. In their spare time in 2003, Jeff Montgomery and the other Union Broadcasting principals had put together a deal to purchase a newly created, "drop-in" FM signal. KZPL ("The Planet") would feature a Triple-A (adult- album-alternative) music format, something that was missing in the Kansas City market. But when some of the Royals brass had voiced concern about the coverage of WHB's nighttime signal, Union Broadcasting added the simulcast to the bid.

On Friday, August 29, 2003, the Royals announced Union Broadcasting and WHB would become the new flagship for Kansas City Royals baseball and its eighty-station network. Kietzman thinks the determining factor was his company's ability to market and sell tickets. Boeger thinks local ownership keyed the deal.

No one announced the actual terms of the contract, but once again the buzz in the pressbox was "they overpaid."

"The loser always says you paid too much," said owner Green.

But Boeger remains confident in what the Royals bring to the station and the entire company in spite of the fact Royals registered a second-straight 100-loss season in 2005. He said he not only looks at the numbers but goes by what his gut tells him.

"It's a Major League franchise," said Boeger. "It's something that brings value to the entire station and station group." Boeger also said baseball helps nighttime and weekend ratings.

Despite the Royals' poor season, WHB claimed the number-one slot for males twenty-five to fifty-four in the Monday through Friday 7 p.m. to midnight time slot with an 11.1 rating. The number 2 station only carried a 7.2 rating. Rival KCSP checked in with a 2.5, good for a tie for fourteenth. WHB even managed a second place finish (5.9) in persons twelve and older and a third place finish (6.5) in persons twenty-five to fifty-four.[23]

WHB also carries Kansas State football and basketball and major events such as *Sunday Night Football* and *Monday Night Football,* the NCAA basketball tournament, college football bowl games, NASCAR, and professional football, basketball, and baseball all-star games and playoffs.

Settling In

As of mid-2004, most of the talent in Kansas City sports-talk radio was under contract. No major-league broadcast rights will be available for bid for a couple of years. So the stations settled into the daily and often unglamorous grind of competition. The spring 2004 Arbitron numbers showed WHB with a significant lead over rival KCSP in every Monday through Friday daypart. It held down the number 2 ranking in the market in males twenty-five to fifty-four, Monday through Sunday, 6 a.m. to midnight and the number-three ranking, Monday through Friday 6 a.m. to 7 p.m. Spring 2005 showed similar numbers.

In a day in which much of sports talk radio is "schtick," WHB has built its reputation on "breaking stories," according to Boeger. The station first told listeners about Norm Stewart's impending retirement as University of Missouri basketball coach. WHB also beat the competition in reporting pending criminal charges against Tamarick Vanover and Bam Morris of the Chiefs. The station spent most of the month of July 2004 reporting on the August election in which Kansas Citians could vote on the financing package for a new downtown arena. That vote failed, so they repeated their extensive coverage in 2006 when the Jackson County Sports Authority went to voters with a $575 million package of renovations for Kauffman and Arrowhead stadiums.

"Before you read it in the morning newspaper the next day or see it on the ten o'clock news, you're going to find out first from us," said Boeger.

To do that requires a significant collection of on-air talent—make that journalism talent. Kietzman, Renshaw, Petro, Bukaty, Fescoe, Clinkscale, and Leabo all have college degrees in journalism or mass communication. So when the time comes to track down a story, the station can unleash a herd of experienced reporters. And all of the previously mentioned staff members except Renshaw either grew up in or went to college in the Kansas City area.

"Nobody's going to come back here and tell anybody on the air what they're supposed to say, what their opinion should be," said Kietzman. "All anybody is ever asked is to be *accurate*."

That concept of localism is another reason for the success of the WHB. Remember, the only reason Union even got WHB was because the owners would not sell to an out-of town conglomerate. Kietzman said WHB advertisers also care. He said one family-owned car dealer will only advertise on the locally owned station. Boeger also said he thought one of the reasons WHB got the Royals' rights was because the station was locally owned.

And much of that goes back to Jerry Green, a life-long Kansas City businessman and what he calls his "big advantage." Green, Boeger, and Jeff Montgomery own most of the stock.

"Every decision is made by us. Three of us can make a decision," said Green. Entercom's and Susquehanna's decisions are made by someone who doesn't live in Kansas City, added Green. Plus, those companies must make quarterly decisions whereas Green says Union Broadcasting has loaded for the long haul.

"Everything isn't dollars and cents in radio and TV," said Green.

However, he added that radio is just like all of the other businesses in which he's been involved.

"You have to make more than you spend," said Green.

Kietzman and Boeger agree Green lets them do their respective jobs. Green said he has made it a point in his career *not* to be a micromanager.

"I think I know how to recognize talent," said the principal company owner. "And Chad is the smartest young guy I've ever been around."

Kietzman echoes that praise of Boeger. "He is one of those businessmen that *just gets it*. He knows how to bring people together, to keep the group focused." He calls Boeger the most honest, hardworking leader he has ever seen.

Kietzman noted that when Boeger married his long-time girlfriend, the couple honeymooned in Bora Bora. It was Boeger's longest time away from the station since he first started working in radio. When Boeger found out his cell phone would not work in Bora Bora, he panicked. Kietzman said Boeger looked into finding a satellite phone to take with him.

Boeger said, as far as getting away from the station, "I've gotten better at it."

But he did not deny the satellite phone story.

Kansas City is one of the smallest markets trying to support two all-sports formats, so the question of whether both can survive moves front and center. Green said he thinks if KCSP does not improve its ratings, it will change formats.

"It's gonna be tough," said Green. "But I think we'll be the winner."

NOTES

1. Boeger, Chad. President and general manager, WHB. Interview by author. Tape recording. July 14, 2004. Unless otherwise noted, all comments from Boeger come from this interview.

2. Machado, Linda M. "The WHB Station Collection." Library of American Broadcasting, The University of Maryland Libraries, July 1999, www.lib.umd.edu/ LAB/COLLECTIONS/whb.html. Accessed June 12, 2004.

3. Machado.

4. Author unknown. "Biography of Count Basie." The John F. Kennedy Center for the Performing Arts, (date unknown), www.kennedy-center.org/calendar/ index.cfm?fuseaction=showIndividual&entitY-id . Accessed June 12, 2004.

5. Machado.

6. Ibid.

7. Burnes, Brian. "KC station pioneered Top 40 format 50 years ago," WHB, World's Happiest Broadcasters, June 5, 2003. www.kansascity.com/mld/kansas city/entertainment/6015315.htm?template-content. Accessed January 19, 2004.

8. Burnes.

9. Ibid.

10. Ibid.

11. Kietzman, Kevin. Part owner and afternoon host, WHB. Interview by author. Tape recording. July 14, 2004. Unless otherwise noted, all comments from Kietzman come from this interview.

12. Green, Jerry. Owner, WHB. Interview by author. July 14, 2004. Unless otherwise noted, all comments from Green come from this interview.

13. Lacerta, Phil. "Letting investors own, run show fuels union securities," *The Business Journal,* June 21, 1999. www.bizjournals.com/kansascity/stories/1999/ 06/21/focus6.html?t=printable. Accessed June 12, 2004.

14. Davis, Jim. "Green-led group buys WHB-AM for conversion," *The Business Journal,* June 9, 1999. www.bizjournals.com/kansascity/stories/1999/09/06/story8 .html?t=printable. Accessed June 12, 2004.

15. *Broadcasting and Cable Yearbook 2001,* Ellicott City, MD: American Media Services.

16. Davis.

17. Flanagan, Jeffrey. "Top of the morning," *Kansas City Star,* D-2, August 13, 2001.

18. Cookson, Brian. "Money where the mouth is," *The Business Journal,* November 5, 2001, www.bizjournals.com/kansascity/stories/2001/11/05smallb1.html ?5=printable. Accessed June 12, 2004.

19. Whitlock, Jason. "Changes needed in sports talk radio," *The Kansas City Star,* p. 1-D. June 22, 2003.

20. Roth, Stephen. "WHB prepares to fight for listeners with Entercom," *The Business Journal,* June 30, 2003, www.bizjournals.com/kansascity/stories/2003/ 06/30/story7.html?t=printable. Accessed June 12, 2004.

21. Arbitron, Spring 2004, ARBITRENDS Trends Report, 2004 Arbitron, Inc. July 30, 2004.

22. Ibid.

23. Ibid.

Chapter 10

WWLS, Oklahoma City: Unleashing "The Animal"

Shelley Wigley

"AAAAAAAAAAAAAAAYYYYYYYYYYYYYYYYYYYY!!! !!!!!!!!!!"

A man's deep voice bellows over the airwaves lasting several minutes. It's not a cry for help or a burst of anger. It's simply sports-talk radio host Jim Traber, also known as "the Ultimate," opening his afternoon show on WWLS *The Sports Animal* in Oklahoma City.

At half-past the hour, a young boy phones in to ask Traber his thoughts on the struggling Dallas Cowboys. After a pleasant exchange in which Traber asks the young man his name (Brandon) and age (eleven), the boy hangs up and the Ultimate is off on one of his familiar tirades:

> Shaping the minds of our youth! That's what I do here on the Sports Animal. No need to sit your kids in front of the TV with Nintendo. No, no, no, no, no! Put them in front of the radio between four and six p.m., and they will LEARN! Back to the phones. You're on the Sports Animal. Go ahead!

The next caller accuses Traber, a former Oklahoma State University football and baseball player, of being a "homer"—a broadcaster who never criticizes the home team—for the OSU Cowboys. Two calls later, an Oklahoma State University fan tells Traber he tries too hard to please the thousands of University of Oklahoma (OU) fans that listen to the station.

Sports-Talk Radio in America
© 2006 by The Haworth Press, Inc. All rights reserved.
doi:10.1300/5335_11

"When I first got started I knew that I was going to be controversial," said the former Baltimore Orioles' first baseman.[1]

Controversial? Absolutely. Traber "screams" his mind, and rarely, if ever, backs down from an opinion. He says things most hosts are afraid to say, and perhaps worst of all for some University of Oklahoma fans, he played both college football and baseball at a rival school—OSU.

"They (OU fans) don't hate him. They love to hate him," said Chris Baker, operations manager for Citadel Communications, the company that owns the Sports Animal.[2]

"Traber can't win for losing," said Randy Heitz, executive producer and sports director at WWLS.

> OSU fans get mad and tell him "You're just a back stabber," and OU fans say "You're an OSU homer," but he's not either one of those. Some fans still picture him in his OSU baseball uniform being the OSU guy. Admittedly, when he first got into sports-talk radio, he talked more OSU because that's where he had more connections. He had his friends at OSU, but he's developed them at OU, so he can get information from both sides, so I actually think Traber is our best well-rounded guy when it comes to knowing both OU and OSU.[3]

Perhaps that's why so many callers can't resist debating with the Ultimate Sports Mind. "I'm a lot more in your face, and I never, ever say anything I don't believe," Traber said. "I was the first in this market to say that John Blake (former OU head football coach) should be fired, and I had people cuss at me at remotes." Despite his controversial style, Traber insisted he is not a host who says things to light up the phone lines. "I say what I feel, and I don't care about the consequences."[4]

Baker said he appreciates Traber's style.

> People don't want to hear anyone who doesn't have an opinion. People who don't have opinions aren't remembered very well. I would much rather have someone say how he truly feels about something then someone who is fair-weathered and whichever way the wind blows is how he's going to have his opinion go.[5]

In addition to his outspoken nature, Traber's playing experience also is a key to his success.

> I think a lot of listeners like the insight Jim is able to bring to the game because he played football at a Division I school, he's gone to the locker room and he's done the training, and the same thing for his professional baseball career. Jim offers our listeners something unusual, which is to have someone here in Oklahoma City who's got this great insight.[6]

Traber's insight isn't lost on listeners—it extends to players and coaches as well. "Jim doesn't throw out softball questions," said Baker. "And you can tell the coaches don't mind it because Jim asks the right questions, and I think he gets a lot of respect because of that."[7]

Traber may be the most well-rounded host, as Heitz described him, but the man who joins Traber on the air for the *Dominant Duo* at 4 p.m. and the *Total Dominance Hour* at 5 p.m. each day is the most experienced. New Jersey native Al Eschbach has been talking sports on the radio for twenty-eight years. "Someone with KTOK Radio called me up and wanted to know if I was interested in doing a one-hour sports show, and I asked, 'Does it pay?' and he said, 'Yeah,' and I said, 'Okay.'"[8]

At the time, Eschbach, a 1968 journalism graduate of the University of Oklahoma, was the sports editor of the now-defunct *Oklahoma Journal*. The one-hour show eventually grew to two hours, and in 1985 Eschbach was hired by John Fox, general manager of WWLS Radio in Norman, to do an expanded sports-talk program that was sandwiched between oldies music. By 1988, the station had become an around-the-clock sports-talk radio station. At the time, New York City's WFAN was the only station with an all sports-talk format.[9]

"Al sounds like he doesn't belong here, but he does," said Baker. "He's so endeared here, and he has a following that is just unbelievable. When we travel with the team and go to out-of-town games, it is interesting how Al can draw a crowd no matter where he goes."[10]

"There is a reason why Al is so popular and so loved and adored by Sports Animal fans and OU fans," said Baker. "He recognizes what people want to talk about (OU football), and he's made a great living at it."[11]

Heitz attributed Eschbach's success to his brash personality. "He's so different from people in Oklahoma."[12]

Baker agreed. "It truly is a phenomenon."[13]

"With my voice the last thing I ever thought I would be doing would be radio in Oklahoma City,"[14] said Eschbach, whose style has been described as "sandpaper rough,"[15] one in which he spits and sputters, "sometimes sounding like a rusty Cadillac whose engine won't turn over."[16] In fact, Eschbach, who refuses to discuss soccer or NASCAR with callers, sometimes gets so excited that his words are no longer understandable. He's been known to shout at callers who give what he considers stupid opinions and has on occasion banned callers from his show.

Want to set him off? Want to hear him spit and sputter? Just call in and say that OU Head Football Coach Bob Stoops should have benched 2003 Heisman Trophy Winner and OU quarterback Jason White during the Sugar Bowl. Or tell him that Bob Stoops hasn't proven he can win a national championship with players he recruited. After spitting and sputtering through a heated argument, the caller who started the debate is gone, and Eschbach replies with one of his favorite phrases. "Give me a physical break!"

The short, fuzzy-haired Eschbach, who doesn't go anywhere without his famous Fedora hat, is well-known for his sports knowledge and his strong ties to the OU football and basketball programs. "He's got his claws into the Oklahoma program and can get you any information," said Heitz. "I think that's one thing that has made him such a success, especially early on because it got to a point where people would say 'oh my gosh what's happened at OU? Let me flip on Al.'"[17]

So how did a Seton Hall Prep graduate such as Eschbach wind up at OU? Simple. Because at the time, OU had been named one of the Top 10 party schools in the country.[18] "I never want to lose the crazy side of me," says Eschbach, who was fired twice from sorority houses for spitting in the ice tea, and caught red-handed attempting to paint over the "B" in Bass House, a dorm on the OU campus.[19]

Indeed, the man whose favorite movie is *Animal House* has transferred his orneriness from the dorms to the airwaves. Just listen to some of the common exchanges between Eschbach and his callers:

CALLER: "What's up Al?"

ESCHBACH: "That's a pretty personal question, don't you think?"

CALLER:"Have a good day."

ESCHBACH: "Why would I have a bad day? That would be pretty stupid."

When he goes to a phone line and no one is there, Eschbach replies with, "You're like Abraham Lincoln. You're History!"

His favorite historical figure? Albert Einstein. His favorite food? Beer and radishes. His favorite game? Tie between Free Cell and "Stump the Chump," a trivia game in which callers try to stump Eschbach with a trivia question on Friday evenings. If they succeed, Eschbach gets to ask them a trivia question. If they miss, they are instantly met with Eschbach's familiar "See ya!" and a dial tone.

Eschbach doesn't talk about just sports, especially when he and Traber share the microphone between 4 and 6 p.m. each day. They often go off on tangents about family, food, and politics. "Everybody who listens knows about my wife, my children, my ex-wife," said Traber. "They feel like they know me, and that's the key—to relate to listeners because they're the reason I'm here."[20]

Baker agreeed: "The more the listeners know about you, the more comfortable they're going to be listening to you."[21]

Both Eschbach and Traber said their on-air personalities are no facade. "I try not be a phony," said Eschbach. "I'm just me. I think some people in this business don't really try to paint the picture of who they really are, but I'm not phony. With me what you see is what you get."[22]

Heitz, who's worked in Oklahoma sports-talk radio for thirteen years, agreed.

These guys are who they are. They use their real names. They aren't false about anything. We all know that Jim's a die-hard Republican, there's no doubt about it. He's not going to hide it. The hosts don't put up fronts. Whoever they say they are on the air, that's who they are. That's why it's funny when I see people out, and they say "Oh, you work with Al. How is that?" and I'm like, "Well, what you hear is what you get. If you hear Al being loud and talking about something, guess what? When he gets off the air he's doing the same thing."[23]

It may seem strange to some that two of the Sports Animals' most popular hosts are originally from outside Oklahoma. Said Heitz:

> Our drive-time team of Al Eschbach and Jim Traber are both from the East Coast, but both of them went to college in Oklahoma. So they know what the fans are like, and they see how passionate they are about their sports, for their football especially.[24]

That knowledge has translated into high ratings for the duo's *Total Dominance Hour.* According to Baker, the program is usually ranked number 1 in the market for men eighteen and older.[25]

In fall 2001, the Sports Animal had its best ratings book ever recorded and finished first among men ages twenty-five to fifty-four for the first time in its history.[26] The station's 5.0 rating topped the station's fall 2000 ratings, when OU won the national championship in football,[27] and the station's summer 2003 Arbitron ratings were up 36 percent over spring 2003.[28]

"We've been trending very well," said Baker. "We always seem to pace ahead of last year's numbers, which is real important to us. We always want to continue to grow."[29]

In fact, Baker said, Citadel's vice president of news talk/sports programming told station executives in 2003 that the Sports Animal was the highest rated sports-talk radio station, per average quarter-hour ratings, in America. "I think we are usually in the top three to four," added Baker. "The station does very well."[30]

Said Heitz:

> Fall is just a blowout ratings-wise. But what is nice is that we're at a point now to where our lowest low in the fall is now our lowest low in the winter (our slower time) which is good. We're pulling up everything. Instead of just becoming a seasonal station, we're starting to become a year-round station.[31]

Admitted Baker:

> Growth didn't come that quickly for us. It took a year or two for it to take off to the level it's at now. When we first started, the success we had then is nowhere what it is now. It's four-, five-, six-, sevenfold from where it was.[32]

One reason for the station's growth, according to Heitz, is the *Morning Animals.*

> The morning show has brought in a variety of people that may have not listened to us before. They may tune into the morning show because they hear their friends talking about it and the next thing you know they get in their car at noon and their radio is still on the Sports Animal. They get in their car after work and the radio is still on the Sports Animal. So really the morning show has been a big contributor to our success and increased ratings.[33]

Mike Steely, Jay Lynch (Lump), and Curtis Fitzpatrick comprise the Morning Animals. Over the years, they have been assisted by a variety of interns they refer to as Bacon, Toast, Pork, Jelly, and Muffin.

"The morning team is a totally different breed," said Heitz.[34]

The Morning Animals often can be found pulling pranks or performing sports-related skits, such as "Thanksgiving at the Stoops'," in which the three hosts imitate the voices of a variety of Oklahoma sports figures who stop by OU football coach Bob Stoops' home for turkey and dressing.

They can emulate anybody, including their boss, General Manager Larry Bastida, who they affectionately call "the corner man." "It's kind of scary," said Baker. "I never want to hear them doing me because they can do anybody and make it sound just like the person."[35]

The trio also has been known to call the University of Texas Athletic Department following an OU football win against Texas and ask them to pay for an uncle's funeral. The reason? Because the uncle had a heart attack following Texas' loss to OU. Other popular segments include an on-air facial given to host Mike Steely, the back waxing of intern Pork, and frequent calls from one of the Morning Animals' favorite listeners, "James the Marvel," who speaks in a low voice and often sounds incoherent as he goes from one bizarre topic to another. One minute he may be discussing an upcoming NFL football game and the next minute he may be discussing a trip he recently made to the moon or Mars. Perhaps his biggest claim to fame, besides the fact that he successfully picked two of the three winning horses in a recent Triple Crown, is his singing.

"There is nothing like James the Marvel's songs to start the day," said Heitz.[36]

The Marvel makes up songs on request from the Morning Animals, and listeners never know what they might get. He composes songs such as "Sooner Land, Sooner Road," and more recently, he sang a song titled "Good Luck America," which coincided with the 2004 Summer Olympic games. It sounded something like this:

"America . . . I love you so much. Won't you stay in touch . . . America?"

"As off the wall as some of his calls are, he is a great caller for the station," said Heitz.

> He's that break when you get tired of talking about who the Dallas Cowboys are going to start this week. James the Marvel calls in with one of his off-the-wall songs and instead of talking sports, people start saying "Wow, do I have to follow that?" Instead of talking sports, the guy on after him is recapping James the Marvel's call for the next five minutes. I think that's a big help because it shows that we have a sense of humor and that we're flexible and really enjoy the callers.[37]

The Sports Animal's midday line-up features what could be considered a slate of kinder, gentler, hosts. Bob Barry, Jr., sports director at the local NBC affiliate, KFOR-TV, hosts *Sports Morning,* while high school football guru Mark Rodgers, who's also sports director at the local ABC affiliate, KOCO-TV, and golf expert Craig Humphreys share duties on the *Middle of the Day* show. They are occasionally joined by *Daily Oklahoman* sports columnists, John Rhode and Berry Tramel. "Craig and Mark are kind of laid-back," said Heitz. "They're like the old guys at the barbershop who sit around and talk sports. Then you've got Bob Barry, Jr. who is really easy to listen to in the morning when you're just trying to get your day going."[38]

"We're lucky that we have a lot of great guys who specialize in their own area of expertise, whether it's golf or high school recruiting," said Baker. "You bring it all together and it's a powerful team."[39]

Sports-talk radio in Oklahoma might not be where it is today if not for a firing, a hiring, a merger, and one man's passion for sports. When Jim Traber's contract was not renewed at Oklahoma's first sports-talk radio station, WWLS Radio, Traber, and Craig Humphreys, a man who loved sports so much he had been purchasing air time on WWLS to do his own sports-talk show, decided to launch their own sports-talk radio station. Humphreys leased time on KXY 1340 AM, and in 1995 SportsTalk 1340 debuted, featuring Humphreys, Traber, and the late Dan Lutz.[40] The station quickly began competing with WWLS, and eventually expanded its programming to eleven hours of sports-talk per day. In 1998, Humphreys sold out to Caribou Communications, which later sold to Citadel Communications, and the Sports Animal was unleashed.[41] Later that same year, Caribou purchased WWLS and merged it with the Sports Animal.[42]

Heitz said the blending of both sports-talk stations into one was fairly smooth.

> Both stations, 1340 and WWLS, had a following, so when the two stations merged, the two loyal followings merged also. It was a little reluctant at first—"Oh, I don't like so-and-so" or "I don't like so-and-so" (referring to listeners' comments about various hosts), but the listeners of both stations have come to know they're one big happy family, and that is one thing that has made the Sports Animal grow to the level it has."[43]

Other factors?
Said Heitz:

> The marketplace we have is a lot different than any other successful sports-talk stations. Most of them are in bigger cities. They have NBA teams, NFL teams, or some kind of pro team. The unique thing about Oklahoma City is the fans are so passionate about their sports, whether it's OU football or OSU basketball, the fans from both schools are just so passionate that all they want to do is talk about their sports.
>
> For example, during the summer when you could be talking baseball, the callers want to talk OU football. I hate to single out one school, but truly it's been Oklahoma football. If Oklahoma football hadn't been so dynamic in the seventies and the early eighties, which is when WWLS Radio started, we probably wouldn't be where we are now. There probably wouldn't be a sports station to this magnitude as far as local sports-talk is concerned.[44]

Baker said part of the station's success can be attributed to knowing what the listeners want.

> It's the heritage of the OU football program. If you want to see
> our ratings go away, let's stop talking OU football. They're not
> going to talk about the Tour de France more than two or three
> phone calls. Callers aren't going to be talking about Wimbledon
> or about golf that much. That's the common denominator.
>
> OU is the "pro" team in Oklahoma. It's got the heritage from
> Bud Wilkinson to Switzer, the whole deal. It's such a strong her-
> itage that the folks here hold onto it.
>
> The fact that OU football is becoming stronger certainly
> drives us, as well as OSU now too. It's just like anything. If you
> have a winning team, you're going to have a bigger following
> and the more you win the more people you have following it and
> wanting to know more about it.[45]

Another factor that has contributed to the station's success, according to Heitz, is its focus on local programming.

> Instead of broadcasting national programs, we try to make ev-
> erything as local as possible, and I think that's been one of the
> selling points to the station.
>
> Most stations especially in non-pro markets and even some
> pro-markets, will have a morning local show, a middle of the
> day local show and a late afternoon drive-time show, but in-
> between and afterward it's all network programming. We make
> a point of doing as many things as we can locally. On Tuesday
> nights we have a local NASCAR show called *Pit Road.* Instead
> of taking the national show, which we could easily do, we said
> "Here's a guy here locally who likes NASCAR and is a
> NASCAR fan." In other words, we try to make it local so the lis-
> teners feel more of a connection than they would to a national
> guy that they're never going to see, and they'll have to wait for
> hours to talk to on the phone.[46]

Other local programs include pre- and post-broadcasts of all OU
and OSU football games, a mid-week program titled *Strictly Football*
and a show focusing entirely on fantasy football.

"Being successful is a lot of hard work," said Baker.

> We just don't turn it on and say "OK, here it is." We go out there and actively solicit people to listen to us by doing things like the Bevo Bash before the OU-Texas game or when we go and broadcast during away games. We actively go out to where our listeners are because we want to be with them during these sporting events.[47]

The Sports Animal also likes to try new things, including shows featuring both current and former OU coaches. The station frequently tries to incorporate former players into its programming by utilizing the insight and expertise of former OU quarterback and Lieutenant Governor Jack Mildren and former OU players Josh Heupel, Trent Smith, and Nate Hybl.

"Where else are you going to hear an NFL quarterback (referring to Hybl who was with the Cleveland Browns in 2003) talking about training and summer camp and stuff? You're not going to get it anywhere else."[48]

"It gets back to trying to make it local," added Heitz.[49]

Said Baker:

> It's like if I wore the same shirt to work every day. I'd be a pretty boring and predictable guy. That's the way we do it with the Sports Animal too. We want to stay contemporary, and contemporary is ever-changing. So if you want to stay contemporary in the sports-talk business, you need to shake it up and change it up a little bit so it's not just the same old thing.
>
> A lot of it is being consistent, but also offering different things. That's why we do change some things. We don't do everything the same every year because we want to stay contemporary and keep it fresh and keep it changing. It's kind of a bit of both. You want to work off your heritage but you don't want to stay on your heritage, because if you stay on your heritage you're going to get dull and you're not going to be exciting.[50]

Baker and Heitz agreed that talent is another reason the Sports Animal has done so well. "I feel like if we were to take our station into a major market we would compete," said Heitz. "Our guys would adjust and we would compete because we know the importance of talking about what listeners want to hear."[51]

Despite the station's talent and knack for innovative programming, the most important ingredient to the station's success may be the callers.

"Callers are what makes the station go," said Heitz. "I don't care how many times we have coaches and players on or whoever, we're not here if not for the callers."[52]

Heitz said callers can sometimes take pressure off the host.

> On slow days, you may get a crazy caller who says one stupid thing and all of a sudden the host is on easy street for the next three hours because our listeners are passionate, and if a caller says something bad about their favorite team or coach, they're on the phone and they're wanting to talk about it and rip the guy who said it."[53]

According to Heitz,

> A lot of OSU fans say "the Sports Animal is an OU station." I tell people who call me and complain that we are not an OU station, we are a station that talks about what callers want to talk about. And we can't control the fact that about 85 percent of our callers want to talk OU football. If the callers call in, then the hosts will talk OSU sports. If those are the calls we have, and we are a caller-driven station, then that's what we have to talk about.
>
> I hope with the more success OSU has that more OSU fans start calling in, and we will sound like a more balanced station.[54]

Heitz said the hosts allow the callers to drive the station, and drive it they do. From "Paintbrush" and his reenactment of play-by-play calls of great Sooner moments to "Doc D" and his criticisms of "Zero U (OU)" fans, "callers are what makes the station," said Heitz.

> I mean, we could have on all the guests in the world, but if we didn't have the caller support we have, our station wouldn't be what it is today. Even if we had the ratings we have, it still wouldn't be as good because it would come down to Bob and

Craig talking to themselves, and you can only listen to that for so long. That's not a slam to anyone, but the callers help add to the entertainment and fun of the station.

You get callers trying to antagonize both sides—OU and OSU fans. It makes the station go in the sense that the calls are entertaining. They make the station lively.[55]

One caller who doesn't mind aggravating the other side is ninety-six-year-old Effie Heil.[56] Said Heitz:

She likes to call in when OU is playing. She's a die-hard Sooner fan. When OU messes up she calls in and says, "Well, they just need to get better." Some people don't like to rip on kids or coaches. But she has no problem. She'll rip the coaches, the players, whatever.[57]

Heil makes no secret about her feelings toward OU's bedlam rival, OSU. "They've had their day. They beat us. . . . So? The sun came up the next morning."[58]

Clearly, Effie doesn't mince words. If the team didn't play well, she admits it. But she always supports them. You can't call her a bandwagon fan because as she says, she's stuck by the team through good years and bad.[59]

Another popular caller is "Rocko," whose handicapping skills have become almost legendary. Said Heitz:

Rocko is your average Joe who does offshore betting on his computer, but he'll call and give his picks and the rest of the day we'll get calls asking for Rocko's picks. It's crazy! He's not an expert, but he does really well because we check his picks every week. We had one guy who was out of town on a business trip, and he actually called in on Friday just to get Rocko's picks.[60]

Most of those involved with the Sports Animal admit they had no idea the station would be such a success. "We knew we had something," Traber said of the station he and Humphreys started in 1995. "But we didn't expect it to become as big as it is now."[61]

Heitz, who started his career at WWLS in 1991, agreed. "It does surprise me a little how far we've come. As far as where we're at ratings-wise, it shocks me a lot. We're showing up with really good ratings."[62]

It's clear that sports-talk radio in Oklahoma has come a long way since Eschbach debuted a one-hour sports-talk program on KTOK more than thirty years ago. Perhaps its evolution can be summed up by one of Escbach's favorite quotes from former OU Head Football Coach Barry Switzer. "I didn't create the monster. Bud Wilkinson did. My job was to feed the monster."

Although a number of people contributed to the creation of the monster that has become the Sports Animal, the station continues to thrive, grow, and be fed.

NOTES

1. Traber, Jim. Telephone interview by author. August 10, 2004. Except where otherwise noted, all comments from Traber come from this interview.

2. Baker, Chris. Interview by author. Tape recording. July 28, 2004. Except where otherwise noted, all comments from Baker come from this interview.

3. Heitz, Randy. Interview by author. Tape recording. August 4, 2004. Except where otherwise noted, all comments from Heitz come from this interview.

4. Traber.

5. Baker.

6. Ibid.

7. Ibid.

8. Eschbach, Al. Telephone interview by author. August 12, 2004. Except where otherwise noted, all comments from Eschbach come from this interview.

9. Tramel, Berry. "Blessing of life: Foxes survive tragedies, see a better tomorrow." *The Daily Oklahoman,* 14-B, February 21, 1999.

10. Baker.

11. Ibid.

12. Heitz.

13. Baker.

14. Eschbach.

15. Capps, Reilly. "Eschbach talks loud game." *The Daily Oklahoman,* 16-D, September 12, 1999.

16. Ibid.

17. Heitz.

18. Capps.

19. Ibid.

20. Traber.

21. Baker.

22. Eschbach.

23. Heitz.

24. Ibid.

25. Baker.

26. Bracht, Mel. "Citadel clinches radio market: Company's five stations finish strong." *The Daily Oklahoman,* 8-B, February 8, 2002.

27. Ibid.

28. Bracht, Mel. "Amnesia will help OSU." *The Daily Oklahoman,* 2-C, November 6, 2003.

29. Baker.

30. Ibid.

31. Heitz.

32. Baker.

33. Heitz.

34. Ibid.

35. Baker.

36. Heitz.

37. Ibid.

38. Ibid.

39. Baker.

40. Bracht, Mel. "Talk show host Lutz dies after battle with cancer." *The Daily Oklahoman,* 3-C, March 11, 2002.

41. Bracht, Mel. "Caribou purchases SportsTalk 1340: Venture expands to 24 hours on FM." 21, *The Daily Oklahoman,* January 17, 1998.

42. Bracht, Mel. "'Sports Animal' buys competitor WWLS." *The Daily Oklahoman,* 25, July 23, 1998.

43. Heitz.

44. Ibid.

45. Baker.

46. Heitz.

47. Baker.

48. Ibid.

49. Heitz.

50. Baker.

51. Heitz.

52. Ibid.

53. Heitz.

54. Ibid.

55. Ibid.

56. DeFrange, Ann. "Sports animal Effie." *The Daily Oklahoman,* 1-B, January 1, 2002.

57. Heitz.

58. DeFrange.

59. Ibid.

60. Heitz.

61. Traber.

62. Heitz.

"Sign Off"

The stations represented in this book run the gamut from the largest and most renowned stations in big-league markets to medium-market stations in college towns. The most successful of them—WFAN in New York, WEEI in Boston, KTCK in Dallas, WHB in Kansas City, WIP in Philadelphia, WGR in Buffalo, WWLS in Oklahoma City—have one very important thing in common: They are very local in their approach to broadcasting. Virtually all of their shows are locally produced and focus almost entirely on local teams. To a great extent, the hosts themselves are either locally born-and-bred or longtime members of local sports media. They not only know the local teams, they know the fans, and so have considerable credibility with the listeners.

For those who fear that localism is fading from broadcasting, the success of these stations is gratifying. But if the reader favors a thoughtful, journalistic approach to sports coverage, he or she may be disappointed by these stations. Although some stations—notably WEEI in Boston and WHB in Kansas City—seem to balance "guy talk" with solid reporting and commentary on the local teams, more often than not, the stations find it more rewarding to aim low. It is not new; American broadcasting has been accused of appealing to the lowest common denominator almost from the beginning. Rarely have broadcasters who do so gone unrewarded. If anything, it's heartening that substantial sports broadcasters such as Norm Hitzges in Dallas, Glenn Ordway in Boston, and Howard Simon in Buffalo still find safe harbor on the sports-talk airwaves.

Laddish guy talk is one thing; recklessness is another. Too often, sports-talk hosts—encouraged by management to swing freely in an effort to keep up the ratings—let fly with comments that hurt their listeners, their stations, and themselves. Examples include a WIP host making Nazi references to the Philadelphia Eagles, whose owner and president are Jewish, and two WEEI hosts apparently comparing an escaped zoo gorilla to minority high-school students in Boston. While reciting the obligatory apology, the WIP host went so far as to invoke the First Amendment to defend his dubious comments.

Under the circumstances, these incidents are unavoidable. When on-air personalities are urged to be outrageous, the occasional pratfall is not at all surprising. Apologies will be issued, promises to prevent the same thing from happening again will be made, and business will continue as usual. The FCC's move to impose much heavier fines for on-the-air indecency has resulted in some fine tuning of what stations allow, but the changes are only a matter of degree, barely noticeable to most listeners. The smart money is betting against anything other than marginal retrenchments of sports-talk radio's slash-and-burn style.

In late 2004, a near riot involving members of the Indiana Pacers, Detroit Pistons, and fans at the Pistons' home arena dominated the news for days. Commentators wondered over the causes of such a flagrant breakdown of order. Sports-talk radio showed up on some lists. Drew Sharp of the *Detroit Free Press* observed:

> Anything goes now. The interactive world of the Internet and the proliferation of sports-talk radio have given too many fans a false sense of empowerment.

The players, Sharp wrote, are expected to take the fans' abuse because "through some warped rationalization," the abuse is seen as the price of earning multi-million dollar salaries for playing a game.[1]

How much of the blame shoot-from-the-lip sports-talk radio deserves for incidents such as the Motown Melee really can't be measured. But it stands to reason that some fans who hear "smack" (in Jim Rome's terminology) day after day on sports-talk radio may take the loose talk too seriously. They may then find themselves on the court confronting a very large and angry pro athlete. If for this reason alone — in the increasingly volatile world we live in — sports-talk program directors should keep tighter reins on their rambunctious on-air talent.

Whatever its effect on popular culture, sports-talk radio long ago proved itself as a viable commercial radio format. WFAN, while only ranking in the middle of the ratings in the cutthroat New York market, became the top-billing station of all-time in 1997,[2] and more than a dozen major-market sports-talk stations were billing more than $10 million per year as of early 2004.[3] As KTCK General Manager Dan Bennett in Dallas says, the format has moved beyond the days when the primary advertisers were sports bars and strip clubs.[4]

It is notable that some sports-talk stations, such as WFAN, rely heavily on play-by-play of local teams, while others, such as KTCK, have enjoyed years of success despite having no major-league sports broadcasts. Few observers would have predicted when the format started that a sports-talk station could survive without holding the broadcast rights to a local major-league team.

A book of this nature can only be a snapshot of a moment in time; change is the only certainty in radio, and change will come (no doubt it already has come) to these stations, for better or worse. One development on the near horizon that may have an effect: digital radio.

AM stations using new digital broadcasting technology will, from all accounts, upgrade the fidelity of their signals to FM quality. If that's the case, it seems likely that some stations now airing news, talk, or sports-talk formats may return to music programming. But radio has become a medium that is targeted at ever smaller niches of the mass audience. In major markets, with as many as fifty stations competing for listeners, a station that can pull even a rating of 2.0 can be profitable. It seems certain sports-talk radio will always be able to find such a niche, and given that the American public's now more-than-a-century-old fascination with sports shows no sign of abating, it's a safe bet that sports-talk radio will be around for a long time to come.

NOTES

1. Sharp, Drew. "Unruly fans must pay a price." *Detroit Free Press,* November 20, 2004. Availabe at http://www.freep.com/news/latenews/pm1489_20041120.htm. Accessed January 4, 2005.

2. Battema, Douglas L. "Sports on radio." In *Museum of Broadcast Communications Encyclopedia of Radio,* Volume 3, edited by Christopher H. Sterling, 1320-1323. New York: Fitzroy Dearborn, 2004.

3. Adams, Russell. "Sports Talk Radio: On the Air and On a Roll." *Street and Smith's Sports Business Journal,* February 2, 2004, 15.

4. Ibid.

Index

Page numbers followed by the letter "f" indicate figures; those followed by the letter "t" indicate tables.

University of Washington, 97, 99-100,
    101, 107
  basketball, 104
  football, 104, 106
Unsportsmanlike Conduct, 81, 84-85,
    90
Urban (hip-hop, R&B) radio stations,
    10, 15
Urination as radio topic, 142
U.S. foreign policy commentary, 27-28,
    59

Vanover, Tamarick, 177
Variety shows, 96
Vedder, Christian, 159, 160
Verbal attacks, 118
Verizon Amphitheater, 168
Veterans Stadium, 116
Viacom (Firm), 60
Viola, Frank, 73
Voice imitations, 27, 36-37, 47, 187

WABZ, 148
Wade, Ed, 111
Waitt Media, 81
Wall, Kevin, 165
Wall, Marty, 175
Wallace, Ben, 75
Walt Disney Company, 56
Walt Disney Florida Classic, 66
Walt Disney World's Magic Kingdom,
    67
Walton, Bill, 29
Wander, Art, 131
War on terrorism, 79
War Paint (horse), 171-172
Warsaw Sports Marketing Center, 101
Washington Redskins, 131
Water cooler topics, 47-48
WBEN, 130, 131, 133, 135, 141, 142,
    144
WBZ, 44
WCBS, 60

WDAE, 2-3, 69
WDAF (Fox 4), 45, 166, 167
WDBO, 76
WEAF (later WFAN), 8, 54
Weather, discussions about, 90
Weather reports, 100, 137
Web sites, 4, 78, 84, 90, 122, 137, 148
Weber, Stan, 170
WEEI (Edison Electric Illuminating)
  community involvement of, 50
  criticism of, 48-50
  debut of, 44
  hosts and programming on, 43-44,
      45-48, 50
  management of, 3
  ratings, 10t, 43, 45
  success, factors in, 45, 50, 197
  target audience of, 43, 44-45
Weekly sports shows, 44
Westwood One Radio Network, 60, 88,
    174, 175
WEVD, 56
WFAN
  criticism of, 59-60
  debut and history of, 8, 53, 55-56
  growth of, 8-9
  hosts and programming on, 55,
      56-60, 199
  precursors of, 8, 54-55
  ratings, 10t, 56, 61, 198
  revenue generated by, 93
  as sports-talk format pioneer, 7, 44,
      53, 63, 79, 97, 111, 183
  success, factors in, 55, 56-57, 59,
      60, 61-62, 63, 197
WFI, 112
WFLF, 68
WFLL, 77
WGL, 112
WGR
  changes in, 148-152
  hosts and programming of, 128, 129,
      131-132, 135-138, 148-149,
      148-152, 150-152
  pre-sports-talk period, 130, 132, 133
  ratings, 144, 145f, 146f, 151